WHEN
FORESTS
RUN
AMOK

WHEN FORESTS RUN AMOK

War and Its Afterlives in Indigenous and Afro-Colombian Territories

Daniel Ruiz-Serna

Duke University Press   *Durham and London*   2023

© 2023 Duke University Press
All rights reserved
Printed in the United States of America on acid-free paper ∞
Project Editor: Lisa Lawley
Designed by Courtney Leigh Richardson
Typeset in MinionPro Regular, Alegreya Sans by Westchester
Publishing Services

Library of Congress Cataloging-in-Publication Data
Names: Ruiz-Serna, Daniel, [date] author.
Title: When forests run amok : war and its afterlives in indigenous and
Afro-Colombian territories / Daniel Ruiz-Serna.
Description: Durham : Duke University Press, 2023. | Includes index.
Identifiers: LCCN 2022034126 (print)
LCCN 2022034127 (ebook)
ISBN 9781478016878 (hardback)
ISBN 9781478019503 (paperback)
ISBN 9781478024149 (ebook)
Subjects: LCSH: War and society—Colombia—Pacific Coast. | War—Environmental
aspects—Colombia—Pacific Coast. | Black people—Colombia—Pacific Coast—
Social conditions. | Indigenous peoples—Colombia—Pacific Coast—Social
conditions. | Ethnoecology—Colombia—Pacific Coast. | BISAC: SOCIAL SCIENCE /
Anthropology / Cultural & Social
Classification: LCC HN310.P33 R857 2023 (print) | LCC HN310.P33 (ebook) |
DDC 305.896/0861—dc23/eng/20220923
LC record available at https://lccn.loc.gov/2022034126
LC ebook record available at https://lccn.loc.gov/2022034127

Cover art: *Flow*, Bajo Atrato, Colombia, 2016. Courtesy of the
author.

To the women I love the most:
Diana, divine custodian of all beings animating the forest,
and Silvana, the forest herself.

Contents

Acknowledgments

One day on a very rainy morning while I was walking through the thick forest near the Tamboral River, an unexpected surge of joy made me feel I could carry out this research. I want to thank that place and those who were walking with me that day. To José Omar, for sharing his story with us and showing me that despite our willingness to heal, our hearts carry wounds from which we never completely recover. To Ernesto Ramírez, a friend and a community leader who walks at ease in both *Chocoano* forests and the urban jungle where we first met, at the time when he had left his river and his people to protect the life of his family. To Abel Gutiérrez Copete, who with good humor showed us how to come to terms with the sadness around us. To Luz Derly Peña Cabezón, a smiling and energetic woman whose gaze conveys the strength of the Wounaan people. To Luna, my wife and steadfast supporter, who agreed to make that journey with me even if I did not deserve her company. I am also thankful to the territory of Bajo Atrato itself for taking care of me during all these years of work and providing conditions that inspired my way of thinking.

My work in this region was possible only because of the support of many wonderful people in Apartadó, Riosucio, Carmen del Darién, Turbo, and Belén de Bajirá. I feel deeply humbled by their generosity. It would be impossible to name them all, but I cannot forget César Acosta and Zenaida Rodríguez; Ana Luisa Ramírez Flórez for the many hours of company and good conversation; Jailer, Luisfer, Elian, and Eliseo, who shared their *chocoanidad* with me; the Claretian Missionaries, especially the priests Armando Valencia, Dagoberto Ayala, Sigifredo López, and Francisco Rodríguez, who made their house mine; Leonarda Lara, Gloria Isabel López Lara, and all the children of their family who adopted me; Dania Palacios and her daughters; María Eleuteria Perea, Claribel Sierra Ramos, Digna Mercedes Murillo, Mélida Mena, and Benilda Rentería Córdoba for sharing their arts with me; Humberto Lara, Carlos Andrés Potes, Sebastian Mena, César Moya, Oiben Mena, Nicomedes Maquilón, Fausto and Faustico Palacios, Wilfrido Mendoza, Amancio Valoyes

Córdoba, Ismael Mena, Domingo Marmolejo, Calvo Edilberto, Emna Córdoba, Florentino y Ricardo Allín Córdoba, Marino Denis, Glenis Asprilla, la seño Edith Mena, and Omilsa Robledo Martínez, whose work and lives are proof of their profound political engagement; everyone from the Asociación de Consejos Comunitarios del Bajo Atrato (ASCOBA): José Ángel Palomeque, Zenaida Martínez, Fernando Álvarez, Alfoncito Feria, Abraham Mosquera, Emilsón Palacios, Jesús Antonio Rodríguez, Ana Dionisia Murillo, Luis Enrique Moya, Eider Martínez, Jorge Quinto, Humberto Paz Romaña, Jackson Romaña Blandón, Frey Tuberquia, Antonio Mena, Francisco Salas, Rosmira Rodríguez, and Marledis Mena. I am especially grateful to Narciso Ramos and Eustaquio Polo; La Negra, Isabelina, La Gorda, and La Tocayita; Carmen Rosa, Félix, and his family; as well as Edgardo Gómez, Jerónimo Martínez, Libia Correa, Ever Arias Correa, Elpidio Hurtado Quinto, Martín Morelo, and Mamerto. I was exceedingly fortunate to share my life with all the people who over the course of the last eighteen years have welcomed me into their homes and communities along the Atrato, Cacarica, Salaquí, Truandó, La Larga, Domingodó, and Curvaradó Rivers. To my dear *tambeadoras* in La Grande, Carlitos Mena, Elvis Paz; to Carlitos in Alto Yarumal for sharing his knowledge and gifts of *jaibana*; to Danielito for believing I could become an inheritor of his healing arts; and to all elders who have made rivers and forests into enchanted places. To all of those who are no longer in this world because of the violence that war and poverty have brought to their lives: my dearest friends Ives Palacios and Miguel López, without you I would have not become the kind of person I currently am. To Eberjo, Moyita, Conce, Ramona, Danae Mena, Erasmo, Josefina, Palomino, Primitiva, Calixto, Antenor, and Don Benja.

This book is the modest result of a tremendous effort, and although I am its author, I did not do it alone. This ethnography would have not come to light without the support, guidance, and teachings of my mentor, Eduardo Kohn. He showed me how to make of anthropological research an act of the finest and purest creation. His careful thoughtfulness has been a tremendous source of intellectual development, and I know his enjoyment of thought will continue informing my own career.

Several colleagues and friends engaged with different chapters of this work and provided crucial ideas for their improvement. I want to thank Mónica Cuéllar Gempeler and Doña Katty LeGrand, who channeled my ideas in the right direction. Gastón Gordillo, Sophie Chao, Amélie Ward, Cristina Yepez, Iván Vargas Roncancio, Pilar Riaño-Alcalá, Arturo Escobar, Colin Scott, Nicole Couture, Marisol de la Cadena, Camilo Gómez, Natalia Quiceno, Alejandro Camargo, Lina Pinto García, Diana Ojeda, Diana Pardo Pedraza, Claudia

Leal, Kristina Lyons, and Ann Farnsworth-Alvear all made the research and writing of this book a wonderful experience. Thanks also to the two anonymous reviewers: their thoughtful reading helped me polish my arguments.

I am deeply grateful to the inspiring scholars I met during my time at McGill, Concordia, and the University of British Columbia, particularly Lisa Stevenson, Kristin Norget, Ismael Vaccaro, Ronald Niezen, Alberto Sanchez, Daviken Studnicki-Gizbert, Carolyn Samuel, Wade Davis, Erin Baines, Kevin Gould, and Luis Carlos Sotelo. I hope I have done justice to the example they set. In Colombia I also benefited from the crucial support of Eduardo Restrepo, Margarita Chaves, Carlos Del Cairo, and Claudia Howald.

This book draws on research I first conducted while I was part of the Centro de Investigacion y Educación Popular (CINEP). My colleagues there gave me the value of melding compassionate listening and intellectual creativity. *Muchas gracias* to Eduardo Vega S.J., Natalia Segura, Carlos Ossa, Stellio Rolland, Luis Guillermo Guerrero, Fernán González S.J., Ingrid Bolívar, and Alejandro Ángulo S.J. The pursuit of my anthropological career and the conditions of academic writing would not have been possible without the faith given to my project by those anonymous people behind the granting of the federal and provincial fellowships I have enjoyed in Canada, particularly the Joseph-Armand Bombardier Canada Graduate Scholarship from the Social Sciences and Humanities Research Council of Canada (SSHRC-7672-0141-566), SSHRC Postdoctoral Fellowship (7562-0180-469), and the Bourse Postdoctorale du Fonds de Recherche du Québec—Société et Culture (FRQSC 2019-B3Z-255273).

Many people worked very hard to make my ideas intelligible: Patrick Quin, Marcela Guzman, Marina Murphy, Amelie Wong, Mona Marchand, and Esteban Alzate. A very special thank you to Jessica Little, who worked very hard on this, line by line.

Finally, *muchas gracias* to the women of my family for believing in me and for looking after me: La Mamá, my sisters Adrianita and Sandra, La Abuela Ana, and my tía Gloria. They gave me the opportunities they didn't have. And to my brother, whose absence still haunts us.

In the forests and rivers of Bajo Atrato, a multitude of abrasive presences now disrupt the proper rhythms of life and death. The spirits of those who were violently killed and whose bodies were not appropriately buried wander through the forest, as do wicked jaguars, drawn by the taste of human flesh. There are large logjams that resemble floating cemeteries of trees and prevent people from pursuing the very journeys that keep their rivers alive. It is not uncommon to encounter snakes capable of injecting into their victims' wounds a poison that pollutes the former villages and forests that warlords have transformed into oil-palm plantations, and it is known that the forest is peopled by evil beings who, after having been released by powerful shamans in their attempt to protect communities from the raids carried out by guerrilla and paramilitary armies, are now wreaking havoc, drowning people and devouring their noses and their fingers.

These are some of the wounds that irregular warfare has engraved upon the territories of Afro-Colombian, Emberá, and Wounaan peoples living in Bajo Atrato, a region located in Chocó, on the northwestern Colombian Pacific coast. Besides the most flagrant and immediate effects in terms of human rights violations and environmental degradation, war has also compromised the web of relations through which these peoples and myriad other-than-human sentient beings weave their lives together. War, as this book discusses, is seldom an exclusively human experience, and we must begin to take seriously the violence perpetrated against the animals, the spirits, and the other-than-human beings that forests and rivers harbor, as the communities of Bajo Atrato already do.

How to bear witness to, and be accountable for, forest and river ecologies running amok and causing damage that cannot be easily tackled with the language of human rights or environmental degradation? This book approaches the question through an ethnographic investigation into the violent transformations that war has produced in the relations that Afro-Colombian and Indigenous peoples weave with their territories, including the relations they cultivate with the other-than-human beings that make up forests and rivers. In our understanding of war and its afterlives in other-than-human worlds, what is the place that concepts such as human rights, trauma, reparation, and damage have? There is a form of violence perpetrated against Indigenous and Afro-Colombian territories that exceeds that which often is conceptualized as environmental damage (e.g., depletion of natural resources, pollution of ecosystems, transformation of land use, and loss of biodiversity). I call this violence *ecological* as it encompasses world-making relations between different kinds of sentient beings—including animals, spirits, rivers, and forests—that are all endowed with some degree of personhood and conscious intent. This ecological violence compels us to look attentively at other-than-human forms of suffering and at those worlds in which humans are not the only actors, worlds in which the allocation of events to either natural or cultural domains is no longer simple and neat. Who or what has been harmed, for instance, by the air strikes which infuriated the spirits that protect wild animals and who, following these attacks, decided to keep game inaccessible to people? Is this harm locatable in the world itself, or does it reside within the so-called cultural representations that certain peoples have forged about nature?

We must also consider the deaths of those who were never buried and whose pain, in the parlance of local communities, taints the land and thus accentuates people's struggles to have successful harvests. Do these deaths express a form of collective trauma, or do they go beyond that, transforming the very qualities of places? These types of harm force us to reconsider what constitutes justice and what the material grounds of reparation might be, particularly because these collective and intersubjective experiences of war challenge assumptions regarding selfhood, bodies, the elements of life, the distinctiveness of humans, and, of course, the possibilities of reparation, recovery, and the regaining of agency in contexts of blatant violence.

My aim is to move our understanding of violence, suffering, and justice out of the human rights framework and of modern multicultural dualisms (e.g., humans and the environment, subjects and objects, reality and beliefs) and to bring it into a broader web of human and other-than-human relations that are emerging from, and making possible, what communities in Bajo Atrato experience as a *living territory*. The spectacle that is so often associated with warfare (massacres, humanitarian crises, power dynamics among the actors involved) often receives more attention than its delayed and dispersed forms of devastation and how these affect ecologies emerging from human and other-than-human entanglements. These events through which this violence is made tangible have world-making power—that is, they induce encounters, reveal attachments, and create horizons of possibility. These events may sometimes echo the acts of annihilation carried out by irregular armies, but they might also at times align with the practices that Afro-Colombian and Indigenous peoples employ to foster life in their territories.

What I propose is a kind of epistemic shift regarding armed violence, one that enables us to see its destructive drives in terms of its world-making effects, for it is not only peoples and their cultures that are at stake when war strikes but also the cosmos itself. Without recasting violence as creative, it is important to see how war enters into the composition of *Bajoatrateño* territories in the guise of a twofold movement—destruction and production—that plays out in a specific manner in this region. To show this, I bring attention to the relational constitution of peoples and their surrounding worlds or, more precisely, between *Bajoatrateño* communities and what they conceptualize as their traditional territories, a notion that encompasses a physical setting as well as the emplaced practices through which humans and other-than-humans hang together in order to create a broader community of life and death. This co-constitution renders porous the divide between natural and cultural realms as two distinct ontological domains, a divide that is embedded in the legal system and that has an effect on the possibility of understanding the experiences of war and therefore on the possibility of redressing its damage.

Inspired by the resurgence of ontological, posthuman, and relational thinking in anthropology, and standing on the shoulders of thinkers who have shown the fallacy of abstracting humans from other forms of life, this book centers relationships of human and other-than-human entanglements in a context of war, describing a variety of socially interwoven relations in which the privileged role of humans as the only actors capable of generating, embodying, and making sense of violent actions is decentered. Such an approach takes into consideration that human interactions with other-than-humans are a condition of being and not a choice that one makes (Bingham 2006; Latour 2004), that worlds inhabitable by humans are always constituted in relation with different kinds of other-than-human Others (Haraway 2008; Tsing 2013), and that such a relationality creates particular connections that both demand and enable particular responses (de la Cadena 2015; Ogden, Hall, and Tanita 2013; Stengers 2005b). Although ontological anthropologies have been criticized for tending to reify ethnic and sociocultural identities (Ramos 2012; Turner 2009), exacerbating issues of incommensurability among peoples that embody different cultures (Graeber 2015; Ramos 2022), overinterpreting and decontextualizing concepts such as animacy, personhood, or agency

(Hornborg 2017), and overemphasizing Indigenous onto-epistemic concerns to the detriment of the political and socioeconomic problems that these peoples face (Bessire and Bond 2014; Todd 2016), in this book I rely on posthuman thinking while, at the same time, remaining attuned to the historical and political nature of Indigenous and Afro-Colombian experiences of place and violence. Posthuman and relational perspectives are particularly useful when thinking about justice in Indigenous and Afro-Colombian territories because they help blur the divides between the animate and the inanimate, subject and object, and beings and their environments—splits that have often characterized studies of war and its aftermath, particularly when it comes to Indigenous peoples. Relational, posthuman, and ontological approaches are also convenient for understanding the expressions of violence in these territories as well as the entangled nature of associations that people in Bajo Atrato forge with beings such as snakes, jaguars, rivers, spirits, and forests. The coming chapters describe how these associations between humans and other-than-human actors generate actions, create obligations, and provide logic to the vital practices through which *Bajoatrateño* communities foster life within their territories. Concretely, I ask this: what kind of justice is conceivable when armed violence results in an experience shared by multiple kinds of human and other-than-human beings? Can an understanding of war that extends beyond human losses and environmental damage establish the conditions for a form of politics that includes the diversity of beings that constitute a shared world? If so, what would this look like?

My work draws from Indigenous and Afro-Colombian philosophies, as well as from the practices of their social organizations to defend their lives in their traditional land. Inspired by their struggle to transform traditional ideas of politics, political representation, and governance in Colombia, as well as ideas of land ownership and property rights, I use Indigenous notions that debunk human exceptionality as compared to other living agents and delve into how these ideas might help us rethink the scope of justice. More specifically, I rely on *Bajoatrateño* onto-epistemologies that situate territory as something other than a physical enclosure and that have successfully pushed for the legal recognition of Indigenous territories as victims of the armed conflict. The remainder of this introduction examines local conceptions of territory, as well as a particular legal instrument that has been designed by the state and Indigenous peoples, and that aims to redress the damage that war has wrought upon these territories. But first a brief description of the ethnographic setting for my work.

A Frontier Zone

The scene occurs outside a nightclub situated in an exclusive neighborhood in Bogotá, the capital of Colombia. It took place some weeks before I traveled to Bajo Atrato in 2015, and it later became a viral video. An angry and visibly drunk man argues with two policemen. They had been called because the man in question was threatening to come to blows with a bar employee. The man taunts the police officers and pushes them repeatedly while they remain unusually stoic and unmoving. Then, the defiant man stands in front of one of the police officers, face-to-face, and slaps him. "Don't you know who I am?" he cries. The man slaps the policeman again. "I'm President Gaviria's nephew. If I make a call and talk to the General, you will be working in Chocó." The man's accent and the family ties he claims to have with a former president reveal his socioeconomic status. Perhaps the policemen really fear the loss of their jobs, for they decide not to react to the abuse. In a country where power is still associated with lineage and skin color, the family name of this haughty individual assures him privileged treatment before the law, or at least that is what both the policemen and this young upstart believe. The drunk man continues to utter his insults and threats while the submissive officers just ask him to calm down. But, as I prepared for my departure to Chocó, what really upset me was the fact that, despite being one of the most biodiverse places on Earth and a cradle of peerless cultural wealth, going to this region is considered a severe punishment. "I will send you to Chocó," declares the arriviste several times. The threats uttered by this man (who turned out to be a liar, for former president Gaviria denied any relationship with him) bring to mind the designation of some regions of the world as places of exile and punishment for those who refused to recognize authority. The British imprisoned Napoleon on Saint Helena, a volcanic tropical island in the middle of the Atlantic Ocean; the French did the same with their undesirable political adversaries on L'île du Diable during the nineteenth and twentieth centuries; Siberia and its infamous gulags were instruments of political repression during the Stalinist era.

The very idea that Chocó might be an adequate location to serve a prison sentence points to the role that this region occupies in the Colombian social and political imagination: a dreadful place to be avoided at all costs. One hundred years before this incident, a local official described Chocó as a "miserable" and "stunted" place "inhabited by wretched people who live far from God or the Law" (quoted in Leal 2018, 172). These ideas are stubbornly persistent, as evidenced by the kinds of news that circulated during the week this man hurled his curses. Several newspapers documented the Department of Chocó's high infant-mortality rates: between January and March 2015, more than twenty children died from diarrhea and malnutrition (*Espectador* 2015). It was no coincidence that, subsequent to the video, the United Nations Office for the Coordination of Humanitarian Affairs reported that at least 655 Indigenous and Afro-Colombian peasants were expelled from their land as a result of constant skirmishes between paramilitary and guerrilla armies (*Tiempo* 2015). Although it is true that violence and malnutrition are part of daily life in Chocó, the way in which these stories are reported—through the threats of an unscrupulous man, or news naturalizing poverty and violence rather than identifying their root causes—helps us understand what makes this region, according to non-*Chocoano* people, an unviable location. Chocó seems to possess all the attributes that city people consider the opposite of a desirable nation: backwardness, isolation, poverty, disease, violence (Serje 2005). These characteristics are constantly overemphasized by an elite class of wealthy entrepreneurs and corrupt politicians who see the region as a place to be exploited and depleted rather than cherished; as a former deputy of the Provincial Assembly of the Department of Antioquia (Chocó's affluent neighbor) declared, "Investing money in Chocó is like applying perfume to crap" (*Colombiano* 2012). It is in Chocó, more concretely in the region of Bajo Atrato, where my ethnography takes place.

Colombia comprises thirty-two administrative and political divisions called departments, which can be understood as equivalent to US states or Canadian provinces. Chocó is one of these departments and one of sharp contrasts indeed. Alongside accounts depicting the exuberance of its tropical rain forests, there are abundant portrayals of poverty, violence, and corruption. For instance, Chocó is one of the world's most important biodiversity hot spots and home of numerous endemic life-forms (Gentry 1986; Groombridge and Jenkins 2002; Mittermeier et al. 2005; Proyecto Biopacífico 1998; Rangel 2015), as well as the poorest department in the country. According to various socioeconomic indicators elaborated by the Colombian National Administrative Department of Statistics (DANE), 80 percent of its population lives on much less than a dollar a day; 75 percent of the people, mostly in rural areas, lack access to basic services such as safe drinking water, sanitation facilities, and schools; its infant mortality rate of 43 per 1,000 is three times higher than the national average (DANE 2018).

Chocó has been considered, historically, a frontier zone: a volatile, lawless place of unrestrained nature (Appelbaum 2016; Roldán 1998; Serje 2005). As early as the second half of the sixteenth century, Spaniards knew about the existence of alluvial gold deposits along the streams of the upper San Juan and Atrato River basins. For the exploitation of said deposits, Spanish mine owners relied, initially, on the forced labor of Indigenous populations and then of enslaved African peoples. However, attempts at colonization encountered several obstacles. The Emberá, Wounaan, and Kuna Indigenous populations furiously resisted the Spanish presence and, even in the cases when they agreed to establish commercial relations with the newcomers, never agreed to relocate to the kind of urban settlements (*reducciones*) that the Crown wanted to impose to enable evangelization, collection of taxes, and tribute (Leal 2018; P. Vargas 1993; Werner 2000). Geographical isolation and lack of transportation routes also proved to be challenges to the Spaniards, for Chocó is covered with dense tropical forests.

Besides the military resistance of the Kuna, Wounaan, and Emberá peoples, other factors, such as their high mortality rates, their patterns of dispersed settlement, and official mandates forbidding certain kinds of coerced labor of Indigenous populations, obliged the Spanish Crown, at the beginning of the eighteenth century, to import African slave labor to pan the streams for gold. The presence of these enslaved peoples increased exponentially in only a few decades: from six hundred slaves in 1704 to two thousand in 1724 and to more than seven thousand in 1782 (Sharp 1976, 21). Thereafter, official censuses show a significant decrease of this population, and although disease was one of the reasons, scholars (Leal 2018; Sharp 1976; Williams 2005) agree that manumission and marronage were the predominant factors. Before 1851, when slavery was legally abolished in Colombia, slaves could purchase their freedom by negotiating with their masters for a price. In Chocó the practice was quite common, for enslaved peoples were allowed to work independently in the mines. In 1782, for example, an official census noted almost four thousand of this kind of *libres* (freedmen) (Sharp 1976, 22). Slave runaways, for their part, established a group of maroon settlements along the headwaters of the different river basins, away from the colonial gaze, where they formed all sorts of economic, ritual, and kinship alliances with Indigenous peoples.

Unlike other colonial mining centers in the Americas, Chocó was not really settled by European descendants. Throughout the colonial period there was not a single Spanish settlement large enough to be considered a city, so the Crown never appointed a mayor or a town council in this region. The few settlements that did exist were scattered far apart, and they looked more like mining camps or commercial warehouses than like centers from whence to launch a permanent colonial dominion (Sharp 1976, 14). As late as 1782, one of the *visitadores*, or Spanish royal inspectors, noted during his visit to Chocó that there were only eight Catholic priests serving a population of about twenty thousand inhabitants (1976, 130), something that, in his eyes, jeopardized not only the conversion of Indigenous and enslaved populations but also the very attempt to civilize these territories.

In regard to the permanence of peoples of African descent in Chocó, historians have argued that the existence of immense forests, wetlands, and rivers, along with the limited presence of colonial authorities and settlements, and the existence of an extractive economy heavily dependent on the commodification of natural resources such as gold, platinum, rubber, and vegetable ivory, contributed to the emergence of a "rainforest peasantry" (Leal 2018, 12; Offen 2018)—that is, a post-abolition Black society that, unlike others in the colonial Americas, attained high levels of autonomy. The capacity of these Afro descendant communities to decide how to use "their bodies, their time, and the spaces they lived in without having to follow orders" (Leal 2018, 12) hinged to a large extent upon the exchanges they forged with Emberá and Wounaan Indigenous peoples (Losonczy 2006a) and upon the knowledge they accumulated about forests, soils, rivers, and wetlands. This in turn allowed these communities to develop their own subsistence practices in crop cultivation, fishing, hunting, and timber harvesting.

Chocó is known today as the Afro-Colombian department, although *resguardos* (communal territories of Indigenous peoples) constitute almost 29 percent of this department's land area (Instituto Colombiano de Cultura Hispánica 1992). It is inhabited by about 550,000 people, 13 percent of them belonging to Indigenous communities, whereas 81 percent are Afro-Colombians (DANE 2010). Geographically speaking, it is important to note that although Chocó is one of the four departments that make up the Colombian Pacific coast (the others are Nariño, Cauca, and Valle del Cauca), its most important river and artery, the imposing Atrato River, does not belong to the Pacific basin but runs through the department from south to north, disemboguing into the Caribbean Sea at the Gulf of Urabá (see map Intro.1).* The lower or northernmost course of this river is what I refer to as Bajo Atrato, a region close to where the isthmus of Panama and the South American continent connect. Characterized by the presence of several rivers, swamps, tropical forests, and freshwater swamp forests, Bajo Atrato comprises three large *municipios* or counties (Belén de Bajirá, Carmen del Darién, and Riosucio) and

---

* Valle del Cauca, Cauca, and Nariño comprise areas of the lowland Pacific Coast but also major areas of interior highlands with primarily mestizo populations. Chocó is the only entirely lowland, tropical-forested, majority Afro-Colombian coastal department.

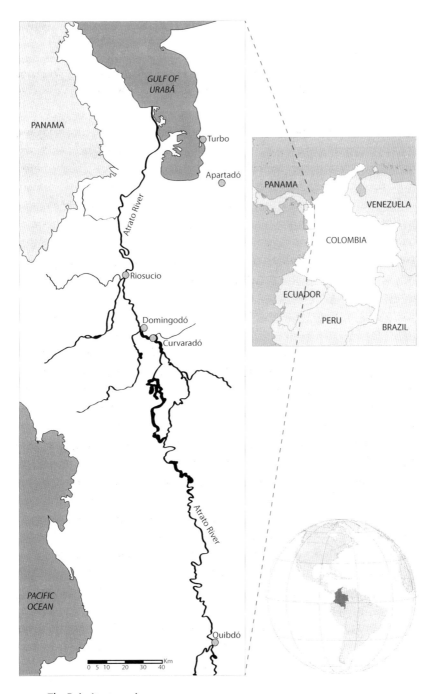

MAP I.1. **The Bajo Atrato region.**

eight different river basins (Cacarica, La Larga-Tumaradó, Salaquí, Truandó, Pedeguita-Mancilla, Domingodó, Curvaradó, and Jiguamiandó). It is along these rivers and their tributaries, which constitute the main transportation routes, that Afro-Colombian, Emberá, and Wounaan villages are located.

In Bajo Atrato, like in most of the Pacific region, both Indigenous and Afro-Colombian communities legally enjoy collective land tenure as part of their *resguardos* (Indigenous reserves) and *territorios colectivos* (collective territories of Black communities). This land is imprescriptible (it cannot be taken away), inalienable (it cannot be transferred), and nonseizable (it cannot be sold to repay creditors), which are three key features that reinforce collective forms of use, enable its protection and management, and guarantee intergenerational permanency. In Bajo Atrato alone, the collective lands belonging to Afro-Colombian communities comprise more than 6,400 square kilometers (4,000 square miles), an area as large as the territory claimed by the State of Palestine. This region is also characterized by the presence of large communities of mestizo peasants or *chilapos*, a local term used to describe the peasant population that migrated from the Sinú River region, in the Department of Córdoba, to the greater Urabá region during the first half of the twentieth century and that in Bajo Atrato settled principally along the Salaquí and Curvaradó Rivers (Ruiz-Serna 2006; Villa 2013). The settlements of these mestizo peasants have been incorporated into the collective territories granted to the Afro-Colombian rural populations, which means that these mestizo peasants are members of *consejos comunitarios* or community councils, local administrative bodies that watch over the protection of the rights of collective property and regulate social relationships according to customary rules. Because *chilapos* in Bajo Atrato enjoy collective land tenure and its concomitant territorial and cultural rights, I do not disaggregate these communities when I refer to Afro-Colombian territories. In recent years the name Bajo Atrato has been gaining popularity in both specialized literature and media because the historical, economic, and social processes of this particular region differ from those of the rest of Urabá, an area mainly located in the affluent department of Antioquia. By speaking of Bajo Atrato instead of Urabá Chocoano, local grassroots organizations also seek to characterize this region as an ethnic territory: an existential place where Indigenous and Afro-Colombian communities have set in motion alternative models of society and different ways of being that have been legally recognized by the Colombian state as Indigenous reserves and collective lands of Black communities. In legal terms these reserves and collective lands are what Indigenous and Afro-Colombian communities refer to as their territory.

The Land Is Not the Territory

Territory is a complex concept, the meaning of which depends on the sociopolitical and cultural contexts in which it is used. One way of grasping its intricacies is to consider the way that territory is conceived of by the Colombian Constitution: a group-differentiated right protected by law. Colombian jurisprudence has made the right to territory the cornerstone of the protection of Indigenous and Afro-Colombian peoples. According to the Constitutional Court, the supreme guardian of the national Constitution, territory is "the material possibility for ethnic groups to exercise their rights to cultural identity and autonomy, insofar as this is the physical space in which their culture can survive" (Corte Constitucional de Colombia, Sentencia T-380–1993, §12). Understood as "material possibility" or "physical space," territory evokes the conceptual elements of a substantialist ontology: it comprises the assortment of places that a given community inhabits and renders socially meaningful, as well as the natural resources the community appropriates for its livelihood. But as environmental and economic anthropologists have long made apparent (Douglas and Isherwood 1979; Halperin 1994; Leal and Restrepo 2003; Wilk 1996; Wilk and Cligget 2007), this appropriation is a historical and cultural process, embedded in the wider array of practices and institutions that make up a society. This means that even in its very material or substantial dimension, territory and what is usually conceptualized as natural resources are not given but constructed: they do not precede the set of social relations and cultural values that render them meaningful.

Since the early 1980s, several Afro-Colombian organizations have successfully espoused a definition of territory that emphasizes the economic and material resources needed to secure social reproduction. Initially, these organizations identified themselves as peasant movements and demanded that the government halt the predatory activities of several timber companies that were depleting forests in Chocó (ACIA 2002; Asher 2009; Escobar 2008; Perea 2012). In Bajo Atrato, such grassroots organizations called into question the extractivist economic models fostered by national authorities, making land claims and conceiving of strategies for securing land tenure under a premise other than that of individual private property, mainly because private ownership was at odds with the customary use of what Afro-Colombian communities have historically considered to be communal forests (E. Restrepo 2013). Although the government considered this land idle and regional environmental authorities were granting it to private timber companies (Leal and Restrepo 2003), *Chocoano* organizations made a twofold demand: legal recognition of the lands that Afro-Colombian communities had been historically occupying and using, on one hand, and the implementation of sustainable development policies, on the other. Implicit in these demands was an alternative notion of territory as a place where communities had been developing unique local economic practices that challenged the rapacious models which were fostered by the forestry industry and supported by national governments.

Another definition of territory emerged in the early 1990s, a period marked by the rise of biodiversity conservation in Chocó through Proyecto Biopacífico (PBP). This was originally a million-dollar initiative founded by the World Bank as part of the agreements reached in 1992 during the Earth Summit. The PBP was initially conceived of within a conventional scientific framework for environmental conservation and sustainable use of the region's biological resources (Escobar 1997). However, during its implementation and following tense negotiations with Afro-Colombian and Indigenous activists, the PBP had to reformulate its initial goals and take into consideration local forms of knowledge and cultural practices as legitimate sources of biological conservation (Escobar 2008). For local organizations, biodiversity could not be conceived of, and even less managed, as distinct from the defense and promotion of traditional production systems, food security, and cultural practices regarding nature. Within this context, the equation Biodiversity = Territory + Culture was first enunciated (Escobar 1997). Based on the tenet that the knowledges, values, and experiences historically cultivated by Indigenous and Afro-Colombian peoples are what have favored the very existence of the diverse forms of life that the international community wanted to protect with their environmental projects, this alternative conceptualization dethroned scientific knowledge as the ultimate guide when tackling pressing ecological problems. From the perspective of local social movements, even the most tangible aspects of biodiversity (ecosystems, species) had to be understood in tandem with the history of the resistance of Indigenous and Afro-Colombian communities and with their struggles to maintain and develop life projects distinct from those of the larger surrounding society (ACIA 2002; Proyecto Biopacífico 1998). From this perspective, territory and all its variety of life-forms emerge as the outcome of local environmental attitudes that were nested in, and favored by, people's historical and cultural practices.

The production of the new Constitution of 1991 could be considered the pinnacle of the struggle for territory and environmental conservation because the nation recognized itself as a multiethnic and multicultural society for the first time. Accordingly, different measures for the protection of ethnocultural minorities were set into motion, including Law 70 of Colombia (1993), which granted collective land tenure to the Afro-Colombian communities inhabiting the Pacific basin. These lands were hitherto considered *baldías*: vacant, barren, or idle lands without owners. Some scholars (Asher 2009; Pardo and Álvarez 2001; E. Restrepo 2013; Ruiz-Serna 2006) have pointed out that, besides the recognition of rights to lands historically occupied by Black rural communities, the granting of these lands contained a heavily prescriptive component, for the law assigned to this collective property "an inherent ecological function," meaning that land grantees were required to "develop conservation and management practices" compatible with the principles of environmental protection and sustainable development (Law 70 of Colombia (1993), Art. 6). In political terms the constitutional reform led to official recognition of these communities as ethnic groups, which means that they collectively became subjects with special rights, including that of maintaining their culture and securing their economic and social development. With their land and rivers protected by law and with their cultural ancestry dignified by the state, the land traditionally inhabited by Afro-Colombian communities became an ethnic territory—that is to say, the quintessential component of their collective identities and the focus of their political actions for the defense of their particular modes of being. Within this context, in the late 1990s and after, peasant movements from Chocó turned into ethnic organizations, and former struggles over land tenure and control of natural resources gave way to demands for territorial rights. The Constitution of 1991 allowed Afro-Colombian communities to gain political, legal, and cultural visibility, and it has led *Chocoano* social movements to articulate further political demands such as autonomy and self-determination in the attempt to strengthen their authority in matters of decision making regarding land and resource use.

The recognition of these new ethnic identities and cultural rights did not, however, have an immediate impact in Bajo Atrato, for the legal multicultural turn coincided with the escalation of violence against Afro-Colombian communities in a dramatic way. Some scholars (Alves and Costa Vargas 2017; Wade 2016) have argued that there was a sort of sinister agenda to displace, terrorize, and murder Afro-Colombian rural peoples to prevent these communities from enjoying any newly acquired rights. Before the titling process through which communities legally delimited their collective lands could even begin in Bajo Atrato, the region became a major theater of war. The fact that violence erupted at this juncture, effectively preventing the titling process from occurring, was certainly not a coincidence. In 1997 thousands of families were forcibly banished from their lands by means of threats, forced disappearances, and assassinations carried out by military, paramilitary, and guerrilla armies. During the time that *Bajoatrateño* communities were demanding that the state support the return to their land, the allocation of legal titles became a crucial point in the agenda of local organizations: having these titles meant securing a safe return to their homelands. Armed conflict and forced displacement were threatening not only the newly gained cultural rights but also the very lives of these communities. In such a context the defense of territory overlaps with the defense of basic human rights. This confluence becomes evident in the motto of the regional Afro-Colombian organization I worked with, ASCOBA (Association of Community Councils of Bajo Atrato). It was established in 2003 (see figure I.1), shortly after most communities returned to their lands, assuming as its principal task "the defense of life in our territory." Territory emerges then not just as a socially meaningful place invested with specific cultural values but also as a place central to people's existence. As a leader recently stated in relation to the presence of agro-industry and mining corporations in ancestral territories, "Territory is our life and life is not for sale. [Our interest is] to defend the right to be in these places because that is what makes us to be who we are" (quoted in Alves 2019, 662). In this sense the political project of *Bajoatrateño* communities is articulated around the defense of their territories, which are conceived of as the only setting in which their collective identities can fully flourish. ASCOBA's motto also exemplifies the transition that local organizations made from a struggle based on class identity for the use and allocation of natural resources—before the reforms of 1991, grassroots organizations identified themselves as peasant organizations—to an identity based on ethnicity in which at stake is the protection of their existential places: Afro-Colombian organizations defending their traditional territories.

I first arrived in Bajo Atrato at the juncture of the humanitarian crisis that followed the forced displacement. It was 2003, and I was working with CINEP (Centre for Research and Popular Education), a nonprofit foundation whose mission was to support local grassroots organizations, strengthening their leadership, documenting serious violations of human rights, and accompanying the communities that were progressively returning to their land. For almost four years I lived in Bajo Atrato and had the privilege of working hand in hand with several leaders, traveling with them along all the river basins in order to design what ASCOBA then called an "ethno-development plan": a charter depicting the main aspects of economic and social development based on the preservation and strengthening of the unique lifestyles embodied by these peoples. After realizing that local ideas of development

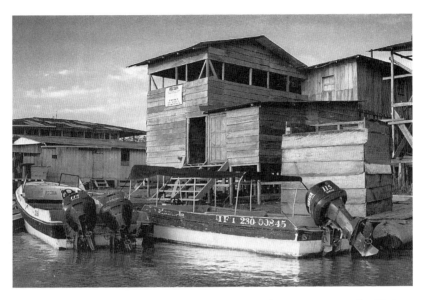

FIGURE I.1. Former headquarters of ASCOBA (Association of Community Councils of Bajo Atrato), located on the banks of the Atrato River in Riosucio. Photo by author.

emphasized a notion of living well that tied humans into wider living networks, and having witnessed multiple instances of violence that extended to the animals, plants, and other sentient beings that inhabit rivers and forests, I decided to stop my work there, let these beings make their way in my thought, and find the conceptual tools (mainly pursuing graduate studies) to better learn to listen to and account for a form of suffering embedded in a larger context that was not necessarily human. This book brings that effort to fruition and is the result of my years of work as a human rights organizer and the more than twenty-four months of fieldwork I carried out between 2009 and 2019. As a Colombian, I have anchored to this region my dreams of a country where the rough and crooked places shaped by war will be made serene and balanced. The ties I have woven with Bajo Atrato are also organic. During a trip I took in 2020, just before the COVID-19 outbreak, my wife and I, along with some *Bajoatrateño* friends and relatives, buried the umbilical cord of my newborn daughter under the roots of an *árbol de pan* tree at the shores of the Salaquí River. That ritual, aimed to strengthen her body, attune her forming self to the sylvan forces of the region, and root her history to that of her ancestors, epitomized the long process of mutual care between me and the *Bajoatrateño* territory. Although I was not born there, I have lived experiences and dreams that make me kin with this territory, while it has shown me its own kindness from the first moment I set my feet there, expanding my thought and gifting me with the health, will, and predilection to describe what the reader will find in the following pages.

A Tapestry of Human and Other-Than-Human Entanglements

At the heart of collective identity as an "existential space of self-reference" (Escobar 2008, 53), territory, as we can now see, is a crucial element of the political struggles around the defense of ethnic identities and cultural rights. It represents different but interconnected objectives: the securing of the livelihood of local communities, the maintenance of traditional and sustainable economic practices, the political projects of regional social movements, the defense of collective rights, the development of proper forms of governability, the local experience of place, and a deep sense of belonging. Thus, what is at stake when defending territory is an alternative model of society and life, a form of being that is often at odds with the values embodied by certain modern institutions and practices. This is why for local communities, Bajo Atrato constitutes not only a territory of life but also a living territory. Let me explain this in more detail. In 2005, on the verge of a crucial decision from the state regarding ownership rights over the lands that oil-palm companies had violently seized from the titled collective territories, leaders from ASCOBA and one of my mentors—a priest and local intellectual whose social commitment draws from the theology of liberation—delineated some key principles about territory and its meanings:

> Territory is the space appropriated for our physical, social, and cultural production. It is the physical space, the plants and the animals; it is the space we name, use, walk, and travel. It is the way villages and households are placed, the economy, our ways of living and working, the days for cultural and religious celebrations, the social relationships, our traditional authorities, and our worldview. All these actions unfold in the space and they create territoriality, which[,] in turn, helps build the territory. . . . The territory is a space to produce life and culture, it reflects our worldview. In the fields we work, in the social and family relations we keep, in the symbolic aspects of our thinking, the territory is materialized. . . . Territory is not only land because it extends far beyond the physical space granted by the law. (Valencia 2005, 15–20)

I would like to emphasize three aspects of this beautiful and powerful definition. First, social practices and relationships (e.g., "ways of working," "cultural and religious celebrations," "traditional authorities," and "social and family relations") are not only developed in the territory but also contribute to the creation of the territory. Second, territory and communities are mutually linked and reciprocally constituted: many practices express the attributes of particular places, and the territory itself reflects the qualities of its inhabitants ("in the fields we work, in the social and family relations we keep, in the symbolic aspects of our thinking, the territory is materialized"). Third, territory cannot be understood as abstracted from the experience of being and belonging to an Afro-Colombian or an Indigenous rural community ("it is the space we name, use, walk, and travel"). This sophisticated conceptualization underscores the way that territory participates essentially and not just contingently in the generation of a collective sense of being, how it provides a particular placement to social experiences, and, most importantly, how territory does not always precede the relations and practices that take place there but, instead, is what results from these relations and practices. In other words, the definition applies a relational approach: territory is enacted and experienced rather than provided, and it emerges as such by virtue of people's practices, while those practices are in turn affected by the territory itself. This definition of territory does not just imply some sort of intimate interconnectedness of people and their places but also comprises the conditions through which both territory and communities come into existence.

Hence, what communities in Bajo Atrato experience as their traditional territories are in fact a heterogeneous cluster of relationships: sentient landscapes, emplaced experiences, local knowledges, the quality of places, and the characteristics of their human and other-than-human inhabitants. In this sense territory might also be conceived of as the possibilities of being and becoming in a shared, living place. This includes the practices of care, reciprocity, or even animosity that people maintain with beings such as *avichuchos* (bugs), trees, spirits, soils, crops, mines, ancestors, the rain; places like villages, gardens, *plataneras*, swidden plots, and the wilderness; the knowledge guiding decisions about what, where, and when to plant; the technique behind the *trasmallos*, fishing nets whose threads and shape fit the geometry and movements of fish; ritual practices such as the burial of newborns' umbilical cords; the places where the afterbirth rests; the understanding of diseases, their treatment, and the summoning of forest spirits that enhance shamanic powers; the culinary and medicinal herbs cultivated by women in their *azoteas*, raised-bed gardens made of decayed dugout canoes; the funerary rites and the *alabaos*, songs that appease the souls of the deceased; when children swim or women do laundry in the river; when leaders meet to discuss their response to the implementation of neoliberal policies promoted by both private companies and the state; celebrations to La Vírgen del Carmén and the *bundes*, dancing processions performed in the wee hours to the rhythm of drums that used to be made of peccary skin. These practices, these ways of living, are not just embedded in the territory: they also act upon it and contribute to its creation. In other words, territory does not merely serve as a setting for the modes of being that people create in close proximity to forests and rivers. Instead, territory is what emerges from these relations; it is what renders possible the specific manner in which Afro-Colombian and Indigenous communities exist in the world.

In order to better understand the co-constitution of people and their territories, I build on the aforementioned tenets delineated by Afro-Colombian intellectuals and draw from streams of philosophical and anthropological thought that stress the ontological preeminence of relations and practices over ontologically derivative entities and substances (see, for instance, Barad 2003; Deleuze and Guattari [1980] 2004; Ingold 2000; Latour 1999; Mol 2002; Rose 1992; Tsing 2013; Vilaça 2005; Viveiros de Castro 1998; Wildman 2010). However, this co-constitution needs to be explored beyond the human aspects of the socio-material world (Kohn 2013) and must include a wider assemblage of beings that also participate in the generation of sociality in *Bajoatrateño* territories. Here the word *assemblage* refers not so much to a collection of beings as to a socio-material ordering of entities connected together to form a new whole (Blaser 2013a; Latour 2004). In an assemblage the properties of the collectivity exceed the properties of its constitutive elements. Another way of putting this is that the constituents of an assemblage partake in relational and dynamic associations, and they do so in such a way that what comes out of these relations actually exceeds the properties of the elements when individually considered (Ogden, Hall, and Tanita 2013). Along these lines, I see that the constantly emergent associations between human and other-than-human entities contribute to bringing the territory into existence, which is another way of saying that in Bajo Atrato to live is always to live with other-than-human others and that territory is always in the making (Escobar 2016): it is the outcome of intimate but asymmetrical relations between heterogeneous entities (Ingold 2011; Kohn 2007; Latour 2005). In this sense territory can be understood as the creation and flourishing of emplaced relations between human and other-than-human beings. The concept of territory also entails that these assemblages of beings do not occur in the abstract but always in a particular place and under specific sociohistorical conditions. Territory, to expand the terms of relational thinking, might be conceived of as a sort of emergent property: it arises out of the contingent relations that human and other-than-human beings establish in particular places, and these relations do not just depend on the territory to exist but constitute the building blocks of what a territory comes to be.

Roughly speaking, *emergence* refers to the relational effects of a given assemblage: an emergent property is what arises out of the specific relations maintained by the constituents of an assemblage (Georgiou 2003; Mitchell 2012). What results from these relations is not reducible to the elements of the assemblage, which means that when the beings that make up an assemblage are taken independently or separately, they do not have the properties the assemblage has. Now, when they emerge as such, assemblages establish their own territories. "Territories" is how Gilles Deleuze and Félix Guattari ([1980] 2004) describe the sets of emplaced processes through which the entities that make up a given assemblage meet, organize, and stay together. Therefore, territory is not given but constituted; it is a force holding things together rather than a substance or a setting. Territory, in other words, is what results from a particular ordering. In this ordering, Deleuze and Guattari argue, it is possible to track processes of deterritorialization and reterritorialization: the breaking of conditions or habits that favor the organization of assemblages and the formation of new conditions or habits to bring together said assemblages. In this fashion war becomes a force, a powerful one indeed, capable of bringing about processes of deterritorialization and reterritorialization, which produce different versions of territory, some of which might be at odds with those other versions that Indigenous and Afro-Colombian communities consider estimable and rightful.

When territory is conceived of in relational terms, it becomes apparent that the existence of the myriad entities with which people relate cannot be reduced to a stream of transcendent materialities or substances. But the opposite—that those entities exist only in terms of the relations they sustain with humans—is not true either because this would simply deny that entities such as forests, rivers, and even spirits possess some kind of ontological core that cannot be exhausted by their relations. Rather than stressing a type of subjective or anthropocentric idealism, the relational approach I adopt underscores that relations between entities are ontologically more important than, but not necessarily prior to, the entities themselves (Wildman 2010). In the context of war this simply means that the transformation of conditions engendering human and other-than-human relations creates new kinds of territorialities—and even new kinds of entities. Another way of understanding the relational features of territory is by noticing that certain beings are rendered possible by virtue of the particular relations or ecologies that nurture their emergence. This means that in *Bajoatrateño* territories, beings, their environments, and their relations constitute one another's conditions for existence (Ingold 2011). When thinking about justice, the nature of these entangled associations renders insufficient the dominant legal system's continued compartmentalization of human rights violations, environmental harm, desecrations, damage to cultural property, and the like. This means, as this book shows, that the effects of armed conflict cannot be framed within an *either-or* structure (de la Cadena 2015) but that they are always hybrid and multiple.

The Suffering of Territory

In Bajo Atrato, some elders claim that the continuous presence of armed soldiers has frightened away the *encantos*, the enchanted creatures that used to live in the forests of this region. Indigenous leaders of the Emberá-Katío communities from the Alto Andágueda in Chocó report the risk to their food sovereignty caused by air strikes launched by the Colombian Air Force: the bombs dropped during these attacks allegedly infuriated the *jaïs*, spirits that protect certain game animals, to the point that these spirits decided to keep agoutis (*Cuniculus paca*) inaccessible to people (J. L. Quiroga, personal communication, Bogotá, August 2015). In the San Juan River region, also located in Chocó, Indigenous Wounaan leaders say that battles between guerrillas and paramilitary armies have displeased Êwandam, the creator of people, who is no longer capable of distinguishing between those who wage war and those who do not. As a result, no new heralds of this divinity have been born in the last twenty years, meaning that the community now lacks traditional healers capable of communicating with godly forces (*Espectador* 2017a). An Indigenous Wiwa leader from the Sierra Nevada of Santa Marta, in the North of Colombia, says that the presence of armed groups has abused and butchered their sacred territories: "Because of the violence, our spiritual fathers who live in the water, the trees, the plants, and the rocks cannot be felt as much as before" (CNMH 2015). These examples demonstrate that, for some Indigenous and Afro-Colombian communities, the experiences of war are not restricted to the damage caused to people but that war's consequences are also engraved on their territories and the myriad beings that cocreate them, in a way that the wounded lives of humans and other-than-human beings cannot be understood solely in terms of human rights. Accordingly, an understanding of war in these territories can hardly be attained without taking into consideration the damage that violence has provoked in the web of emplaced relationships these peoples weave with wider communities of life in which humans are not the only actors.

Given these far-reaching effects of war, which cause forests and rivers to run amok, we need to refine our understanding of justice and cultivate new forms of responsibility and accountability. By this I mean we need new ways to respond to (Haraway 2008) and to account for (Barad 2011) the relational worlds that human and other-than-human existences generate. In order to begin to imagine what this other form of justice might look like, this ethnography explores some of the overwhelming latent effects that violence produces in the manifold beings and relations that constitute *Bajoatrateño* territories. Attending to beings such as spirits provoking havoc or rivers that are being prevented from flowing properly, I adopt a relational perspective that seeks to understand the intersections among war, ecologies made of human and other-than-human entanglements, and Indigenous ontologies. This book is then my humble response to the challenges that Indigenous and Afro-Colombian communities have presented in their insistent call for the construction of a more capacious kind of justice in their traditional territories, which is a concern that Indigenous organizations successfully addressed when they managed to forge a series of laws with the state for assistance, reparation, and restitution of their rights as victims of war. In particular, the Decree-Law 4633 of 2011, also known as the Victims' Law for Indigenous [Peoples], incorporates the notion that their territories should also be considered victims of armed conflict: "The territory, understood as a living entity and foundation of identity and harmony, in accordance with the very cosmovision of the Indigenous peoples and by virtue of the special and collective link that they hold with it, suffers a damage when it is violated or desecrated by the internal armed conflict and its underlying and related factors" (Congreso de Colombia, Decreto-Ley 4633, Art. 45).

The raison d'être of the recognition of the territory as victim is based on several interconnected facts: the existence of a special legal regime for collective land ownership; territory has a fundamental importance for the physical existence, cultural survival, and autonomous development of Indigenous and Afro-Colombian peoples; armed conflict has hit these peoples disproportionately and in ways that require different measures of rectification than those the government provides to other kinds of victims; and the presence, in the parlance of the law, of a "special spiritual relationship . . . that indigenous peoples have with their territory" (Art. 8). However, it is important to point out that if this law seems to express a certain sensitivity on the part of the legal system, it is because of the unflagging efforts of Indigenous organizations that contested the initial scope that the government meant to give to the Victims' Law—namely, that the measures of attention to Indigenous and Afro-Colombian peoples would be the same as those applied to victims from the rest of society.

From a certain perspective, the recognition of territory as a victim might be considered a kind of legal fiction: a proposition or a "technique of make-believe" (Moglen 1990) through which certain facts are assumed or created in order to apply a legal rule. The classical example of a legal fiction is the way in which corporations are treated as persons by many nations' laws in order to affirm that they have the same legal rights and responsibilities a natural person has. In the Colombian case, it appears that the Victims' Law establishes the territory as a victim in order to advance public policy and preserve the territorial rights of Indigenous peoples. This seems to be achieved by enforcing respect for both the previously recognized collective land rights and the cultural values that these communities attach to their territories. Yet, I argue, conferring statutory personhood on Indigenous territories is something that exceeds traditional multicultural arrangements (e.g., the protection of the worldviews associated with those peoples affected by war), particularly as it takes into account the lively relationalities of people, places, and other-than-human beings that have been compromised by war. If one takes, for example, the harm experienced by masters of game animals, *encantos*, and the spiritual guardians of trees and rocks, the recognition of territory as a victim demands that we question modern practices regarding justice and reparations, for what becomes a matter of concern is not mainly cultural rights (including the right to use and manage lands) but the set of practices through which these peoples share life with a set of beings whose natures transcend some modern divides such as animate and inanimate, sacred and secular, or *bios* and *geos*. Put differently, the idea that territory should also be considered a victim of war renders possible not just a series of actions for the protection of particular cultural frameworks but also, more importantly, for the recognition of diverse groups of beings and emplaced practices whose importance transcends what modern ontology usually relegates to the religious sphere.

To honor the complexities that Indigenous and Afro-Colombian peoples bring to the fore requires a form of ethnographic attention that recognizes that the harm inflicted upon the territory is not just damage to their worldviews. Rather, such harm is in fact an experience related to the very nature of war and its impacts upon the world. This kind of ethnographic attention is different from what, for instance, political ecology or cultural politics might offer in their interpretation of the Victims' Law. For example, from a cultural politics perspective, the inclusion of the territory as a victim can be understood as the recognition made by a multicultural state of the variety of worldviews embodied by Indigenous peoples. From that viewpoint, one would feel tempted to acknowledge the important advances of Colombian legislation and to interpret said inclusion as an achievement of Indigenous organizations in the recognition of their territorial rights. Indeed, the framework of cultural politics would lead to praise for the way that Indigenous organizations successfully challenged the dynamics of state power and contested the initial scope that the government wished to give to the Victims' Law, mainly its emphasis on the restitution of some purported universal human rights. From a political ecology perspective (i.e., the analysis of power struggles in environmental governance), the inclusion of the territory as a victim would provide new ways to understand disputes over the control, use, and protection of rights of ownership of collective lands and territorial resources, as well as the conflicts that emerge when nature is conceived of and experienced in radically different ways by different actors. Even from the perspective of political economy, this recognition would problematize the type of hegemonic ideas that have rendered territory and its constituents a collection of natural resources to be exploited. My point, paraphrasing Marisol de la Cadena (2015), is that the recognition of Indigenous territories as victims of armed conflict addresses all that but not only that. The recognition of the territory as victim entails the recognition of a violence that goes beyond its human and environmental impacts—and thus beyond modern notions of human rights and ecological restoration or, more broadly speaking, beyond the boundaries that state and modern politics have mapped out between the realms of nature and culture. And this requires, once again, an ethnographic attunement to the harm that communities in Bajo Atrato register on the living relationalities that make up their territories, as well as to the way their own humanness is constituted through the various emplaced relations they cultivate with other-than-human beings. Part of what this book seeks to do is to gauge what transpires in this legal recognition of the territory as a victim of war, paying attention to the challenges this event poses to the cultural policies promoted under the banner of multiculturalism, as well as to the implementation of appropriate and effective policies of truth, justice, and reparation for these peoples and their living territories.

Ontological Occupation

Approaching war from a perspective that takes into consideration the harm suffered by wider assemblages of human and other-than-human beings is the way I have found to underscore the ontologically and politically disturbing character of the demands made by Indigenous and Afro-Colombian organizations. The fact that in 2011 Colombian law recognized the territory as victim of the armed conflict is an event without precedent in the national and international jurisprudence of war. It paves the way for local organizations, and for anthropologists like me, to go beyond the modernist, anthropocentric conceptualization of victimization toward a relational and ontological approach centered on the idea that what is at stake is the veritable destruction of the worlds forged by wider communities of life. In this sense the war in Bajo Atrato has not just been a war waged in the territories of Indigenous and Afro-Colombian communities or merely a violence against these peoples and the ways of being they embody. It is all of that, of course, but not only that. This book shows that war is not just a phenomenon unfolding in Bajo Atrato but rather a force producing other versions of this territory. War comprises world-making relations between different sets of sentient beings, relations that do not merely take place in the territory but that contribute to bringing it into existence. What I attempt here is not just to include animals or the environment in our accounts of human destructive acts—to do so would only enact the nature-culture divide—but rather to describe how war reconfigures whole ecologies or relational worlds made of human and other-than-human entanglements. Entanglement, as Karen Barad (2011, 150) reminds us, is not interconnectedness but specific material relations of obligation: "being bound to the other." To put it differently, if war compromises the values, rules of engagement, and obligations through which people and other-than-humans *are* and become the territory, it follows that war becomes a form of ontological occupation of Afro-Colombian and Indigenous territories.

Colombian anthropologist Arturo Escobar (2016, 2020) uses the concept "ontological occupation" to describe the tenacious and continual dominant world-building endeavor of modern institutions to erase other emplaced realities that do not fit within the hegemonic idea of "One-World World" (Law 2015). Drawing from a Western onto-episteme that arrogates to itself the right to be "the world" and to speak on behalf of a monist reality, this One-World World relegates all other worlds "to its rule, to a state of subordination, or to nonexistence" (Escobar 2020, 14). In this sense the most fundamental dimension of the struggles of Indigenous and Afro-Colombian peoples in defense of their territories is ontological: the protection of the conditions that sustain the emergence of their own local, relational worlds. Ontological occupation of the territories and lives of these communities is effectuated through capitalist, colonial, secular, or patriarchal means, war being the most perverted manifestation of this kind of occupation: one that, besides constraining people's possibilities of being and canceling other thoughts and relationalities, pursues not just the submission of local worlds but their actual obliteration. If what is destroyed or affected are relational worlds, then war also destroys worlds that flourish from relations and modes of being different than the ones prescribed by modern onto-epistemic frameworks.

There is little novelty in writing about armed conflict in Colombia. As a matter of fact, war is such a pervasive topic that there even exists a school of thinking and research devoted to understanding it—*violentology*—and for which Colombian social and human sciences are, rightly, internationally known. I can hardly get away from that pervasiveness, yet what I show is that besides the political, economic, environmental, or cultural aspects of war, we need to pay attention to its latent repercussions in terms other than those offered by the human rights framework and its anthropocentrism.

In Bajo Atrato, war takes different forms and is performed by different actors embodying different ideologies and therefore fostering different sets of relations. In this region war has pitted a range of distinct armed groups against one another, but it has been, as a matter of fact, a war waged against the Indigenous and Afro-Colombian peoples and the modes of being that they and their territories embody. By this, I mean that the so-called civilian casualties and collateral damages associated with the actions of armed groups (e.g., forced displacement, land expropriation, resource depletion) have not been incidental to armed conflict but fundamental to the aims pursued by these groups. The numerous loyalties of these groups and the array of their political agendas are implicit in the acronyms they adopt: FARC, ELN, ACCU, AUC, BACRIM, AGC, FFMM. A common interpretation of war in this region is that it initially pitted a communist guerrilla army (the Revolutionary Armed Forces of Colombia—FARC) against right-wing paramilitary armies (initially the Peasant Self-Defense Forces of Córdoba and Urabá—ACCU—which later became part of the United Self-Defense Forces of Colombia—AUC). From that perspective the state, through its military forces (army and police—FFMM), fought these illegal armies in order to fulfill its constitutional duty of protecting citizens' life, dignity, property, rights, and freedoms. Unfortunately, the presence of the Colombian armed forces has rarely had this protective effect: recent local history contains many examples of the involvement of both army and police officials in serious human rights violations for which several top commanders have been found guilty or are under investigation (Salinas and Zarama 2012; J. Vargas 2016). Those cases are not just a matter of a few bad apples but are symptomatic of the role that the state plays in armed violence. The connivance of the state in this violence in Bajo Atrato results in a form of power relying not so much on the discourse and practice of the control and regulation of life—what Michel Foucault (1990) called biopolitics, the distinctive trait of modern states—as on the permissiveness of the state toward death—thanatopolitics, or what Achille Mbembe characterizes as necropolitics: "the subjugation of life to the power of death" (2003, 39). In this way, war—and the chronically entrenched poverty, marginalization, and discrimination that make war possible in the first place—becomes a way of defining "who matters and who does not, who is disposable and who is not" (Mbembe 2003, 27): a practice of carrying death and letting it happen to peoples and places deemed as killable or less worthy of grief (Butler 2009). And this constitutes one of the traits of the ontological occupation fostered by war.

The unfolding of events in Bajo Atrato leaves little doubt about the way that the army and the paramilitary, along with regional political elites, wealthy financiers, entrepreneurs, and companies that for years systematically funded the counterinsurgency war launched by paramilitaries, formed strategic alliances in order to extirpate all guerrilla influence in the region and gain economic power through dispossession of people's lands. The so-called counterinsurgency war was at the service of the social and economic status quo, and it adopted the classic "drain the water" strategy: catching guerrillas (the fish) by polluting or drying out their milieu, in this case by eliminating their alleged supporters—the civil population. The apex of this violence took place between 1996 and 2005, when the campaigns launched by both paramilitary and army forces resulted not in the diminishing of guerrilla power but in the banishment of hundreds of Afro-Colombian communities from their traditional lands. Even more than twenty years after Operación Génesis (1996), the army campaign that allowed several paramilitary squads to take control of the region by means of economic blockades, abductions, torture, and systematic killings, many communities have not succeeded in returning to their land under appropriate conditions of safety and dignity because skirmishes between new paramilitary armies and other communist guerrillas are ongoing.

But the armed conflict has not been a counterinsurgency war only. A more complex image emerges when drug trafficking, gunrunning, land-grabbing, agribusiness, and mining enter the picture. When armed groups promote such activities and earn substantial money from them, war becomes the continuation of political and economic neoliberal agendas by other means. Armed conflict in Bajo Atrato is not a binary conflict, and it eludes any Manichaean interpretation. It demonstrates that politics and economic and military considerations are not always discrete motivations, that some actions undertaken by armed groups are not necessarily aligned to ideological discourses or related to their strategic goals (Kalyvas 2003). This is particularly true when one finds the counterrevolutionary motivations of paramilitary groups conflated with the goals of certain political and economic elites, as well as with the desire of state security forces to "clean up" purported insurgent areas; or when depletion of natural resources and forced displacement of entire communities become instrumental to guerrillas' political agendas.

To further complicate this picture, it is worth bearing in mind that guerrillas and paramilitaries are, in essence, peasant armies. This means that their soldiers often come from the regions that these groups aim to control. Bajo Atrato is no exception, and there, as in many other regions of the country, many young teenagers are recruited as soldiers. Even those who join these armies as legal adults do so constrained by a lack of other viable economic and social opportunities because these armies come to represent a way to earn a living, gain power, and even acquire social prestige. In the same vein, because of the long-term character of this armed conflict, the regular presence of these armies, and the way they permeate different spheres of local life, it would be naive to see these armies as alien, perverted forces overturning a peaceful order of things. This means that there have been instances in which local leaders and some communities have aligned their own economic and political interests with these armed actors, a fact that in some cases has undermined the legitimacy of some local organizations.

Despite the official demobilization of paramilitary forces in 2006 and the peace accord reached between the Colombian government and the FARC in 2016, war has not ceased in Bajo Atrato, to the extent that the region can be characterized as one of the areas entrenched in what Diego Restrepo (2018) oxymoronically describes as armed post-conflict (see also Castaño and Ruiz 2019). After demobilization of top paramilitary commanders, new armed groups occupied the structures of power left behind by the AUC in Bajo Atrato. Although the government insists on calling these groups gangs or BACRIM (criminal bands), they continue exerting the violent power of their predecessors under the guise of a euphemistic name: Gaitanista Self-Defense Group of Colombia (AGC).* Something similar has happened with the FARC. From the very moment the peace talks with the government were announced in 2012, the ELN guerrilla group (National Liberation Army) began occupying the areas that had previously been under FARC influence. The war waged between these armies for the control of crucial points for accessing oceangoing drug and weapon routes has provoked, according to a mission in May 2019 of the United Nations Office for the Coordination of Humanitarian Affairs (OCHA), the forced displacement of at least 1,644 people belonging to Wounaan and Emberá Indigenous communities. What is common to all these armed actors, regardless of their purported ideological affiliations, is that they engage in the economic activities of contraband, logging, drug trafficking, illegal mining, or whatever allows them to fuel their war machines. They also share common strategies for terrorizing and disciplining populations: forced displacement, selective assassinations, extortion, threats, economic blockades.

Even though the armies involved in the conflict have received a wide variety of labels from the state—sometimes they have been called and treated as terrorists, gangs, or drug cartels, and at other times they have received legal belligerent status, which means political recognition of their right to resist what the armed groups consider an illegitimate power—and even though the armed conflict itself has been denied by some governments and understood as a legitimate struggle by others, I maintain that armed conflict in Bajo Atrato is above all an expression of politically motivated aims. This is because each armed group represents a particular ideology and organizes its actions to either modify or perpetuate certain power structures. As politics is partly concerned with power and organizing control over a given population, there is little doubt that armed conflict in this region is a form of political violence: all armed actors aim, by one means or another, to exert power over local communities. But, more important to the argument being made, the armed conflict is an expression of an ontological occupa-

* The Autodefensas Gaitanistas de Colombia, a right-wing paramilitary group, took its name from Jorge Eliécer Gaitán, a charismatic politician and populist leader who was running for president when he was assassinated in 1948. His death led to the historical period known simply as La Violencia, a large-scale political violence instigated by the Conservative party government against opposition parties. That violence claimed between 200,000 and 300,000 lives (Carroll 2011; Hristov 2009; LeGrand 2003). Gaitán was a strong proponent of workers' rights and fought to help the disenfranchised population against the status quo. When a paramilitary group that defends the elitist interests of a powerful economic minority adopts Gaitán's name, we are brought face-to-face with one of the most ironic and oxymoronic political positions in contemporary history.

tion of *Bajoatrateño* territories because the values and practices systematically driven, fostered, embodied, or reproduced by armed actors are usually at odds with the relations and ways of being that are essential to the very existence of Indigenous and Afro-Colombian peoples and their territories.

War maintains and reproduces power-laden relations; it disciplines people; it naturalizes poverty; it constrains agency. This is why the ontological occupation of Indigenous and Afro-Colombian territories affects the horizon of relations that are possible when the values and obligations associated with places and beings are severely altered by instances of power that are at odds with the histories, thoughts, subjectivities, forms of knowledge, and possibilities of being that a territory would otherwise render meaningful. What I underscore is that in the case of Bajo Atrato, the ontological occupation is related not only to the political, economic, environmental, and even cultural aspects of armed violence, but also, and primarily, to the destructive production of human and other-than-human relations and to the struggles these large communities of life undertake for their right to exist. By "destructive production" I refer to the way war enters into—and comes to saturate, to occupy—the composition of *Bajoatrateño* worlds, to the power it has to push cosmological orders beyond their historical, knowable formulas, to the emergence of new kinds of agencies and new kinds of others, and to the arising of new relations and ontological transactions. Without idealizing violence as creative, I analyze war not only in terms of what it prevents, hinders, or destroys; instead, I look at war in order to show, paraphrasing Patrick Wolfe's (1999) conceptualization of settler colonialism, that it is more a structure than an event and that in Bajo Atrato war has produced new presences and forms of agency but also, in some cases, has altered the existences already embedded within the territory. These transformations have compelled communities to establish new kinds of relationships with the places and beings that make up their collective territories.

A word about one of my methodological premises: the understanding of the harm inflicted upon *Bajoatrateño* territories is the means I found to dislodge human-centered approaches from current policies of justice and reparation. This implies not only a focus on the kinds of harm in which the human is merely another agent but also a reconsideration of agency within practices rather than discourses, as well as attention to the politics of knowledge and practices rather than to the politics of identity (C. Hughes and Lury 2013). In other words, rather than examining the role that social categories such as ethnicity, ancestry, or, more broadly speaking, indigeneity play at the moment of experiencing the territory as a victim, I focus on relationality, on events and forms of engagement within the territory. This means that what people experience as damage does not necessarily map onto assigned ethnic or cultural identity categories because what renders intelligible the experiences with, for instance, wandering ghosts, wicked spirits, or evil animals is not so much group ascription as the kinds of practices that take place within a shared place. By underscoring practices, I point to their performative power because, as a great deal of anthropological literature has shown (Blaser 2009; de la Cadena 2015; Escobar 2016; Latour 1999; Law 2007; Mol 1999), practices enact worlds, worlds made up not only of human meanings but co-constituted by assemblages of other-than-human existences. This is why this book should not be considered as an ethnography of Afro-Colombian or Emberá and Wounaan communities but rather as an ethnography of place or, even better, of crucial events that have reconfigured a territory treasured by some Indigenous, *chilapo*, and Afro-Colombian peoples. If what defines damage to the territory is its world-making effects, then group ascription (i.e., ethnic or cultural collective identity) is not a condition for tracing the kind of harm that extends beyond people and their human rights. Moreover, my preference for focusing on practices and engagements within particular places becomes a means of seeing the harm inflicted upon *Bajoatrateño* territories not so much as the outcome of particular cultural representations of reality but rather as a set of possibilities that are experienced when people engage in a particular way with their territories.

Chapter Overviews

I have arranged this book into seven chapters. Each of the first six conveys attributes of a territory that is interpreted in relational terms. They also include the conceptual and methodological premises that should guide an understanding of war and its afterlives in worlds made of human and more-than-human entanglements. Chapter 1, for example, illustrates the instances of coproduction between rivers and people and how war affects, in accretive and incremental ways, the practices through which people's and rivers' lives are mutually nurtured. Given that Bajo Atrato is above all an aquatic universe, here I describe the prevalence of water, paying attention to rivers and to the ways that their flow and movement support particular modes of existence. Called "The Flow of Selves," this chapter describes an array of local practices that show how human actions, paraphrasing Karine Gagné and Mattias Borg Rasmussen (2016), are done with rivers and not just to them. I pay attention to how forced displacement and the rapacious economic interests of paramilitary armies and timber companies proliferated a form of damage that, besides provoking serious environmental impacts, undermined people's possibilities of traveling and taking care of their rivers, which ended up hindering the very practices that help communities bring their territory into existence.

The violent transformation of rivers cannot be addressed only through the ethics of environmental conservation. Conservation, at least in dominant legal systems, supposes the enactment of rivers as natural resources: entities external to and detached from people, whereas the practices of care undertaken by local communities imply the flourishing of different forms of lives, including other-than-human lives, that not only inhabit the rivers but that *are* and become with them. This is the main argument developed in Chapter 2, "Still Waters Run Deep." I examine how war has changed the relations that different aquatic beings engage in. Concretely, I describe *fieras*, a set of often colossal and extraordinary beings whose existence cannot be understood as disconnected from the specific material forms and ecological constraints that rivers propitiate or from the affective embodied dispositions through which people meet these *fieras*. This means that more than discrete beings endowed with a kind of reality independent from people or places, *fieras* are forged within relational fields. I explore how war has compromised the existence of these beings in order to raise questions about how to understand damage and the possibility of its reparation once the harm is situated within a world made of entangled relations between beings and places whose contours are not always neat. In this chapter the emergent properties of territory—territory being an aggregate of assemblages whose associations generate bigger unities—become more evident, showing that the violence of war propagates in ways that involve relations between multiple assemblages. Therefore, its effects are better traced when paying attention to said relations.

In Chapter 3, "Imperishable Evils," waterscapes and the worlds of spirits meet, showing how violence ramifies in many directions and how in a territory of multiple entanglements war becomes a "threat multiplier," something that does not "simply impact existing forms of life in obvious ways" (Khan 2016, 190). Here I describe the powers of an evil being, known in Spanish as *madre de agua*, that assaults people in the rivers. This being, whose name I have roughly translated as Water Mother, embodies a form of shamanic aggression set in motion by *jaibanas*, the traditional Emberá healers. Although they are more ancient than warfare in the region, Water Mothers have participated in the armed conflict and its afterlives. When the violence exerted by the official armed forces, guerrillas, and paramilitaries attained one of its highest peaks in the period 1996–2005, some powerful *jaibanas* mobilized these evil spirits in an attempt to protect their communities from the attacks of these armed groups. However, the very nature of armed violence caused many of these spirits to run amok, to the extent that some of these beings are still wandering the rivers and causing indiscriminate damage because they are no longer capable of distinguishing between those who make war and those who do not. In this chapter I tell the story of one of these attacks in an attempt to depict what I consider to be the rhizomatic nature of war and its afterlives in Bajo Atrato, meaning that events apparently disconnected in time and place might share heterogeneous bonds whose repercussions spread in ways that resist single directions and causalities.

In the second part of this book I shift my gaze from rivers to forests. In chapter 4, "Awakening Forests," I depict the afterlife of forced displacement in order to show the processes of ruination associated with war. I focus on the abandonment of villages, gardens, and trails to stress some forms of power inherent to forests, particularly their perseverance in continuing to grow and propagate. However, forests' generative power represents to people in Bajo Atrato a process of rot and decay. I then describe how multiple kinds of other-than-human agencies are involved in processes of ruination and how the entanglement of rubble and animal and vegetal species might help us reconsider the material and analytical grounds of concepts such as forced displacement or dispossession. Ultimately, this chapter conveys the idea that territory is always in the making because ruins and other-than-human presences show how places are in motion or, better, that they can be conceptualized as moments in the arrangements of things (Ingold 1993).

The intricate role of sylvan agents in the decay of people's livelihood, on the one hand, and the proliferation of forces that produce more than material effects during processes of ruination, on the other, complexify certain legal definitions regarding territorial damage, which usually only speak to material losses. This means that we need to look closely at the transformation of the intangible qualities of places, which is the topic I address in chapter 5, "The Shared World of the Living and the Dead." Here I depict the kind of harm associated with the hauntings provoked by the presence of the restless spirits of some soldiers who experienced a violent death. Whereas the first chapter discusses the importance of flow and how rivers propitiate particular values and modes of being, in this chapter I deal with the flow of life and death or, more precisely, the problems associated with those spirits that remain stagnant within the spatial and temporal contours where their human lives ended. Given that, for local communities, coming to terms with these ghostly presences is a condition for healing their land, I am interested in showing the important role that spirits play in attaining peace and justice. This chapter explores how war is not always bounded within bodies and how being in a territory presupposes being vulnerable to others that can make us and unmake us, that can transform us "into something other than what we are" (Clark 2010, xxi).

Chapter 6, "A Jaguar and a Half," delves into how territory is made of heterogeneous encounters whose outcomes can rarely be taken for granted. Here I describe the events unleashed by a man-eating jaguar and the assorted misunderstandings and responses this provoked among different people involved. I track the deaths caused by this jaguar to show the pervasiveness of war in Bajo Atrato and the perversity of certain warlords who managed to involve sylvan beings in their deadly business. I show how the man-eating jaguar epitomizes a form of excess that renders it a hybrid figure capable of dislocating multiple borders: between human and other-than-human forces, between environmental and social processes, between predation and warfare. Ethnographic attention to this excess sheds light on the instances of hybridization and multiplicity that render war a phenomenon that extends beyond the human.

After having built an ethnographic argument about the form of harm that decades of war have wrought on the large communities of life that constitute *Bajoatrateño* territories, in the final chapter I explore to what extent the legal recognition of Indigenous territories as victims makes a difference in how the conflict itself, its multiple impacts, and the measures to redress it (including reparations) are understood, and how it could be otherwise. I show that despite the progressive deepening of the state's multicultural discourses evident in the law, it remains trapped within realist languages of science, rights, culture, and rationality that, emphasizing an ethics of environmental conservation, deflate the ontological dimensions of the events and beings discussed throughout this book.

A word about the book's title: the war waged in Indigenous and Afro-Colombian traditional territories has produced vast harm. As I will demonstrate, this harm extends beyond people and threatens the very worlds that are both constitutive of and constituted through the social relations which Indigenous and Afro-Colombian peoples cultivate with other-than-human selves. The harm of armed conflict has not ceased, and what is left in the wake of destruction, killing, and forced displacement still reverberates in the lives of the myriad beings that constitute these territories. In this sense the afterlives of war are the kinds of lives that humans and other-than-humans must undertake in the wake of the cumulative deaths caused by an ongoing violence.

Inspired by Christina Sharpe (2016), I understand this wake as a track, one left in this case by a war machine, as well as the state of being awake, being vigilant in the context of unending violence. By being in this wake, Afro-Colombian and Indigenous peoples are reaffirming their insistence on living the kind of life that renders their territories a place for worlds otherwise (Escobar 2007; Povinelli 2012). The afterlives of war are not simply trauma or environmental degradation, and they are more than ongoing violence. Instead, afterlives are the effects upon the vital relationalities that make up territories, which at times give rise to certain versions of said territories that can be wrong in the sense of constituting worlds "in which or with which [people] do not want to live" (Blaser 2013b, 552). At stake in *Bajoatrateño* territories is life itself and the possibilities of fostering a life lived in worlds different than the one John Law (2015) refers to as the "one-world world," that epistemologically and ontologically flat world that modernity presents as superior, leaving other realities out of the picture. A form of violence still reverberating, that overturns entangled continuums of human and other-than-human relationships, and that has the power of shaping territories: these are the afterlives of war. When forests and rivers run amok, their ecologies become erratic and often unpredictable, but more importantly these ecologies alter the properties of beings, such that these beings may begin to cause havoc. When rivers and forests run amok, a violent form of indeterminacy permeates the places and beings that render life meaningful in Bajo Atrato. When forests and rivers become so intermingled with armed violence, one wonders to what extent these militarized ecologies can be fully dismantled. Let us then embark on this journey up the rivers and along the muddy trails that cross *Bajoatrateño* territories in order to cultivate a form of ethnographic attention capable of perceiving an ecological violence that extends beyond environmental impacts and human rights violations.

1

THE FLOW
OF SELVES

In his novel *The Magic Mountain*, German writer Thomas Mann describes space as wielding the powers that we generally ascribe to time. Time, he says, is Lethe, the river of the underworld that, according to Greek mythology, provoked forgetfulness in all those who drank from it. During travel, argues Mann, space rolls and revolves, "setting us bodily free from our surroundings." But if space brings about changes in a less thorough manner than time, it "does so more quickly" (Mann [1924] 1958, 4). I find that Mann catches the essence of what travel is: going from one place to another only to find oneself captivated by and even lost in one's experiences and discoveries en route. This experience of betweenness, of letting space engender its own changes, is what makes the journey as important as the destination itself. In Bajo Atrato, that betweenness, that space linking different surroundings and making transformation possible, has a particular materialization: rivers.

Rivers are the main transportation route in the Bajo Atrato region. They epitomize flow and movement, bringing together distinct realms of social life, connecting towns and villages, making possible the circulation of people and goods, permitting all kinds of journeys—from family visits to pilgrimages—as well as social processes, including economic activities and political organization. Just as a society might be described as a network of social relationships, the landscape in Bajo Atrato might be conceived of as a network of

FIGURE 1.1. **Flow. Photo by author.**

rivers. Of rivers but also of torrents, streams, creeks, canals, natural levees, floodplain lagoons, lakes, swamps. People constantly move through both social and aquatic networks. Relationships among people living in different hamlets or among communities belonging to different river basins are often determined by the mobility of the actors, by the connections they can establish. And in a landscape made up of large aquatic networks, rivers are what provide said mobility, opening up the possibility of connection. In this fashion, social relationships are established, maintained, and reproduced thanks to the journeys that rivers allow. To clarify: rivers are not simply associated with social ties; they in fact permit such ties. Rivers do not just represent flow or movement. Rather, their actuality, their thereness or very presence, renders them flow and movement (see figure 1.1).

A river is how the territory teaches people to flow; by flowing a river creates courses, and by traveling via these watercourses people learn about their territory and their own possibilities of being and becoming within it. Bearing this in mind, I see the everyday social relationships in Bajo Atrato as an entangled network of people and rivers or, better, of people and what geographer Ulrich Oslender (2004) calls "aquatic spaces," meaning the manifold aquatic elements associated with the specific tropical rain-forest environment of this region: intricate river networks, high levels of precipitation, seasonal inundations. Following Tim Ingold, I use the word "entanglement" to describe a meshwork of interwoven "lines of growth and movement" through which "beings are instantiated in the world" (2006, 14). This means that flow is essential to understand the processes—or lines, as Ingold calls them—that set the conditions of possibility and of becoming (movement and growth) through which communities and aquatic networks constitute each other. In other words, by describing social relationships in Bajo Atrato as an entangled domain of people and rivers, I highlight the fact that both are mutually constituted through outward practices and that their possibilities of mutual flourishing are defined by the relations that constitute them (Escobar 2016, 18).

This chapter focuses on rivers in order to highlight the main social practices that they allow as well as the values associated with said practices. One of these practices has to do with traveling and with the maintenance and creation of social connections. In Bajo Atrato to travel means to use the river networks as a transportation route, and to travel by river means, inexorably, to embark, which etymologically means to go aboard a barque, to get on a boat. Locals use the word *embarcar* to mean "to embark," which in this context means to travel, and to travel is, needless to say, to move. This chapter is then about river travel, particularly about the possibilities and impossibilities of embarking in times of incessant war. I show that part of what defines a river is people's use of river networks to embark and that this use of the waterscape has been seriously hindered by war. Inspired by the works of Marilyn Strathern (2005) and Marisol de la Cadena (2015), I see rivers as affording particular relationships but also as being constituted by the relations that people weave with them. Through rivers, one might not only "perceive relations between things but also perceive things as relations" (Strathern 2005, 63). Thus, besides being geographical features, rivers are also produced and enacted: they are brought into a particular mode of being through a specific set of practices.

The chapter is divided into three parts. The first depicts the role that rivers play in the region, placing particular emphasis on the way they favor certain relationships—from kinship and social exchanges to the development of economic and political networks. As I describe the multitude of ways in which rivers connect people, and given the importance of what I call their thereness—by which I mean their nearness to people, their quality of being there, the state of being present and participating in manifold social activities and relations—I have included some photos that help harness certain aspects of their actuality: flow, movement, ubiquity. Although photos are, by definition, a capture of light in a determined space and time or, as John Berger (1980, 86) puts it, they "arrest the flow of time in which the event photographed once existed," through the use of the chosen images I show some everyday water practices and how attributes such as flow and movement contribute to the maintenance of both social and aquatic networks. Sometimes these photos are not intended to merely illustrate my arguments but are intended to convey other meanings via their own way of telling.

The second part describes a common kind of work: *la limpieza de los ríos*, literally "the cleaning of rivers," the maintenance of their navigability. I show how through cleaning, people engage in a practice of care, working in and with their territories as stewards. This practice is what allows travel and what maintains, ultimately, the social life of rivers. It also brings into evidence that in Bajo Atrato, and here I am paraphrasing Mattias Borg Rasmussen (2015, 207), many activities are done with the rivers rather than to them. After having described how people take care of rivers, the third part explores *palizadas*: logjams or river blockages that create the need for said care. Inspired by the work of Gastón Gordillo (2004) on landscapes and memory, I see that rivers, their meanings, and the interactions they favor are often based on relations of contrast and opposition to another aquatic feature: *palizadas*. They divert flow and convey the idea of stagnation, so they may be seen as the antithesis of rivers, yet *palizadas* are important in the process through which practices and modes of being in Bajo Atrato become waterlogged.

The Actuality of Rivers

There are nine main rivers in the Bajo Atrato region, each comprising a river basin: Cacarica, Pedeguita-Mancilla, Salaquí, La Larga-Tumaradó, Truandó, Domingodó, Curvaradó, Jiguamiandó, and Atrato. The suffix *dó* comes from the Emberá language, one of the two languages that still survive from the Chocó language family, and it means "river." The paradigmatic river in the region is the Atrato River. The origin of its name is unclear. Some scholars suggest that the name started to be used in 1536 (IGAC 1992) but that it became popular at the beginning of the eighteenth century. *Atrato* could mean "the river of the Citará people" (Isacsson 1975), an interpretation based on the fact that the word *Atrato* may be decomposed into the suffix *to*, a Hispanicization of the Emberá word for "river," and *atara*, a contraction of the name that the Spaniards gave to some Indigenous peoples they found in Chocó: the Citará people, who are also referred to as Tirabará or Atará (Isacsson 1975, 97–98). Thus, if we treat *atara* as an ethnonym, *Atrato* would simply mean "the river of people" (see figure 1.2).

FIGURE 1.2. The river of people. Photo by author.

This imposing, incredibly muddy, and slow-moving river has more than 3,000 different tributaries and is considered the river with the highest volume of water in the world when compared to its length, which is 650 kilometers (404 miles) (IGAC 1992). It has an average discharge of 4,000–5,000 cubic meters (2.49 cubic miles) per second (IGAC 1992, 23), and it is estimated that it discharges about 344 million cubic meters (213,752 cubic miles) of brown water every day into the Gulf of Urabá (see figure 1.3), where its eighteen mouths form a large, swampy delta (Proyecto Biopacífico 1998; West 1957). Throughout all its course, the Atrato River barely descends 43 meters (47 yards), a fact that led some of the travelers that visited the region in the nineteenth century to describe it as "a large lake in slow motion" (Leal 2018, 20). A friend and I used to call it "The Silent Giant": I tried as hard as I could to tune my ear to its sound, but its flow is so silent and my hearing so poorly trained that I never was able to hear it at all.

Many scholars have pointed to the importance that rivers on the Colombian Pacific coast have had as the setting and condition for an array of different social processes (see, for example, Escobar 2008; Hoffmann 2004; Leal 2018; Oslender 2016; Quiceno 2016; Sharp 1976; Werner 2000; West 1957; Whitten 1974). Historically, rivers allowed exploration, economic exploitation,

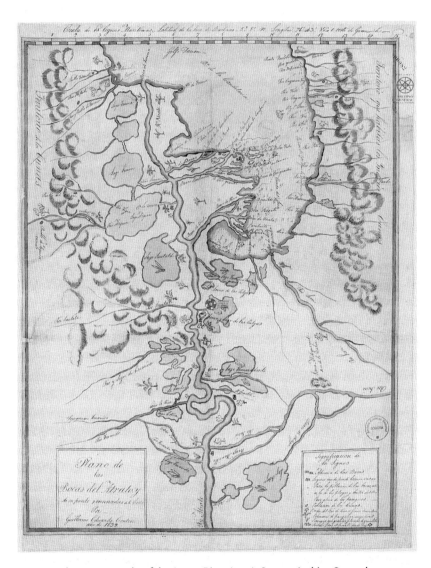

FIGURE 1.3. The many mouths of the Atrato River (1832). Source: Archivo General de la Nación, Bogotá.

and settlement of the region. For instance, during the colonial period Chocó was a mining frontier, and for the exploitation of the alluvial gold deposits, as throughout the Americas, Spanish mine owners relied on forced labor of Native Americans and enslaved peoples of African descent. The gold-mining work was mostly organized around *cuadrillas*, groups of African slaves and

Indigenous peoples under the command, at least in theory, of a Spanish *capitán*. These *cuadrillas* lived in camps established along different watercourses where they could easily get access to food—fish, manatees, but also crops and game animals—and to transportation and communication with urban settlements.

Unlike other colonial mining centers in the Americas, Chocó was not truly settled by European descendants since mine owners and officials showed little interest in establishing permanent residence in the region (Leal 2018; Sharp 1976; Werner 2000). During the eighteenth century, royal officials often complained about the climate, describing it as fever-ridden, incredibly humid, and so hot that it was not healthy for white settlers (Sharp 1976). Many officials resigned because of these conditions, and the Spanish Crown had to offer better pay to its functionaries in order to foster white presence in the region (Werner 2000; Whitten 1974). Chocó was seen by Spanish officials as a place to make a quick fortune in order to retire later to what they considered to be more suitable areas than the hot, moist forests. With time, major alluvial gold sites came to be owned by absentee Spanish proprietors, headed by free Black "captains," and operated by enslaved Africans and their descendants (Leal 2018; Sharp 1976; Werner 2000; Williams 2005). In this way, mine exploitation relied on the establishment of fixed quotas of raw gold calculated on the assessment of each mine's likely productivity (Restall and Lane 2011, 162). Under such circumstances, once their quotas were reached, enslaved peoples in Chocó enjoyed a certain autonomy. They could work independently, whether in other mining camps, where they collected gold in order to purchase manumission with their own funds, or on their own farms, where they tried commercial agriculture, mainly of maize and plantains, for supplying sufficient food for workers was always a problem for the *cuadrillas'* overseers (Leal 2018; Sharp 1976; Werner 2000).

The connection of the Atrato River with the Caribbean Sea and the weak presence of royal authorities created a major problem for the Spanish Crown: contraband. Dutch, Scottish, French, and English pirates and filibusters constantly navigated the Atrato River in search of gold, establishing military and commercial alliances with Indigenous and maroon communities, which often received from these contrabandists all sorts of commodities—clothing, machetes, axes, alcohol—that the Spanish officers were reluctant to offer (Whitten 1974). In order to counter the danger of such alliances, in some instances the Spanish Crown ended up exempting free slaves and Indigenous communities from tribute in exchange for their agreeing not to ally themselves with these foreigners (Restall and Lane 2011). Contraband was such a serious problem that the Atrato River was closed to maritime commerce between

1698 and 1784 (Leal 2018; Werner 2000). However, the closing of the main transportation route only rendered the problem worse, for necessary goods and staples became scarce and therefore expensive. The situation forced mine owners, maroons, and Indigenous communities alike to find new ways of pursuing contraband trade with the myriad merchants and marauders who were always willing to exchange supplies for gold. The Atrato River, despite the ban of Spanish authorities, always remained the main economic connection between the goods produced by local communities and the opportunistic merchants who had the capital to trade for and transport these commodities.

In addition to having an important influence on the economic development of the region, the river network also shaped local settlement patterns. Both runaway slaves and *libres*—freedmen who managed to buy their freedom from their masters—took advantage of the immense forests and the weak presence of official authorities in order to reach lands located upstream, away from urban settlements and the colonial gaze. To go up a river meant, and still means, to move toward less inhabited areas, to reach untilled lands and abundant forests. Whether as maroons or as freedmen, settling upriver was a way to attain enough lands for crops, to access rivers to fish, to approach woodlands to hunt or get supplies of wood, to create a place to raise one's own family, and to share life with others who had gone through similar experiences. From the very moment that maroons and *libres* began traveling the rivers of their own accord and in search of lands for their own autonomous projects, they started another kind of journey: from enslavement to freedom. According to environmental historian Claudia Leal (2018), the access that enslaved peoples gained to wide forested lands, wetlands (*ciénagas* and mangroves), and rivers set the conditions for the flourishing of a post-emancipatory Black society that enjoyed much more autonomy than its peers elsewhere in Latin America. Historically speaking, mobility along watercourses opened up the possibilities for a life free from colonial authorities. Even today in Bajo Atrato, many communities are able to trace their historical foundation to the journeys undertaken by their ancestors many years ago, when they settled new lands and traveled up the local rivers in order to exploit vegetable ivory palms or trade maize, plantains, bushmeat, and fish.

The pattern of settlement following watercourses produced in some regions what pioneer Colombian anthropologist Nina S. de Friedemann (1974) identified as *troncos*, literally "trunks." *Troncos* are defined as groups of families with rights to live and work in a specific territory inherited from ancestors who had previously taken possession of the land (de Friedemann

1985, 204). Although *troncos* as defined by this author are specific to mining communities located elsewhere on the Pacific coast, some characteristics of these *troncos* are nevertheless present among communities that, as in Bajo Atrato, were settled during a more recent period. These settlements, simply called communities (*comunidades*), are villages inhabited by people who control land and inherit property under a set of rules of descent. Whether by patrilateral or matrilateral affiliations, members of a community maintain a connection to the group, as well as to land rights, by virtue of being considered a descendant of someone who demonstrates historical ties to the territory. In sum, a community is a group of families sharing a common territory and, most of the time, kinship; who live in a village along a given river; who develop a sense of belonging strongly associated with a particular river; who share collective rights to land and resources; and who identify themselves as being part of an organizational and political unity called a Community Council to which the state has granted full land tenure rights.

In Bajo Atrato, when one asks elders about their history in the region, they always talk about the *arribeños*, ancestors living somewhere upstream on the Atrato River and who traveled downstream in the first half of the twentieth century in order to settle these lands and rivers. The origin of most current communities in this region is then traced back to the voyage undertaken by a forebearer, to their will to embark and travel down the Atrato River and up one of its tributaries in order to enhance their economic possibilities and enlarge their social ties. To communities living in the lower Atrato, the people living upstream are seen as possessing a certain ancestry, as having a kind of primal knowledge developed during the historical time of the first maroons and freedmen. The lands located upstream on the Atrato River are somehow seen as containing the strength and skills developed by these first *libres* (Quiceno 2016). Accordingly, to come from upstream on this river constitutes a historical and existential experience qualitatively different from that of being from downstream on this watercourse. Importantly, travel in this region was not only a means to settle new areas and eventually to found a village or become part of a new community; travel was also a way to move through the kinship network of relatives who had established themselves on other rivers. To voyage via the rivers was and still is to participate in social and economic networks. To travel, in short, is both to enlarge and to actualize one's territory, to foster a particular sense of place in which emplaced memories, practices, and experiences are entangled with kinship ties, economic practices, social organizations, symbolic manifestations, and even political identities.

Some scholars (Hoffmann 2004; Losonczy 2006a; Wade 1990) have pointed out that on the Pacific coast mobility has also influenced the constitution of kinship groups or extended families, which in turn links various portions of a river and aids access to and exploitation of different resources. Extended families are often the result of what Norman Whitten (1974) characterizes as "serial polygyny," a practice in which a man may have different wives and overlapping households at the same time. Extended families constitute a flexible kinship network that may be used by individuals to assert social ties and rights within a particular territory, as well as to mobilize affective ties or influence within a given community. Parents, sons, siblings, grandparents, grandsons, and godparents all weave a web of relationships that enlarge social and territorial ties. At the same time, the definition of family is often extended to include the entire community to the extent that classificatory kinship terms such as cousins, uncles, aunts, nieces, and nephews serve to describe an extended number of people with whom one shares some kind of kinship ties, even fictive ones. It is not unusual to hear someone who arrives in a village greeting everybody by simply calling them family, even those who are not actually blood relatives. As noted by anthropologists Anne-Marie Losonczy (2006b) and Natalia Quiceno (2016), kinship networks and the act of traveling through them contribute to creating a sense of territory, as much as the pattern of rivers, watercourses, and settlements is what shapes the experiences that people cultivate with their own families, lands, and communities.

In Bajo Atrato each community is situated on the shores of a particular river and has adopted the name of said watercourse. For example, the communities of Chicao or La Madre are situated near the mouths of the Chicao and La Madre Rivers, small rivers that disembogue into the Domingodó River, which is a tributary of the Atrato River. Some other communities, such as La Grande or Pedeguita, are located along the Atrato but have taken their names from the swamps and lakes located near their villages. Rivers provide a strong sense of individual and collective belonging. People often identify themselves as belonging to a particular river—"I'm from the Curvaradó River," "My community is located on the Truandó River"; alternatively, communities may identify as being part of a specific basin: Chicao and La Madre each has its own community council, but both communities belong to the Domingodó basin, which has its own great council, an organizational instance that brings together and represents all communities living along this river basin. In Bajo Atrato collective property titles were distributed in 1996 and 2000 by the government to the Afro-Colombian communities of river basins, which were organized into both community councils and great councils. Both community councils and great councils constitute administrative and political organizations responsible for the use and protection of these collective lands.

As it has been described by Oslender (2004, 2008), the geography of the intricate river networks in the region constitutes the spatial organizing structure of Afro-descendant communities on Colombia's Pacific coast. This is true on different levels, from the most pragmatic (settlement or economic exploitation, for instance), to social (for example, kinship alliances or group solidarity based on affiliation with a specific place), to political (communities have created community councils along river basins). Oslender shows how the mobile nature of many of the social practices of these communities and their daily interaction with rivers has helped forge local and regional connections: "The aquatic space can be thought of as providing the specific place-based context in which social movements are generated and consequently mobilized" (2004, 962). Drawing on social movement literature, Oslender shows how on the Pacific coast the Afro-Colombian organizations that fight for the defense of their territories consider the rivers to be the place-specific context of their mobilization (2004, 2008), so the aquatic geography has shaped collective organizing practices as well as activist subjectivities.

Since the very first time I set foot in this region in 2003, I bore witness to what it meant to conceive of rivers as main referents of collective identity and territorial attachment. At that time many rural communities were organizing the means for returning to their territories after they had been forcedly displaced by guerrilla and paramilitary armies. I recorded in one of my field diaries the way people often described that return: they were going back to their rivers. What they were yearning for was not only their lands—their hamlets, their gardens, their fields, and their forests—but their rivers and with them their possibilities of embarking and bringing the territory into existence through their manifold travels. If homeland is the name many people give to the place they regard as home, maybe in Bajo Atrato one has to invent a compound word like *homeriver* to describe people's place of birth, residence, and deep attachment.

Rivers also constitute a privileged place for daily social interactions. Key domestic activities such as bathing, laundering, and dishwashing take place there. The washing of clothes and the cleaning of dishes and cooking utensils are activities relegated almost exclusively to women, who rarely go alone to perform such tasks. Even if they do, they usually find someone else at the river. These domestic activities are thus performed publicly, and they take place on

FIGURE 1.4. **Rafts. Photo by author.**

the rafts located near the shore of rivers. Rafts or *balsas* are multipurpose devices made of the soft and light wood from the *balso* tree (*Ochroma pyramidale*). Given their use for matters of housekeeping (for example, the washing of clothes and dishes), they are often considered by local people to be female places. Paola Mameli (2014) sees rafts as a spatial extension of kitchens: whereas the latter are private domestic places, the former are public (see figure 1.4). Rafts do not have owners, and in towns they are usually built and maintained by the neighborhood men. Rafts are indispensable devices, and they are visited all day long, starting in the wee hours, when women arrive to wash up cutlery, pots, and dishes used the night before. The morning is usually the rush hour because everyone bathes there, and as it is also the favorite moment for doing laundry because the air temperature is still cool.

Although rafts are public places, a given raft is frequented by the same group of people living in a given vicinity. Rafts are divided into two spaces: one used for washing and the other used as a toilet. The toilet area is recognizable because there is a hole in the floor. Through that hole one can often see the *cagas*, fish without scales that eat up people's excrements. The best rafts have a roof and a small enclosed room made of wood or zinc corrugated roofing sheets that explicitly divide the toilet from the rest of the space. The quality of a raft may

FIGURE 1.5. **Playground or play-river? Photo by author.**

ease the work of women: roofed rafts protect them from sunlight, just as those rafts with an enclosed toilet ensure greater privacy for their users.

Rivers are also children's favorite places to play, although they may become dangerous, particularly to little kids. Despite the constant supervision of adults, accidents are always possible on or near the rafts (see figure 1.5). Occasionally, children who are not yet good swimmers may fall and be dragged underwater by the current. I remember one weekend when the streets of Riosucio were full of posters of a missing boy who had been sent to run errands. In those days there were also rumors about two foreign people kidnapping children for the organ trade, and everybody was expecting the worst, which indeed happened but for other reasons: the kid had wanted to buy some candies with the money left over from his errands, and he had made a detour on his way home. The last time he was seen, he was crossing a bridge from a raft. His little body was found on Monday, close to the river shore, turning and turning in a kind of whirlpool where most of the garbage thrown into the river ends up.

Rivers shape life in Bajo Atrato, but on occasion they may also take life. During the summer or dry season, when there is a wind that blows all the time, the surface of the otherwise quiet and calm Atrato River becomes a field of small, pointy, but persistent waves that complicate navigation. Therefore,

FIGURE 1.6. **Cemetery of Riosucio. Photo by author.**

accidents are frequent. On one occasion, a small fiberglass boat going at full speed capsized, and two men were dragged underwater by the deep currents. In accidents such as this, drowned bodies drift downward until they reach the bottom, and they emerge on their own when gases from decomposition cause them to rise to the surface. Only then can the bodies be found. The day after this fatal accident had an unusually cloudy sky and quite cold weather during what was otherwise a normal summer day. Many people explained to me that the reason for that change in the weather was the death of those two men. Their bodies drifted by two days later on the surface of the water a couple of kilometers downstream. From the moment the bodies were found, the waves and wind calmed down. The river, I learned, is sentient, and people explained to me that with these two drowned men it had satiated its fury and that it would be peaceful for the rest of the season. There were no more drowning victims that year (see figure 1.6).

FIGURE 1.7. *Trasmallos*. Photos by author.

The waterscape also plays an important role in the economy of the region. For instance, fishing is a subsistence practice that provides crucial food to many people, although everybody in Bajo Atrato holds that fish is not as abundant as it used to be. Mostly undertaken by individual fishing households, this activity is carried out by men in the lakes and swamps near the villages. It is an artisanal practice involving the use of gill nets known as *trasmallos*, which are set in areas frequented by fish (figure 1.7). Fishermen commence their fishing trips very early in the morning, before dawn. They embark either in their motorboats or in their dugout canoes (*champas*), make the trip to their fishing spots, check the gill nets, harvest the fish, set their nets again in appropriate places until the next day, and go back to their villages to gut, wash, cure, and store all the harvested fish.

Despite the decrease of fish attributed to pollution caused by mining exploitation farther upstream the Atrato River, fishing still produces some surplus for local trade. There are about 118 different species in the Atrato basin,

FIGURE 1.8. *Bocachicos*. Photos by author.

and at least 50 percent of them are endemic (Jaramillo-Villa and Jiménez-Segura 2008). The most frequently captured species are *doncella* (some species from the *Ageneiosus* genus), *quícharo* (*Hoplias malabaricus*), *guacuco* (*Hypostomus hondae*), and mainly *bocachico* (*Prochilodus magdalenae*), a migratory freshwater fish that feeds on the fine organic material suspended at the bottom of the water (figure 1.8).

Logging is also a river-based activity: the driving of logs is possible only by using watercourses. Indeed, timber rafting is the main method of log transportation, and it heavily depends on floods, tides, and other changes in the river's flow. Some other economic activities like cash-crop farming also depend indirectly on rivers not only as a means of transportation but also because rivers' flow and flooding cycles determine which lands are suitable for cultivation.

I need to point out another manifestation of rivers or, better, the way their rhythmic materiality shapes the very form of towns and villages. Given the fact that the Atrato River overflows with some frequency, all settlements located at its shores are made of stilt houses. This kind of technology has allowed people to coexist for centuries with the periodic floods of the river, as well as to extend their dwellings to the swampy grounds surrounding towns like Riosucio. Besides protecting against floods, the shady space under these houses render them fresher as the airflow from underneath the floorboards increases, which constitutes a great adaptation to the hot environment of this region. But because of the height of these piles, houses lose stability, and their floors and walls tend to smoothly move to the rhythms of the wake left behind by boats or as the result of heavy footsteps. The slight but rather constant movement of the very floor on which one grounds herself evokes to some extent the bodily dispositions required to travel on boats and paddle dugout canoes. These embodied skills become even more indispensable when walking the streets of some of these towns. In places like Riosucio, most houses and neighborhoods are connected by flimsy, precarious planks that are used as footpaths. I prefer to describe these thin, unsteady wooden bridges as trails rather than as local versions of sidewalks because many of these bridges do not necessarily connect to adjacent neighbors or extend throughout all the streets of the town. Instead, these shaky bridges may follow winding paths that end up in front of a single house without reaching other contiguous dwellings. The art of walking on these bridges requires that bodies harness some of the properties of rivers, for balance on these planks is reached not through a solid grip on the ground but with a fluent movement of the body (figure 1.9).

To sum up, by virtue of being the main transportation routes, rivers bind together villages, communities, and towns but also connect regions. People have to travel for multiple reasons: in order to access their crop plots because cultivated areas are rarely adjacent to the villages, to visit relatives and friends, to go to any of the annual patronage festivals, to participate in meetings or soccer tournaments, to look for healers or midwives, to fish or to log, or simply to go to the towns in order to take care of business affairs. Rivers, in sum, provide different social possibilities, which in turn give rise to a particular trait of the Afro-Colombian ethos: mobility and the importance these rural communities give to the act of embarking. To embark, as I have pointed out, is to travel, and to do so is to set things in motion: to link different communities together, to expand kinship and social networks, to enhance economic opportunities, to spread one's sense of belonging, and to situate oneself within historical processes and community patterns (Almario 2001; de Friedemann 1974; Escobar 2008; Hoffmann 2004; Losonczy 2006b; Oslender 2016). As beautifully captured by Quiceno (2016), to embark is an everyday practice through which people let life, and everything that gives strength to this life,

FIGURE 1.9. **Bridges. Photo by author.**

flourish. When embarking, people are not just traveling around their territories; they are also bringing them into existence, cultivating a mode of being in which mobility, flow, and connection are indispensable to the creation of strong social, economic, symbolic, and riparian networks. Embarking conveys the idea that rivers and movement or, even better, that territory and flow are simultaneously produced "in and through relations" (Escobar 2008, 26). There is so much life happening in the river—bathing, working, playing, resting—that even if people do not travel, a river does not cease its embodiment of movement: flowing, changing its current and form, flooding over lands, carrying things. Just as this flowing allows communities in Bajo Atrato to attain what they consider to be a good life, the counterpart of flowing—in this case, stagnation—threatens the very practices that allow people to bring their territories into existence.

Working the Land, Working the Water

In Bajo Atrato, local community councils hold meetings on a regular basis. I remember the agenda of one of these meetings in a community on the Salaquí River, when one of the points discussed was the imperative need to convene all men to a collective workday. These workdays are intended to be used to do whatever work the community may need: to improve and keep up trails; to maintain the school or its soccer field; to look after collective crops; to repair boats, outboard motors, electric generators, or any other collectively owned equipment; to prepare the hamlet for gatherings or celebrations. This time the goal of the collective work was to clean the main transportation route. As I myself had taken that route on my way to that meeting and endured the difficulties of transportation, I agreed that the route urgently needed cleaning and maintenance. All the men in the community were supposed to attend that workday, for it would involve a lot of hard work. I volunteered, but I warned people that my skills might not be the most suitable for the required tasks: I knew that unlike an ordinary cleaning using brooms, rakes, trash pickers, and garbage cans, this work would require machetes, axes, chainsaws, and sharpening steels. During the collective workday our goal was to take away the tons and tons of woody debris—broken branches, sticks, fallen trees, rotten tree trunks, stumps, log blocks, and all kinds of driftwood—that the flow of the Salaquí River had been dragging downstream over the course of recent weeks and that because of its accumulation near the river's shores was now blocking the access for motorboats and dugout canoes.

These *palizadas*—logjams or river blockages provoked by heavy rains and the constant overflowing of rivers—are huge groups of woody debris that obstruct navigation. *Palizadas* are not a banal issue in a region where it may rain from twenty to twenty-five days each month and that receives an average annual rainfall of 11,770 mm (463 inches) (Proyecto Biopacífico 1998). In Bajo Atrato water is an overwhelming element that assaults your body and your senses, manifesting itself everywhere: coming from the heavens in the form of clouds, rains, downpours, deluges, dews, drizzles, and *serenos*; flowing through rivers of all sizes and depths or through water bodies of all kinds of shapes, from floodplain lagoons to swamps and shallow lakes; moving down into the ground, permeating the land and saturating soils; steamily floating in the air in the form of a heavy moisture that permeates your clothes, skin, and pretty much everything you touch; or simply coming from inside your body because you sweat so much that your clothes get drenched and can never dry out.

FIGURE 1.10. A *palizada*. Photo by author.

With the huge amount of water flowing in Bajo Atrato, it is common that heavy rains and tides drag with them incommensurable quantities of debris that end up clogging the rivers. There are different kinds of *palizadas*. Every rain, regardless of its intensity, causes some tree branches and logs to get dragged down the river. This debris sometimes gets stuck in meanders or simply entangled on the riverbanks. Other *palizadas* are the result of heavy rains and sudden floods, especially in the headwaters of the rivers, when the torrent drags a large pool of organic materials, including soil, plants, fallen trees, and even dead animals, down the river. These *palizadas* may cause trouble if for any reason they become jammed and block the flow of the river. Once they get stuck, they are more likely to grow in size either because of the accumulation of more materials always being naturally dragged along by the river or because of new rains, torrential downpours, or floods tugging more and more debris downstream (figure 1.10).

Floodplain lagoons and swamps are another important source of materials that become part of river blockages. These places are populated by aquatic plants such as *arracacho* (*Montrichardia arborescens*), *lechugas*, and *orejiburros* (both from the *Pistia* genus), plants that have roots barely submersed beneath the water's surface and that may easily break away from

FIGURE 1.11. A sea of *arracacho* plants. Photo by author.

their root system when the water level increases. I have seen entire forests of *Pistia* plants blocking waterways and floating islands of *arracacho* traveling down the Atrato River (figure 1.11).

Palizadas are not an exception but rather a normal condition of navigation on the rivers of this region. Depending on the kind and the size of the *palizada*, there are different ways for river travelers to deal with it. The most common *palizadas* are just fallen trees or branches going across from one of the riverbanks to the other. In these cases, and depending on the water level or the weight of the boat and its cargo, boats may simply cross under or above the obstacle, always being pushed and pulled by the people traveling on board. If a *palizada* is not too thick, trees and branches are cut and left to be dragged away by the river. This is why it is so important to carry at least a machete every time one travels. But if the *palizada* is big and has a lot of debris, the boat has to break through it by taking it away and cutting into pieces the most manageable trunks and logs, just enough to make room for the boat. The real difficulty here depends on whether you are going downstream or upstream through these *palizadas*. When going down, as a friend I met in Chocó used to say, "Even the stones roll," but going up, in a boat full of goods, as the boats usually are when people travel from the town to their hamlets, things become harder. Here is when two other instruments become indispensable: paddles (*canaletes*) and a *palanca*, a large, hard wooden stick forked on one of its ends. Both tools are used to propel or to push the boat.

Even if one does not encounter true *palizadas* during one's travels, the rivers are always full of logs, branches, and pieces of wood floating around, sometimes hidden just beneath the surface. This unseen debris is the most dangerous: it might break or overturn boats, or cause serious damage to the lower unit (*pata*) of the outboard motor. These kinds of accidents are quite frequent, and one constantly hears stories of people losing bags, food, animals, goods, and even outboard motors during their river travels. There have also been some fatal accidents caused by these unseen tips of branches stuck in the riverbed. Even the most experienced boat drivers are not exempt from these accidents, and in order to avoid any breakdown of their outboard motors they always carry a set of nails to repair the propeller drive-shaft or an extra propeller, which are the pieces that break most often when navigating the rivers of this region. Boat drivers are very dexterous, and even if the wooden boats that navigate these rivers are rather slow, drivers must react quickly to the presence of any debris and constantly tilt the engine out of the water in order to avoid the gearbox hitting a tree trunk or other debris. When a driver is navigating, there is usually a *puntero* on board, a person who sits in the front and indicates to the driver the presence of any obstacle or debris and who, with the *palanca*, helps the boat to turn quickly in the most pronounced river curves (figure 1.12).

Now let us get back to that call from the local community council to perform the *limpieza* (cleaning) of the *palizada* in the Salaquí River. Most men residing in the community attended, and those who did not had to pay a fine. The work started early in the morning, and men were carrying their indispensable tools: sharpening steels, machetes, and axes. There were also a couple of chainsaws as well as some ropes. The procedure for unblocking the river seems simple in its logic, but it involves a lot of hard, physical work. Branches and small logs must be taken away and put on the riverbanks, but not too close to the river: the idea is to avoid tides or sudden floods dragging all that wood downriver again. In order to take all this debris out of the water, some men jumped into the river while others, including myself, formed a human chain on the riverbank and started to pass logs from one to another, accumulating a pile of wet and rotten wood. Sometimes those in the water had to dive in order to better push the heavy stump pieces out of the water. But this was not always possible because the depth of the river might render it difficult to find a fixed point from which a person could lift said stumps in order to get them to the riverbank. When the strength of a single man was not enough

FIGURE 1.12. A *puntero* holding a *palanca*. Photo by author.

or the piece of wood was too heavy to be lifted, men dove in order to tie a rope around the stumps, which were then pulled by the men onto the shore and later cut into pieces using chainsaws. In this way, these pieces became manageable and could then be placed beside the piles of wood. By cutting wood into small pieces, people made sure that if this debris was dragged away again by the water, it would not get easily stuck.

Meanwhile, the chainsaw operators worked on the bigger logs: those that, because of their size, impeded the rest of the debris from going downstream. As rafts of debris continue to accumulate every day with the force of the river, these logs become more and more jammed together, and the rafts themselves become very thick. Indeed, it is often possible to walk over these *palizadas* without sinking. Standing on those stumps, chainsaw operators proceed by cutting the big logs into pieces. It is not an easy task, for operators have to avoid getting their chainsaw's engine wet. Also, when the chainsaw's bar hits the water, the saw chain starts to splash water violently, so the operator has to know very well where to stand in order to avoid getting excessively wet or blinded because of the splatter. It is hard and very noisy work, especially when there are three or four chainsaws working at the same time. Once a main log has been cut and released, the whole raft starts to loosen, and branches and small logs are more easily taken away. Finally, the small debris is left to be dragged along by the stream.

That particular *palizada* in the Salaquí River was about one kilometer long, and it took four days for more than fifty men to make the river, if not totally clean, at least navigable again (figure 1.13). When performing this task, people are constantly wet because they are repeatedly getting splashed by the water or getting themselves soaked while pulling logs onto land. To be wet while you are overheated or sweating is a condition that people in Bajo Atrato avoid as much as possible because it makes them sick. This is particularly true for the chainsaw operators, who are carrying a heavy machine, getting overheated because of the proximity of the hot engine, and soaked because of the water splashing them. Nothing is worse, people hold, than the cold of water, whether from rain or rivers, when one is *enfogado*: literally "on fire, full of heat." This threatens the appropriate thermal balance the body must have in order to be in good health. In Bajo Atrato most illnesses are associated with some thermal properties and classified as either hot or cold. Therefore, their treatment involves plants, medicine, or procedures that are intended to control the excess of one of these temperatures. In the case of people getting cold because of the water while working, they experience, in the short term, headaches, fever, and cold. But in the long term, the accumulated exposure to changes between heat and cold provokes joint pain and stiffness, just the kind of pain that senior lumberjacks complain about. Other risks involved with working in the *palizadas* are stepping on a stingray and being stung by its tail or being bitten by a snake hidden in the debris because, according to local accounts, *mapana* snakes (*Bothrops atrox*) like to sun themselves on branches and logs near the water's edge and they even use this debris to travel downriver and migrate to new areas.

The work of taking away *palizadas*, which makes navigability possible, has to be done on a regular basis. Sometimes this work is the result of an individual initiative, as when someone traveling or transporting plantain or timber needs to cross and decides to clear debris. On other occasions, the work is done by members of a local community council because the *palizada*'s size requires more effort. In the case of a vast *palizada* like the one found on the Salaquí River, the intervention of the great community council, a council that brings together all the seventeen local councils from this basin, was necessary. The great council took charge of all the required logistical aspects for

FIGURE 1.13. *Palizadas* dragging dead animals. Photo by author.

this communal work, from fuel for transportation and chainsaws to food for all workers. Men who were not available to work contributed with some of the fuel and food. To some extent, the cleaning of rivers also demonstrates how *palizadas* build a sense of community. Collective forms of labor around the cleaning up of this debris also contribute to processes of place making:

FIGURE 1.14. A cemetery of trees. Photo by author.

through this kind of work, people foster a version of rivers more aligned to local meanings and needs, which at the same time contributes to creating territory from the bottom up.

Through my experience in Bajo Atrato, I came to realize that the cleaning of rivers is part of the work that characterizes rural life. Navigability is not always an intrinsic feature of rivers but is, at least in this region, the result of people's work and their engagement with their waterscapes. Rivers are subject to systematic human intervention, and just as people prepare land for cultivation, they also take charge of the preparation of the rivers for transportation. In order to plant crops, the land needs to be cleared and cleaned: woodlands have to be slashed and left to rot or be burned. This work, as well as that of caring for and maintaining the crops once they have been cultivated, is also considered a form of *limpieza*. Something similar happens to the rivers. They need to be cleaned, to be maintained, and to be cared for. *Limpieza* helps produce the flow of rivers, allowing said rivers to be allies in people's lives.

Big *palizadas* clog riverbeds and streams, affecting the direction of the water, altering flow velocity, forcing water out of its natural stream, and flooding lands that people need for crops (see figure 1.14). *Palizadas* can also increase the intensity and duration of floods; they can make the river overflow its banks, increasing sedimentation but also erosion problems that lead to undercut banks, more flooding, and loss of cultivable lands. *Palizadas* can create wetlands, increase turbidity, and jeopardize water quality; they change the distribution of the soil and of the organic sediment carried in the water, for when there are huge *palizadas*, this sediment tends to settle to the bottom of rivers. In brief, if they are not dealt with appropriately, *palizadas* may become major ecological troublemakers, affecting social and economic relations and contributing to issues such as the undermining of food sovereignty (because of the destruction of crops or loss of livestock) or the clogging of communication and transport routes. *Palizadas* and the difficulties they create may be seen to represent stagnation: the antithesis of both the values that rivers embody and the practices they normally favor.

In her work on how social organizations resist armed conflict in Chocó, Quiceno (2016) describes how people conceive of "the good life" (*vida sabrosa*) as one of frequent embarkations, as a life where it is possible to travel in order to visit family, meet people, and go to work, as well as to incorporate new patches of land into agricultural production. Through all these voyages by river, people travel across their territory, and in the process, they create a unique sense of place: "To live is to embark and to embark is a way of bringing the territory into existence" (Quiceno 2016, 102). As I have pointed out previously, in Bajo Atrato to embark and to travel tend to be conflated. To embark not only means to travel via a river but also to move through social networks of kinship and collective work. In other words, rivers open up the possibility of attaining diverse social, political, and economic ideals—in sum, of living the good life that communities from Chocó aspire to. *Palizadas* impede this good life, blocking the appropriate flow of both rivers and people, making water stagnant, inactive, lacking freshness and, therefore, without life. *Palizadas* leave people without the possibility of embarking and without the chance of pursuing the journeys and activities that contribute to bringing the territory into existence.

Along with all the social meanings that are derived from river travel, the amount of work, energy, and resources put into an ordinary activity such as the cleaning of rivers leads me to believe that rivers are not just natural flowing watercourses found out there in nature but that they are enacted or brought into a particular form of being through different human practices. One such practice is that of cleaning *palizadas*. In a sense that is not completely figurative, when people take care of rivers, they work the water just as much as they work the land when they grow crops. *Palizadas* are then part of a double social bind: on one hand, they convene people to work collectively, and they rouse manifestations of solidarity between neighbors and between communities; on the other hand, they accentuate the practices of stewardship by convoking people to take care of their rivers. But if there are instances in which the indispensable *limpieza* cannot be done, *palizadas* might also harm the territory. This is exactly what happened in the Truandó, Salaquí, and Jiguamiandó Rivers, where paramilitary and guerrilla armies alike coerced entire communities to move away from their traditional *homerivers* and livelihoods.

Stagnation

Adam Ferguson, a Scottish philosopher in the Enlightenment era, described humankind as endowed with a perpetual capacity to invent and improve. "We mistake human nature," he wrote, "if we wish for a termination of labour, or a scene of repose." To him, "a passing stream, not a stagnating pool" was the emblem of humanity (Ferguson [1767] 1995, 13). Flowing streams and still waters are two powerful images: one evokes progression and improvement; the other evokes deterioration, rot. The imagery of rivers has been very useful when thinking about a vast array of human concerns, from the irreversibility of time to the everlasting nature of change. No doubt, the actuality of rivers, their presence and existence, their thereness renders them, if we employ the well-known Lévi-Straussian formula, "good to think with" (Lévi-Strauss 1962). The move from stagnating pools to passing streams conveys the idea of progression as an increase, as a process of developing toward a more advanced state. The opposite, passing from streams to stagnant waters, seems to imply deceleration, inactivity. However, between flowing streams and stagnant waters, or between rivers and *palizadas*, there is a "zone of exchange" (Deleuze and Guattari [1991] 1996) in which something of one passes into the other: even if a *palizada* conveys stagnation, this stagnation cannot occur without the constant flowing of debris carried by rivers; after crossing through *palizadas*, water changes its quality and the river some of its properties. *Palizadas* are a component of waterscapes, yet they do not partake of the flowing properties of rivers; *palizadas* are an unrooted, unstable form of forests that by virtue of their solidity amid the waters produce a version of rivers that people have a hard time dealing with. *Palizadas* are thus a point of confluence in which properties of rivers and forest meet, where their qualities become relational and the life of Indigenous and Afro-Colombian territories is in dispute. In this section I depict the conditions that favored the emergence of some epic *palizadas* in order to show that their presence and growth are related to some absences: the lack of people to take care of their rivers and the lack of boats circulating because of the forced displacement endured by many communities. *Palizadas* might also seen as a form of dispossession: the loss of rivers and hence of the possibilities of embarking and undertaking the kinds of journeys that bring the territory into existence. A last way of seeing *palizadas* is to conceive of the apparent decrease of activity they embody as representative of the acceleration of another kind of action: warfare and its predatory economies.

As mentioned in the introduction, the armed conflict in Bajo Atrato reached its peak during the 1996–2005 period, when the paramilitary forces from the ACCU (Peasant Self-Defense Forces of Córdoba and Urabá) seized the town of Riosucio and launched, alongside the Seventeenth Brigade of the National Army, a violent military campaign against the rural communities inhabiting the different basins of the region. As entire communities were driven from their lands and had to live in conditions of forced displacement for many years, paramilitaries set the conditions for the exploitation of the forests that make up *Bajoatrateño* territories, establishing criminal alliances with timber companies and fostering the settlement of people from outside the region who helped them carry out the truculent depletion of forests (J. Vargas 2016). During this same period, those communities that managed to return to their lands faced threats and crimes against their leaders and organizations, and experienced all sorts of repressive tactics ranging from economic blockades to confinement. Even ordinary things such as going to work in the crop plots or traveling between communities became highly risky activities. The blockades entailed restrictions on the circulation of boats and people, which, along with forced displacement, contributed to a progressive abandonment of rivers as the people were no longer able to care for them in the way that these watercourses require.

As rivers were less and less traveled and there were not enough people willing to clean them, *palizadas* started to grow and propagate. That was particularly true in rivers such as Cacarica, Truandó, and Salaquí, where, at the same time, the systematic depletion of forests became very noticeable. Along these rivers, the commander of the paramilitaries in Riosucio distributed more than eighty-seven chainsaws and other logging equipment in 2005, sometimes to his own combatants, sometimes to people who were not from the region, to be used in the exploitation of timber. These foreign lumbermen worked under conditions of debt peonage: they received tools and supplies from the paramilitary warlords, who also were timber buyers, paying below the market price and keeping the workers in debt (Ruiz González 2012; *Semana* 2006). Paramilitaries and timber companies took advantage of the abandoned lands and of the vulnerability of exiled communities in order to pursue their own economic interests, leaving a wake of ruined forests wherever their army of chainsaws passed. Indiscriminate logging not only ruined entire patches of forests but also created large amounts of woody debris that led to the apparition of new *palizadas* every time there was a heavy rain and the river overflowed. With forest depletion, *palizadas* just jammed and jammed. In the Salaquí River some *palizadas* grew to two kilometers long, and in Truandó they reached up to four kilometers. Those rivers were partially unblocked by the same companies and people depleting the forests, but only because they needed the rivers to be cleared to transport the exploited timber. Once communities started returning to their territories in 1999, they found several watercourses clogged and even diverted. It was only after the return of people to their own communities that these rivers were finally cleaned. But this was not possible in the Jiguamiandó River, where the *palizada* reached epic proportions.

In order to understand what happened in the Jiguamiandó, let us consider this. Geologically speaking, rivers are significant shapers of landscapes. Their main goal is to get from headwaters to sea level in an efficient way, always taking the path of least resistance. If a river finds any obstacle that cannot be easily broken down by the strength of water, it will simply skirt around it, whether these obstacles be rocks, a mountain, or a *palizada*. If the *palizada* reaches a disproportionate size, the landscape will change radically, and the river may cease to be a supporter of life. That was the case of the Jiguamiandó River, a river that lost about twenty kilometers (more than twelve miles) of its navigable area because of deposition and sedimentation that arose after the forced displacement of the communities living along this basin.

Jiguamiandó, meaning "river of the fevers" in the Emberá language, has a length of 74 kilometers (46 miles) and more than fifteen different tributaries, including the Uradá, Ancadía, Jarapetó, Coredó, and Guamal Rivers. Its headwaters are located in the mountains of the Paramillo Massif, at the northern end of the Colombian West Andes. It has an average width of 56 meters (61 yards), and its basin extends over more than 46,000 hectares (114,000 acres) (Cuesta Romaña 2010; Proyecto Biopacífico 1998). The Jiguamiandó River has what hydrologists call a low form factor—0.46 in this case—this being the ratio of depth to width of a given river, a measure indicating the flow intensity of a basin for a defined area. That means that because of its morphology, this particular river should have a low tendency to flood (Cuesta Romaña 2010). However, after a 7.2 magnitude earthquake took place in 1992, the river started to change. The earthquake produced several landslides that discharged tons of mud and sand that ended up filling some portions of the Jiguamiandó River, creating large patches of sedimentation that severely altered the depth of several pools and meanders, which became much shallower. This of course rendered navigation difficult, particularly during the dry season. Accounts of people having to pull boats for hours and hours or having to wait for rains in order to pass through these patches of heavy sedimentation were common among those traveling this river. But the situation worsened after the escalation of paramilitary violence and the massive forced displacement that left the basin without people who could clear the usual *palizadas* carried there by the rains. According to Manuel Denis Blandón, community leader of this region, in 2000 the *palizada* was 300 meters (328 yards) long, but in 2015 it had reached 13 kilometers (8 miles) (Contagio Radio 2015).

Let me say more about the conditions that contributed to the rise of such an epic *palizada*. After the attack launched by the army and paramilitary forces in 1997, communities from the Jiguamiandó basin had to abandon their settlements and livelihoods. Many simply left the region, and of those who did not, about 2,500, according to some figures (Valencia 2013, 62), chose to live hidden in the wilderness, making forests a refuge from the constant military and paramilitary raids. Very few dared to travel via the river, except some paramilitary boats that continued using that route. As an inhabitant of this region recalls, "We could go to the river only when they [paramilitaries] wanted to let us go. When they did not allow us, we could not even go to do laundry because they used to say that they were not responsible for those of us who dared to be in the river. There were many times when we could not go downstream" (quoted in Comisión Intereclesial de Justicia y Paz 2005, 28). When armed groups impede access of people to their rivers, these armies are not only violating people's freedom of movement; as well, these groups are impeding people from performing the very activities that sustain their sociability and livelihood. Not being allowed to be in the river implies, among other things, loss of access to the rafts and therefore to the possibility of laundering, dishwashing, and bathing; lack of water during the dry season; and the impossibility of freely embarking, which entails the cutoff of supplies and communications. The unfeasibility of embarking and the restrictions regarding the vital activities performed in the rivers are some of the reasons that local communities often refer to armed groups as "those that block the rivers" (Quiceno 2016, 16).

To these communities, transiting the Jiguamiandó River became a very dangerous activity as they knew they could be kidnapped or killed while traveling, just as had happened many times to others in the neighboring Curvaradó River. Communities from the Jiguamiandó basin preferred to avoid this route even if it meant their own isolation. In this way the river was gradually abandoned to its own fate: no one dared to travel downstream, no one could clean its debris, and with every rain there was a new tide; with it, the *palizada* just grew and grew. But to some extent the abandonment of the river became instrumental to the security of people: the *palizadas* also affected the armed groups that used to navigate the river, safeguarding local communities against the raids of military and paramilitary death squads.

Deforestation also contributed to the size of this huge *palizada* in Jiguamiandó. Even before forced displacement began, timber companies were leaving behind all kinds of debris, from stumps to branches and treetops:

> The [Jiguamiandó] River was not as it is today [2005]. The river had a clean course, it was wide and you could travel any time you wanted to. There was no risk at all as it was a clean river. But the Maderas del Darién Company took possession of a place called Calderón and they started there to log all kinds of woods. Once the Company left, the river started to get dry and we think it was because they left many stumps and logs to rot and sink to the bottom of the river. That was one of the reasons there was so much sedimentation. (Comisión Intereclesial de Justicia y Paz 2005, 18)

Deforestation increased exponentially during the years of terror, and the paramilitary armies themselves contributed to the exploitation of all available wood. Forest debris became the feedstock of new and bigger *palizadas* once these residues were dragged down the river by the rains and the usual river tides.

If both forced displacement and forest depletion were key to the rise of the Jiguamiandó River's *palizada*, two other elements have been decisive in its perpetuation: on one hand, bureaucratic indolence and negligence, and on the other hand, and more broadly speaking, the state politics of abandonment. Local and national authorities have shown little willingness to solve the problem even after the demobilization of paramilitary armies in 2006. The Colombian state was compelled to take action after an order of the Inter-American Commission on Human Rights in 2003. In this order, the commission called upon the state to adopt forthwith provisional measures to protect the lives and safety of the communities living in the Jiguamiandó basin, including measures to aid in the recovery of this river's navigability. However, this action was constantly postponed until 2007, when the logjam had reached 12 kilometers (7.5 miles) long. At that time the National Roads Institute—INVIAS—conducted some studies and approved a 100,000 million Colombian pesos (about US $4 million) budget to unblock the river. However, the work was not immediately set into motion because of different bureaucratic procedures, mainly because the Ministry of Transportation, the National Roads Institute, the National Planning Department, and the municipal government were all passing the responsibility for the management of the project back and forth, with no department willing to take full charge (Corte Suprema de

Justicia 2010, *Acta 209 por la cual se resuelve la impugnación formulada por el accionante Manuel Denis Blandón contra el fallo del 22 de abril de 2010 de la Sala Única del Tribunal Superior de Quibdó*). In 2010 communities from the Jiguamiandó River presented a writ for the protection of their constitutional rights, and they obtained a judgment from the Supreme Court of Justice that ordered national and local authorities to quickly adopt concrete, doable, and scheduled measures to unblock the river. In 2013, when the work finally started, the *palizada* had reached a length of 19 kilometers (almost 12 miles), and the initially approved budget was no longer enough. Moreover, whether because of inefficiency, mismanagement, or simply corruption, the contractor hired by the municipal government cleared only two-thirds of the initially projected 12 kilometers. In 2015 the *palizada* had not only returned to its original huge size, but it had also continued growing with each new heavy rain and flood.

The existence of such a *palizada* puts into evidence the politics of abandonment that has been the hallmark of state politics regarding communities from Bajo Atrato and Chocó in general. Government negligence on this issue demonstrates once again the indifference of national authorities to the precariousness that shapes people's lives in this region, perpetuating a state of affairs in which poverty, isolation, and structural violence are normalized. The blocking of the river is not a natural phenomenon even if tides, flooding, or heavy rains are part of the natural world. People in this region have always known how to deal with *palizadas*. However, there is nothing natural in forced displacement keeping people from traveling their rivers, in violence causing people to abandon their daily activities on their lands and in their rivers, in the negligence of a state letting the river die. All these actions not only jeopardize the livelihoods of these communities; they also threaten the possibility of life that the river and these communities embody. In the case of the damming of the Jiguamiandó River, human agency is a determinant, and the outcome reveals not only a failed or fragmented state, as Colombia has been often characterized (Bushnell 1993; Chomsky 2006; Safford and Palacios 2002), but also a state that through "the subjugation of life to the power of death" (Mbembe 2003, 39) deprives inhabitants of their livelihoods and allows death to happen to peoples and places deemed as dispensable.

Today, the landscape of the Jiguamiandó River changes radically as one travels from its mouth to the communities living upstream. In the areas near its mouth in the Atrato River, the water that comes from the Jiguamiandó merges with the streams of the big lakes and swamps where people fish. Here the river is still a part of the life that fishermen have traditionally cultivated. As one travels upstream, the river channel becomes narrower, and its banks become more well-defined. On both sides, the surrounding green forest rises imposingly, and through its leafy canopy the sounds of cicadas and birds emerge. But as you continue upstream, the forest presents a more desolate aspect. Trees are still standing, but their branches are dried and without a single leaf. "It looks like it's been fumigated, or like there's been a forest fire," says one of the inhabitants of this region when describing the ruined landscape (quoted in Comisión Intereclesial de Justicia y Paz 2012). Then comes the *palizada*: so big, so gray, and so thick that it seems to be the forgotten rubble of an exhausted forest. Perhaps this is what a *palizada* is after all: a floating cemetery of trees.

The stillness of the *palizada* creates the effect of the river being a stagnant body of water, but in fact water is being diverted by the *palizada*, uninterruptedly overflowing both sides of the river, where it stays at the foot of decaying trees, leaving a barrenness that seems beyond repair. Dead wood floating on the river, decaying trees on the riverbanks: there is something sinister about that gray landscape. Some leaders calculate there are about 10,000 hectares (25,000 acres) of ruined forests (Contagio Radio 2015), which means that almost one-quarter of the soil in this area is now covered by water. People also say that game animals have withdrawn because of the diverted waters. The damage has extended to both cultivated areas and settlements. There are now muddy areas where people cannot plant anything. Hamlets are now constantly flooded, and not just temporarily waterlogged like they used to be before the forced displacement. Those are just some of the long-lasting effects that war has carved in the landscape, effects that are still interrupting the flow of Afro-Colombian and Indigenous lives and overflowing into their territories with the rains that fall in one of the wettest places on Earth.

The Flow of Selves

This chapter described some of the social relationships favored by rivers, as well as the damage that may result from the impeding of the appropriate flow of rivers and hence relations. When rivers divert or stagnate because of *palizadas*, the possibilities of embarking are at stake. Without embarking, the travels that tie places and people together; the expansion of social, economic, and kinship networks; and the strengthening of collective identities and territorial stewardship cease to be possible. Through the practices of embarking the agentive powers of rivers become more evident, exemplifying the extent to which people, their livelihoods, and their modes of being are simultaneously, to paraphrase Gagné and Rasmussen (2016), subjects and objects of water. But also, without the people that take care of water-scapes through the practices associated with embarking and *limpieza*, other harmful versions of rivers emerge. In this sense one may conceive of terri-tory as being constantly redefined by the flow and quality of rivers. And this compels us to reconsider the prevalence that earthly elements have in the very notion of territory, a word whose etymological sense (from Latin *terre*, "earth") reveals that strong connection with the land. In Bajo Atrato, how-ever, more than the land that constitutes someone's domain, Indigenous and Afro-Colombian territories evoke aquatic elements: territoriality consists of a set of properties, such as fluidity and movement, that make up rivers. Per-haps a portmanteau like *waterritories* or *terrivertories* might better capture the interweaving of lands and rivers in this region.

Although *palizadas* are often linked to the specific tropical conditions of rivers in Bajo Atrato, they are not entirely natural, for human agency is often behind their expansion. This is quite clear in the case of the epic *palizadas* that harmed the Jiguamiandó River. Sedimentation, diverted waters, pollution, the clogging of watercourses, the ruination of forests, and the disappearance of game animals are more than just examples of environmental damage associ-ated with warfare. Instead, they severely affect the possibilities of being and becoming that communities have historically cultivated in and with their *ter-rivertories*. *Palizadas* add another layer to the unpredictability and vulnerabil-ity brought by war. I have suggested that *palizadas* might also be understood as instances of ruination: destroyed forests, flooded crops, compromised water quality, cultivable lands under threat, game animals running away. In this sense and given the constraints that they impose over the practices that help bring the territory into being, epic *palizadas* become a form of dispossession. And this obliges us, as Diana Ojeda (2016) and Kristina Lyons (2019) have pointed out, to expand the material and analytical grounds that concepts such as forced displacement or dispossession have in dominant legal systems.

By exploring the intimate ties between rivers and people, my aim is not simply to stress how the environmental consequences generated by the economic interests of armed groups end up jeopardizing the human rights of the communities living in Bajo Atrato. I rather propose to understand the damage provoked by war in a way that takes into consideration the co-constitutive, existential bind between these communities and their territories. In this manner, what happens to the places that encourage collective, essential practices is not disconnected from what happens to the people who belong to and dwell in said places, and whatever happens to the people hinders the pos-sibilities of the territory to exist. Thus, war not only affects recognized rights, but also, and perhaps more importantly, it affects the proliferation of qualities and relations (flow, movement, connection, social and riparian networks) as well as the existence of beings (rivers, fish, game animals, communities) that help create territory. This realization leads to a different kind of understanding of the destructive human acts associated with war, and as the following chapters discuss, their possibilities for reparation. When territory is seen as a domain of co-constitutive relations and manifold practices with the power of enacting beings and possibilities of becoming, the boundaries between people and their places, or between humans and their environments, are rendered porous. As rivers render evident, territory expresses an occurrence of relations and practices. Territory happens (Casey 1996, 27), and it does so because it is constituted within a relational network in which different kinds of beings— both human and more-than-human—participate (Escobar 2016). When considering the territory to be "more an event than a thing" (Escobar 2001, 143), approaches examining the aftermath of war merely in terms of environmental or sociocultural damage cease to be sufficient.

At the beginning of this chapter I mentioned the possible meaning of the word *Atrato*: the river of people. If *Citará*, which was the name that identified the Indigenous peoples living in Chocó at the time of the Spanish conquest, was how these peoples referred to themselves, *Citará* would not be just an ethnonym but, as in many Amerindian languages, a deictic word (Viveiros de Castro 1998): an expression whose referent changes depending on who says the word. Citará would be an enunciative marker of position, a deictic that, just like the English pronouns, denotes a person. In this case Citará would be a self-reflexive term that identifies the speaker as a subject, as an I or self. Along these lines, Atrato—"the river of the Citará people"—might then be translated as the river of the selves or, even better, the flow of the I. Because flow and movement are not just qualities attributed to rivers, but also social instances aided and made possible by them, *palizadas* constrain the flow of the activities that allow people to cultivate their humanness, their collective self. *To cultivate*, according to its etymological sense, as provided by the *Oxford English Dictionary*, means to prepare for crops, to labor, to care for tilled places; to frequent, tend, and respect. Therefore, to be cultural, to have a culture and to cultivate—which is to devote one's attention to the systematic refinement of the self—is to inhabit a place sufficiently intensively to attend to it caringly (Casey 1996, 34). This is, after all, the kind of relation that epic *palizadas* prevent in Indigenous and Afro-Colombian territories.

2

STILL WATERS RUN DEEP

Ramona loved smoking unfiltered cigarettes, and she used to smoke by keeping the lit end in her mouth. Holding the thick smoke of tobacco and burned paper inside her mouth, she extended to the max the experience of every puff. During one of my visits to her home in Domingodó and while she was lighting up a *peche*, one of the cigarettes that I had given her as a gift, Ramona shared with me her memories of the *fieras* of the Atrato River: those colossal and often voracious aquatic beings capable of causing great havoc (see figure 2.1). She then told me about a giant turtle that dug a hole in a ravine on the edge of the river, taking away a considerable amount of soil and leaving the town of Domingodó completely exposed to floods. She also described fish such as *quícharos* and *pelmás* that become so huge that they can sink dugout canoes and even ships, as well as giant *meros*, similar to groupers, that attract and swallow little fish through their gills and that have even eaten people. "*Meros*," she said, "cry at night. When a *mero* comes across a *champa* [dugout canoe] bigger than it, it goes away crying." Several people in Domingodó told me about one particular *fiera* inhabiting a swirl that forms in the sinuous river's curve located just upstream of the town. When this *fiera* swims close to the shore, it creates waves so high that they shatter the rafts and even reach the houses of Domingodó. Those who have seen this enormous *fiera* say it might be a grouper, although no one knows for sure because they have

FIGURE 2.1. **Ramona. Photo by author.**

only managed to see a section of its black back and a huge dorsal fin. Despite their disproportionate size and the devastation that they can unleash, *fieras* are so elusive these days that many think the constant traffic of boats has frightened them away. According to Ramona, it is not only the increased presence of watercraft but also the past actions of armies that have contributed to the increasingly sporadic appearance of *fieras*:

> *There was a black and ugly* mero *in the Atrato River. It was huge and hunchbacked. But it is either gone or dead because when we had to leave to Pavarandó, I remember there were military aircraft throwing bombs. The river was agitated, and after one of those bombs fell, some dirty water was stirred up. That day the* mero *died. (Ramona Rentería, in discussion with the author, Domingodó)*

When Ramona mentions Pavarandó, she is referring to the forced displacement that affected more than six thousand inhabitants of Bajo Atrato in 1997, when paramilitary and military operations forced scores of communities to abandon their lands. The air strikes were so intense and caused so much damage that, if one listens to what Ramona says and what many others attest to, they left profound traces in the places and on the other-than-human beings, such as *fieras*, that inhabit the rivers of this region. The *mero*'s death compels us to be attentive to the vulnerabilities that humans and other-than-humans share when armed violence hits. More important to my argument, the disappearance of *fieras* exemplifies not so much the annihilation brought about by war as the extent to which armed conflict transforms how local communities relate with their rivers.

As special and often marvelous entities inhabiting rivers, *fieras* embody some of the properties that local people find in their rivers: a river's potential danger, the mystery of what lies under a river's surface, the uncertainty of the travels a river allows. If in the previous chapter I focused on the day-to-day practices of care that contribute to the existence of rivers, here I complete that picture by conveying how some other-than-human beings also participate in the existence of rivers and everything they offer. Attention to the participation of these other-than-human actors is key to shifting our understanding of rivers from being given and transcendent natural resources to being existences that humans and other-than-humans contribute to creating. More particularly, this chapter shows that stories of *fieras* are a kind of knowledge not just *about* rivers but coproduced *with* them. This knowledge, anchored on a set of emplaced practices, bodily dispositions, and affective materialities, arises out of the intimate relations between rivers and their peoples. *Fieras* are more than a meaningful cultural representation of the natural world; they are a phenomenological event whose possibility of emergence resides in the rivers themselves. Through the exploration of these creatures, how they are an intrinsic element of rivers and the terms or conditions under which they come into existence, I show that rivers embody a form of agency that compels us to look again at certain assumptions regarding what a living being might be. Rivers are alive not just because they sustain human and other-than-human life but because they are vibrant, having their own tendencies and propensities (Jane Bennett 2010, viii). That rivers are alive does not mean that their mode of existence should be equated to human life, rather that they should be considered more than simply objects of environmental concern, which is a key consideration when designing ways to redress the damage experienced in Bajo Atrato.

Primarily using the oral stories of elders such as Ramona, but also inspired by the oral traditions of the Emberá and Wounaan peoples, I depict how rivers are experienced as sentient places. Similar to the way glaciers are portrayed in Athapaskan and Tlingit oral traditions, as explored by Julie Cruikshank, people in Bajo Atrato depict rivers as simultaneously "animate (endowed with life) and as animating (giving life to)" the territory where these communities dwell (2005, 3). I argue that people's dynamic ways of knowing in relation to their

Takubanabe

FIGURE 2.2. A *Chocoano* leviathan. Source: Castrillón 2010.

rivers might help us understand that *fieras* are simultaneously the outcome of people's engagement with their *terrivertories* as well as what emerges from the particular, material properties of rivers. Under this premise, understanding the existence of *fieras* as the simultaneous effect of local practices and the actualization of certain properties of rivers—as beings located between the subject-object divide—should affect policies of protection and justice regarding *Bajoatrateño* territories.

Fieras

Fieras may perturb and haunt riverine places. According to Emberá Katío and Emberá Chamí Indigenous peoples, some of these beings are capable of provoking floods as well as storms. Priest Constancio Pinto García, a missionary who wrote one of the most detailed linguistic analyses of the Katío language, describes the *jepá*, a giant serpent (see figure 2.2) provoking swirls, sinking boats, and devouring shipwrecked sailors (Pinto García 1978, 244). Héctor Castrillón (2010, 196–97), another scholarly priest, depicts the *je* and the *takubanabe*, beings that have the shape of a big canoe, that live at the bottom of whirlpools, and that may provoke very strong winds. In her work on how different Indigenous peoples approach nature, Colombian anthropologist Patricia Vargas includes a map designed by some Wounaan elders in which they drew the places inhabited by some mythical *fieras*. According to them, after humanity was created on a beach in Baudó, the Wounaan started their travel in the world by navigating upstream on the rivers of the Pacific region, but in some places they were stopped by "monstrous animals" (figure 2.3) that prevented the passage of their boats (P. Vargas 2016, 76).

Roughly speaking, a *fiera* is a special kind of being that lives in rivers and is often dangerous and willing to devour whatever crosses its path. Sometimes a *fiera* is an ordinary fish, such as *quícharos* or *beringos*, that has grown excessively in size. *Fieras* may also be caimans; stingrays with their sharp barbs; *pejesapo*, fish that cause warts when you touch them; giant turtles that live in river meanders; *sierpe*, enormous snakes that can sink boats; or *vacas de agua*, cows similar to domestic cattle but that live underwater, sunbathe at beaches, and can devour animals that drink water at rivers. *Fieras* usually inhabit swirls, rapids, and sharp bends of rivers. They use trunks or sunken trees to build their lairs deep down in these places. The presence of *fieras* is often indicated by the accumulated foam in these places, by the bubbles breaking from time to time the surface tension of the water, or by changes in the velocity of currents.

Depending on their origin, *fieras* might be classified as types or as tokens. The former are all the individuals of a class that is considered dangerous because its members share pernicious attributes such as a propensity for harming or devouring people, or an unusually large size. That is the case of *meros* and caimans: all *meros* and all caimans are instances of a *fiera* type. This mean that all the individuals of the class *mero* or the class caiman possess dangerous characteristics and exhibit dangerous behaviors. *Fieras* as tokens are the particular individuals from a class that is not necessarily considered dangerous but whose members might develop some features that turn them into menaces. For example, the *quícharo*, a type of fish usually included in the diet of people, is not considered a *fiera*, but an individual *quícharo*—a token— may become one if it grows to an exceptionally large size and becomes capable of provoking huge waves or sinking boats.

Having said that, all *fieras*—whether types or tokens—are born to be *fieras*, meaning that their "*fiereness*" is not a trait acquired over time. For example, the individuals from usually harmless fish types such as *beringos* or *pelmás* that are born to be *fieras* have physical features different than those common to fish of their class. "The bad quícharo," an elder told me, "is born to be bad; you can see the baby fish moves differently from others and produces foam around the mouth." After asking what caused some individuals to become *fieras*, Macario, another elder participating in the conversation, answered:

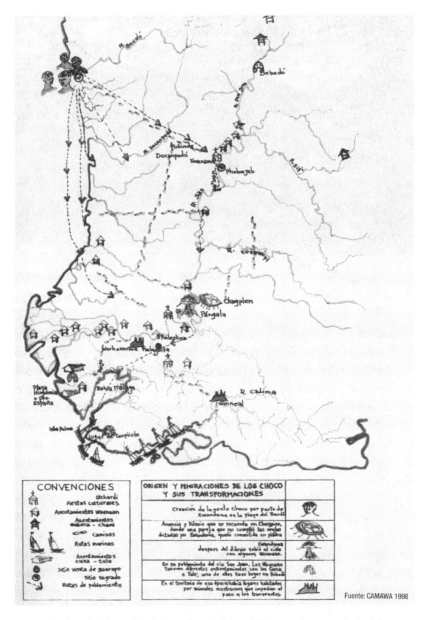

FIGURE 2.3. Historical *fieras*. Worhokormie and Guineal (the two places marked with an orange house-shaped irregular polygon) were inhabited by *fieras*. At the bottom of the map the legend says: "In the territory of the old times there were places inhabited by monstruous animals that prevented people from passing." Source: P. Vargas 2016.

Some become fieras *because each one faces its doom; they become huge.*
You can tell the difference between a fiera *and others through their size*
because fieras *grow bigger. They have a different spirit since the very mo-*
ment they are born. It is just like a family where you can find good and bad
people. Siblings belong all to the same family, but each one is born with a
particular spirit, although they all come from the same root. (Macario, in
discussion with the author, Salaquí River)

One last example of *fiereness*: caimans are all deemed to be *fieras*; following the metaphor of good and bad people in the family, Macario explained
to me that caimans were a family in which everyone was born wicked. Several people told me that some caimans are so huge and so old that plants
may grow on their backs, so they are often mistaken for trunks or branches
dragged along by the water. Caimans prefer living in deep rivers, and a few
years ago it was common to see them sunbathing at the beaches. Chencho,
an elder who used to live in a hamlet on the Tamboral River, told me that
there were two classes of caimans: *agujeto* and *sapo*. Their most significant
difference, he explained, is that the former attacks only on land, whereas the
latter attacks both on land and water. I also heard that caimans keep the jew-
els of the people they have eaten in their stomachs. Some time ago, caimans
were hunted, and former hunters told me that while preparing the caiman
skins, they used to find necklaces, bracelets, earrings, and hair inside their
stomachs because caimans are unable to expel these things.

Because of the importance that rivers and watercourses have in the region,
an encounter with a *fiera* is always a matter of concern. These *fieras* are so
widespread throughout the aquatic network that one hears in every village the
stories of a given *fiera* living near the riverine settlements. For example, some
people hold that in a meander of the Salaquí River there is a huge turtle that
has sunk several boats, but it has not been seen since the *palizadas* blocked
a large part of the river. In the Cacarica River, near its mouth, several people
have seen the huge back of a *fiera* that they have not been able to identify but
that produces massive waves every time it surfaces. In Domingodó, people say
that besides the *fiera* inhabiting a nearby meander, there is another one that
dug a cave on the shoreline, provoking the detachment of soil into the water
to the point that the town has actually lost several meters of its shoreline and
several houses have collapsed (figure 2.4). I was also told that a floodplain
that connects the Truandó and Salaquí Rivers is the lair of a *fiera* that has
taken several fishing nets away. Near a village called Vigía de Curvaradó,
fishermen say that there is a *sierpe* living in a swirl and that this giant snake

FIGURE 2.4. Sinking houses in Domingodó. Photo by author.

has sunk several dugout canoes. *Sierpes* are usually born on the shore of any stream or river, and although they can grow in shallow pools, they need deeper waters when they grow up. So, in order to reach such places, *sierpes* may provoke sudden floods with the violent movement of their bodies. They then go downstream, and because they have become so large, they can drag anything in their way. I was told that sometimes the debris that forms *palizadas* is actually the trees dragged by *sierpes* during their travels down the river.

One of the most common and fearsome *fiera* is the *mero*. Some say that *meros* are giant groupers capable of inhabiting both saltwater and freshwater. According to locals, they are great predators because they devour not only fish but also people. I was told that they can absorb anything they find in their path through their gills, and as Ramona said at the beginning of this chapter, they are known to cry like a little child. Several people told me the story of a woman who was bathing her child in the river by holding him by the arms in order to submerge him underwater. When she pulled her child back up, he had been cut in half: a *mero* had bitten off the child's legs in one single bite. Each person who told me this story added new details, but nobody knew who the woman was, and everyone located the event in a different village.

There is another kind of *fiera* called *vaca de agua*, which literally means "water cow." Pinto García (1978, 247) says that this being is called *dopaca* in the Katío language and that it provokes fever and vomiting in those who see it. *Vacas de agua* look like common cows, but their horns are much more curved, and their sharp ends point to each other. They have very big ears and live underwater. People notice their presence through the sudden formation of swirls. The water cows sunbathe on beaches during certain seasons, and although they do not eat people, *vacas de agua* can drown them if they feel threatened. Few people have managed to see water cows because of their outstanding hearing: as soon as they perceive people around, they dive deep into the river. Many people who live near rivers claim that the presence of *vacas de agua* is more and more unusual because they like living in faraway places, close to pristine forests and far from human settlements. Thus, land occupation and the noise caused by logging in remote areas have pushed *vacas de agua* to live increasingly farther away.

Fieras' Form

Fieras are not always discernible from other riverine features. For example, the *sierpe* is simultaneously a huge snake living underwater and the flood that the snake provokes. Stingrays, *quícharos*, and *pelmás* not only inhabit deep pools or swirls in rivers; they also create such hydrological features with their mere presence. A pronounced, deep meander might be the preferred place of a *mero* but also might be an extension of its own body. It is as if *fieras* and rivers are reciprocally constituted or, to be more specific, as if *fieras*, on one hand, and particular riverine places (e.g., pools, meanders) and some attributes of the water flowing in rivers (e.g., seams, swirls, ripples, riffles), on the other, are intermingled. Perhaps another way of conceptualizing what *fieras* are is by conceiving as a single thing their form and their movements, which means that their bodies and their trajectories are not distinct from each other. A *fiera* is then content and container, figure and ground, entity and milieu: it is a sudden flood and the *sierpe* that moves with the flowing water; it is a deep pool located in a very pronounced meander and also the *fiera* that inhabits it and whose mere presence amplifies said riverine feature. That a *fiera*'s presence is instantiated in swirls, ripples, or pools means that these beings are not supra-realities independent from people or from places, which is to say, they are not well-bounded entities whose bodies are discernible from surrounding riverine attributes. Rather, *fieras* happen, they emerge, and they come into being in time and space in tandem with the forms that rivers contribute to generating. To use some Deleuzian vocabulary (Deleuze 2001), one might thus consider a *fiera* more a becoming than a being or, even better, a form that is emergent within the set of flows that rivers create. An example helps to break these ideas down.

A deep pool formed in a bend of La Honda, a river of the Salaquí basin, used to be inhabited by a fierce *fiera* that, according to some people, was a huge stingray. This *fiera* came out and produced big waves every time a boat passed by or stopped near this pool. One day, some paramilitary soldiers whose boats were being damaged every time they circulated in this zone threw a grenade at this bend in the river. It seems that the grenade killed the stingray because since then no other boat has reported problems in that place. Intriguingly enough, some months after the paramilitary attack, the pool started to dry up. According to locals, this was a consequence of the stingray's death because its mere presence was what had rendered possible the existence of that pool. The attack, in other words, simultaneously killed the *fiera* and transformed the qualities of the riverine place. This implies then an intermingling between rivers and *fieras*, one that goes beyond a simple relationship whereby the river provides the setting for *fieras* to exist. Instead, rivers seem to participate in these *fieras'* coming into being. Or to put it in another way: swirls, rapids, pools, or floods are both the conditions and effects of *fieras*: they are not just the manifestations of a *fiera's* presence, but they also play a part in the generation of its being. Because of the open and fuzzy borders that exist between *fieras*, riverine places, and the flow of their waters, one is compelled to conceive of certain beings as relations and to consider that the way these relations are instantiated is what constitutes a *fiera*. *Fieras* are a gathering force but also what has been gathered; they emerge from the set of flows and relations meeting at a particular place. This way of conceiving of *fieras* might be better understood through the consideration of form, a concept I borrow from Eduardo Kohn (2013) in order to underscore some of the properties exhibited by the riverine phenomena so often associated with the presence of *fieras*.

By "form" I do not mean the *fiera's* shape or size. Instead, following Kohn, "form" refers to the set of configurations that constrain the possibilities that certain phenomena have to emerge and propagate (Kohn 2013, 157–89). In the case of *fieras*, this means that the way certain riverine attributes meet or become arranged within the course of water will lead to the emergence of certain specific *fieras*. One of the examples that Kohn discusses is relevant to the argument being made here: only under the right conditions do water currents moving around obstacles create the patterns of motion that result in the emergence of whirlpools. These whirlpools exhibit novel properties—e.g., a circular pattern of moving water—with respect to the rivers in which they appear. That is, they come to exhibit a set of features that, even if contained within the flow of rivers, are not totally reducible to said flow. Consider this: whirlpools need the flow of water to exist, and this flow is what makes them continuous with that stream from which they come. Yet that continuity does not mean that whirlpools' geometrical flowing pattern is reducible to the type of flow one finds in the river, mainly because in whirlpools water flows in a novel way that is different than the riverine flow configuration on which said whirlpools depend. From a certain point of view, Kohn argues, this different way of flowing is "something less": "Water flowing through a whirlpool does so in a way that is less free when compared to all the various less coordinated ways in which water otherwise moves through a river" (166). This "something less," explains Kohn, these constraints on possibility of water's flow that result in the emergence of whirlpools, is what accounts for their form. Similarly, I see the presence of *fieras* in places such as bends or pools, where water flows in specific ways, as a type of form or, better, as what emerges as a result of the constraints or conditions particular to said places.

Being a kind of emergent form—an entity that has properties that its constitutive parts do not have on their own—*fieras*, as well as swirls, deep pools, or pronounced bends created by the characteristic flow of water in the Atrato basin, are not just something that humans impose on the world; rather, *fieras* are part of a set of riverine properties that contribute to their coming into being. Take, for instance, the foam lines, the bubbles that congregate and break the surface tension, the rip currents, the riffles, the mud, the pools, the animals, the plants, or whatever other components that may affect the velocity, flow, and shape of water in any of the riverine places where *fieras* emerge. I do not pretend to exhaust the sum of elements and relations involved in the emergence of *fieras* because, as emergentist scholars have made evident, it is empirically and conceptually hard to ascertain when and why the intermingle of a system's components is sufficient to produce novel effects (Clayton 2006, 4). But I do want to emphasize that a lot of these elements and relations do not have their origin in the realm of human ideas that are imposed upon the materiality of rivers. This means that rather than merely reflect a sort of prefigured, local belief about some kind of abstract nature, stories and accounts about *fieras* convey, in an imaginative way (Cruikshank 2005), the properties of the aquatic worlds with which people engage. In other words, in order to exist, *fieras* do not just need to participate in a network of beliefs shared by people, but their coming into being is also heavily dependent on a set of certain riverine, material conditions. My point is that *fieras* are a challenge to the social constructionist paradigm, by which I mean that their existence is not reducible to the sociocultural representations that Indigenous or Afro-Colombian peoples have forged of their rivers.

That *fieras* are born out of rivers' form means that to some extent they *happen*. But in order to happen or emerge, *fieras* require something else for their completion—namely, the embodied dispositions of people, by which I mean the culturally learned perspectives and practices that people in Bajo Atrato employ in order to sensually know about and engage with the material attributes of their aquatic worlds. However, my point is that such dispositions do not just create *fieras* out of nothing but that these dispositions help capture, so to speak, the eventfulness or coming into being of these beings—an eventfulness contained within a set of riverine properties that, only under specific conditions, become *fieras*. In this sense *fieras* are a set of affective qualities emanating from but exceeding the assemblage of rivers' properties and people's embodied dispositions. Their elusive nature and the assortment of elements participating in their coming into being render *fieras* something occurring simultaneously beyond, around, and alongside rivers and the culturally emplaced bodies that dwell in river ecologies. In other words, they are a property of rivers as well as a property of people. To stress this point, I rely on Ben Anderson's (2009) ideas on affective atmospheres and on his reading of the work of French phenomenologist Mikel Dufrenne in relation to the aesthetic experience. Aesthetic objects, holds Dufrenne ([1953] 1973), express their own world: they generate their own set of affective qualities or atmospheres that cannot be reduced either to those of a purely intentional object (a material object with an independent and objective existence) or to those of an ideal signification (a mere state of mind that relates with said aesthetic object). Similarly, *fieras* are a collection of certain qualities of rivers, but qualities that do not uniquely belong to rivers because these bodies of water cannot bring *fieras* about by themselves. This means, on one hand, that *fieras* are not entirely independent of people: they require "completion by the subjects that 'apprehend' them" (Dufrenne [1953] 1973, 79). In this sense they belong to the perceiving subjects. On the other hand, *fieras* emanate from the ensemble of elements that make up a given riverine place and the flow of its waters. Therefore, they belong to rivers as well ([1953] 1973, 79). *Fieras* thus simultaneously belong to rivers and to people, yet they are not reducible to either.

A similar argument is made by German philosopher Gernot Böhme (1993) in his exploration of atmosphere as a fundamental concept of aesthetics. Often characterized as a kind of mood that proceeds from objects or environments, atmosphere, according to Böhme, denotes an attribute that can simultaneously be named either from the side of the object or from the side of the perceiver (Böhme 1993, 121). Similarly, *fieras* are indeterminate in relation to the environments from which they proceed or to the subjects who experience them. They are neither something objective—beings that belong to rivers—nor something subjective, reifications of human minds. Rather, they are simultaneously both thing-like and subject-like: "They are something thing-like, belonging to the thing in that things articulate their presence through qualities," and they are subject-like, belonging to subjects "in that they are sensed in bodily presence by human beings and this sensing is at the same time a bodily state of being of subjects in space" (Böhme 1993, 122). In other terms, *fieras* express a set of relations between riverine qualities *and* human embodied dispositions, and this "and," this in-betweenness, is what renders *fieras* something that transcends the subject-object dichotomy.

Like other emergent phenomena, *fieras* are constituted through an interplay of elements. In broad terms, an emergent property is what arises out of the specific relations kept by the constituents of a given assemblage (Clayton 2006; Georgiou 2003; Mitchell 2012). Take a colony of ants, for instance. The low-level behavior of any individual ant is not enough to design an anthill or to explain the organization of a colony as a whole. But as individuals specialize in their task and work cooperatively, higher levels of organization arise and create new components to the whole. In this sense the ant colony with all its behavioral patterns of organization is an entirely new phenomenon that comes from the smaller component traits that individual ants exhibit. The ant colony is then an emergent property because it is novel in and of itself: what it is cannot be broken down into its component parts. In other words, *emergence* makes reference to the relational effects produced by a given assemblage. What results from these relations is not reducible to the elements of the assemblage, which means that when the elements that make up a given assemblage are taken independently or separately, they do not have the properties the assemblage has. Along these lines, a *fiera* might be conceived of as a kind of emergent property of rivers and the human and other-than-human bodies or components that come together in a given, riverine place.

Far from being temporally homogeneous or permanent beings, *fieras* are always in the process of emerging and transforming; they are, to borrow words from Gastón Gordillo (2019), "a fleeting becoming," a process of coming into being and of "eventual dissipation" that mainly exists as an event. This is why, despite their fierceness, *fieras* are fragile or, even better, ephemeral and volatile because they can emerge only under specific circumstances (Coole and Frost 2010, 14; Deacon 2006, 124; Kohn 2013, 186). When considering *fieras* to be affective qualities emanating from the assembling of human and other-than-human components that make up the kind of everyday encounters that take place in rivers, they should be understood as possessing a sort of "in-betweenness" status in regard to the subject-object distinction: they are a characteristic spatial form generated by bodies—bodies of water but also human and other-than-human bodies—yet they are, nonetheless, a form of being that is not reducible to said bodies. *Fieras*, as Anderson aptly explains in relation to atmospheres, are a set of "affective qualities that express a certain world" (2009, 79). The worlds expressed by *fieras* are part and parcel of rivers. Therefore, whether considered as emergent properties or affective qualities, *fieras'* existence does not run ahead of a material realization (Navaro-Yashin 2012, 15), which means that they have to be understood as actual, tangible beings, too. In their encounters, *fieras*, rivers, and human subjectivities exist and act in a unity that cannot be compartmentalized for conceptualization, even less for their protection, as, I discuss in the last chapter of this book, legal systems pretend.

Bearing Witness to the *Fiereness* of Rivers

Now I can come back to the conditions that have transformed the possibilities of encountering *fieras*. The sightings of *fieras* such as colossal groupers or *vacas de agua* tend to be less frequent nowadays than they were some years ago. On one hand, people say, it seems that the constant traffic of boats and fuel and oil smells may have driven them away. On the other hand, pollution has made them tamer: "Those animals," explained a woman, "have been tamed by the soap one uses when washing as well as by the glass and garbage one throws into the river. It looks like they may get cut, so they have become a bit more docile." This docility has prevented *fieras* from causing the kind of havoc they used to, and it has therefore rendered their presence more and more unnoticed. According to multiple testimonies that I collected, it was easier to meet a *fiera* when the Atrato River was transited only by paddleboats. But nowadays, because of the noise of engines and fuel pollution produced by outboard motors, *fieras* have been progressively driven away and have even left the areas that people usually travel through:

> *Formerly we did not have so much technological stuff. We used to go from the Atrato's mouth to Quibdó by rowing, and in those days the water was not so polluted. I do not know where those* fieras *are going, but if you believe what our grandfathers used to say, there are very few* fieras *today. I remember that there used to be a huge and quite dangerous swirl near*

Tanguí, my hometown, but last time I visited, it had already dried up. It is gone. There used to be a lot of fieras *in that place. (Zurdo, in discussion with the author, Riosucio)*

People assume that *fieras* have moved farther downstream, nearer to the Atrato's mouth or even into the sea. The *fieras* that still inhabit the rivers probably remain in the deepest parts because they cannot inhabit headwaters or shallow waters. From a certain perspective, the increasingly sporadic sighting of *fieras* expresses a kind of disenchantment of the river, a process brought about by the increasing human presence in the waterscape, either in the form of the constant traffic of vessels or the garbage and fuel thrown into rivers. But as Ramona pointed out, the disenchantment of the river has also been accelerated by the military presence. I do not necessarily see this disenchantment as being one of the outcomes of modern and secular discourses and practices regarding nature, because what has eroded is not so much the way people see and interact with their aquatic worlds as the set of conditions that render *fieras* possible—namely the way human and other-than-human relations take place or are instantiated where *fieras* emerge. Outboard motorboats, fuel, garbage, grenades, or bombs change the ways that people might encounter these beings. The enchantment that *fieras* represent for locals is not a matter of the persistence of marvelous creatures that defy an over-explored or over-understood world, nor is it a reenactment of the experiences of elders and the return of more reassuring times. Rather, this enchantment has to do with the sense of awe that an ordinary river can produce; it has to do with the possibility, as Jane Bennett (2001, 4) beautifully puts it, "to participate in a momentarily immobilizing encounter . . . to be struck and shaken by the extraordinary that lives amid the familiar and the everyday."

Let us consider, once again, what Ramona said about the death of the *fiera* that used to live near her village. The disappearance of this occurring as a result of a military strike is substantially different from the dispersion of *fieras* after their travels farther downstream because of human presence on the river. When people describe the fewer sightings of *fieras* as a result of human presence, they are saying that *fieras* are moving away, not disappearing. This difference may be described as one of remoteness versus vanishing or of scarcity as opposed to extinction, which are differences related to the kinds of relationships that people in Bajo Atrato establish with the beings that constitute their territories. Let us contrast the remoteness of *fieras* caused by human presence to the death of *fieras* provoked by war. Several scholars working on the Colombian Pacific coast (Escobar 2008; Losonczy

1993; E. Restrepo 1995) have described a specific "grammar of the environment" (Escobar 2005, 152), or the series of ontological assumptions that guide how rural Afro-Colombian communities classify, sort, and hierarchize different living beings. A basic notion of this grammar is *renaciente*, literally "those who are to be reborn." It is a concept that entails a kind of succession, a continuity between the offspring of different beings. *Renacientes* may be defined as new generations: young people and children, descendants of adults who were, in turn, *renacientes* of the previous generation. *Renacientes* may also be animals' offspring, as well as plantain and manioc suckers, as these plants grow from propagules made from parts of mature stems. "*Renacientes*," as was explained to me by a man from the Salaquí River, "are the living beings of each genera- tion. You know, there is always a bud after a bud. In the same way, there is a time when we old people die and our *renacientes*, our children, take over." The concept establishes a sort of grammar in which life is seen as an eternal re- birth of what exists (Escobar 2008). *Renaciente* implies a constant flow where past, present, and future are tied together (Almario 2001) because the living beings, those that exist now, are but *renacientes* of former beings, those who were before. People are born again through their children, plants are born again through their seeds, and animals are born again through their offspring. *Renaciente* is therefore a genealogical notion (descendance), but it is also historical (the *renacientes* assume, represent, and continue with the legacy of former generations), and teleological (it is the continuation, the projection of something that existed before). In a sense, the term bridges the gap between the history, the present, and the becoming, for the *renaciente* is the perpetual succession of a being throughout time and space, the natural extension of something sharing the same origin, the same root, the same history.

As in this particular ontology beings are constantly reborn, there is little place for concepts such as finitude or even extinction. For example, accord- ing to residents, wild game, fish, and trees never disappear; they simply move away, they leave, they all go to places deep in the forest or move to other riv- ers; they stay in places that are inaccessible or never visited by people (E. Re- strepo 1995). That is exactly the case of *vacas de agua, sierpes,* and other *fieras* that people used to see in rivers: they have moved somewhere else. People's practices such as hunting, fishing, logging, or boat travel are not dooming these beings to extinction: *fieras* are simply displaced or tamed. Conversely, according to people's accounts, war has actually caused such irremediable impacts: it has made *fieras* disappear.

Undoubtedly, *fieras* are dangerous beings because they can devour humans, sink vessels, and even ruin the shores of rural settlements. Local communities are well aware of the risks these beings represent but do not attack them, much less kill them, because that would entail a series of transformations that would drastically alter river ecologies: the disappearance of a *fiera* would change the features of pools, meanders, and bends, disrupting the very flow of the rivers and, of course, of communities and their socialities. Killing *fieras* is not an action that local communities would take against these beings. Rather, killing *fieras* is part of the logic of war. The worldly consequences of armed conflict, by which I mean the power of war to overturn existences and the worlds associated with these, are at odds with the principle of *renacientes*. Although sightings of *fieras* are increasingly rare, people assume they continue to live in rivers since they are an intrinsic part of this aquatic universe. People have learned how to live with these *fieras*; they are able to notice the presence of these beings, and, thanks to the intimate relationship people have cultivated with their rivers, they are able to prevent the harm that a *fiera* could potentially cause. Local communities avoid encounters with these beings and even adjust their routines to favor versions of *fieras* aligned with people's modes of living: throwing glass and garbage, and spilling fuel or oil, are means to tame *fieras*, not eliminate them. *Fieras*, regardless of how dangerous they might become, are accepted as a constitutive part of people's territories. But this is not the way that armed actors see and even less relate with *fieras*. What they did in the case of the grenade that destroyed a pool in La Honda or the air strike that killed a colossal grouper was to attack a being that they saw as disconnected from the river ecology, as having no relation at all with its surrounding world, and even less with the world that they, in their role as military and paramilitary soldiers, attempt to occupy. Perhaps this contempt for relations within forest and river ecologies and this idea that beings and environments can be easily compartmentalized are at the foundation of the logic that guides the development of monocrop plantations or the depletion of forests, projects that fuel the war that regional capitalists and paramilitary armies have waged against *Bajoatrateño* territories.

The presence of *fieras* opens up possibilities of dwelling and being in the world that have now been hindered by war. The harm inflicted to *fieras* is more than a violence against the worldviews of Indigenous and Afro-Colombian communities because when armed actors purposefully killed *fieras*, the attributes of rivers changed as well, just as much as the violent transformation of the places *fieras* occupy transform the conditions that favor their emergence. The logic of war sets the conditions so that the river can never favor *fieras* or their kind again, and if they disappear, the world will be irremediably poorer for it.

Where the Wild Things Are

Either as instantiated attributes of rivers, particular kinds of existence populating the aquatic world, beings capable of provoking havoc, or emergent forms brought into existence by virtue of human and other-than-human interactions, *fieras* upset the distinctions between people and rivers, beings and their environments, figure and ground, singular and vague, relations and substances, ordinariness and enchantment, or that which dwells out there underwater and that which takes place when one's body is permeated by aquatic worlds. This ambiguity, this resistance to being one single thing occupying a familiar place, is somehow conveyed by the etymological meaning of *fiera*: "beast," a wild and ferocious animal. Here I use "wild" to refer to what resists being tamed and to whose mode of being is not bound by the conjunctions *either/or* (which express separation and distinction between two things or domains) but embraces *both/and* as its form (de la Cadena 2016), which are correlative conjunctions expressing the sum or coexistence of several domains.

The connection between *fieras* and certain features of rivers demonstrates that these beings are not discrete entities whose bodies and trajectories can be dissociated from their emplaced manifestations. Rather, these beings acquire form through their eventfulness—an eventfulness that renders them something akin to what Marilyn Strathern refers to as partial connections: relationships that are composed of an assemblage that is "neither singular nor plural, neither one nor many, a circuit of connections rather than joint parts" (2004, 54). Therefore, the protection of Indigenous and Afro-Colombian territories and rights should not be just a matter of protecting places or resources, because what is at stake is not something these peoples have but a set of existences with which they *are* and flourish. Hence any abrupt change in the kinds of relations people ordinarily have with rivers, as may happen in the context of war, may result not so much in a violation of their human rights as in a severe transformation of the conditions that, were it not for war, would favor the emergence of *fieras* and hence of totally new worlds and possibilities of being and becoming.

When considering the effects of war in a region where beings such as *fieras* are part and parcel of rivers, we must overcome the divide between people, other-than-human beings, and their vital places. If *fieras* emerge out of the process of assembling bodies of all sorts—yet they are not reducible to this collection of bodies—an important question arises: how to attend to rivers and *fieras* without reducing them to objects of the natural world or to the culturally affective bodies that bear witness to their existence? This question matters because it forces us to reconsider the appropriate ways to protect the life of rivers as well as the lives that rivers foster. In Bajo Atrato, taking care of the ecological harm embodied by *fieras* should not necessarily conflate with the redressing of cultural rights of an ethnic minority but should instead involve new abilities to respond (Haraway 2008) to other forms of more-than-human distinctiveness. Discussing the existence of *fieras* and what armed conflict has done to them is my attempt to address the differential experiences of war not so much in terms of people's beliefs about the world as in terms of the kinds of worlds that Indigenous and Afro-Colombian communities experience and live within.

3

IMPERISHABLE EVILS

Dead in the Water

Jonas was an Indigenous Emberá who arrived in Blind River fleeing a punishment that he considered unfair. After he had an argument with a neighbor and threatened him with a machete, the Indigenous authorities from Acandí, Jonas's homeland, imposed a sentence that consisted of tying him for eight months to a *cepo* (pillory): a device introduced in colonial times for public punishment and that is still used on some Indigenous reserves. It locks offenders of local laws to a heavy timber frame with holes for their wrists and neck (see figure 3.1). Rather than accepting this punishment, Jonas preferred to leave his land and relatives. After many comings and goings working as a peon, he finally settled down in Blind River, a village inhabited primarily by mestizo peasants who had settled the Bajo Atrato region during the early 1980s. There he came to be known simply as "The Indian," and he lived with his wife and two children in a house with a plastic sheet for a roof, right next to a small Pentecostal church.

The first time we spoke, he had just come from clearing a small area of the forest where he was planning to grow plantains. He arrived wearing a large hat and a red handkerchief around his neck. Soaked in sweat, he told us he had just used his machete to kill a *mapana*, a lancehead snake (*Bothrops atrox*) that he had found while working. He had already had a feeling that he was going

FIGURE 3.1. *Cepos* (pillories). Above: *Négres ào tronco,* watercolor by Jean-Baptiste Debret (1834). Below: Every indigenous village in Bajo Atrato has a pillory. In some cases it may become a seesaw. Photos by author.

to have an encounter of this kind because of the bad dream of the previous night: in the dream he was running through the forest, chasing two people who eventually escaped by climbing a tree. The tree suddenly transformed into a giant rocky crag, and Jonas shouted at the top of his lungs for them to come down. It was only after encountering the deadly serpent that he realized the dream was actually an omen, and having realized the connection between the viper, the crag, and the people he had followed in his dream, he decided to stop his work and return home early. As we started to talk about the *mapana* he killed, Jonas told us about his grandfather: a powerful medicine man (*jaibana*) who was killed by a snake that was supposedly sent by another *jaibana* rival. *Jaibanas* are men of knowledge who have cultivated the powers of curing disease and controlling spirits. According to Jonas, the rival who managed to kill his grandfather had been courting his grandmother, who, before she died years later—also the victim of an act performed by another *jaibana*—made Jonas promise that he would escape that land in order to live in a community not infested by evil.

A few weeks after our conversation, Jonas was found dead in the river, floating facedown in front of the family house where I used to stay. He was found in the wee hours of the morning at the bottom of a somewhat shallow pool, along with his harpoon and lantern, still turned on. Jonas had left that night to fish, as he often did, using a technique that consists of using a diving mask in order to harpoon big fish while submerged in the water. When they found him, his body was already rigid, and his face had the pallor that only death provides. There were five small but deep marks on his forehead, like the ones that serpents leave with their eyeteeth. He also had a cleft in one of his cheekbones, the kind someone might receive from a mighty blow with a stick. I saw these wounds myself in photographs that someone else took the day he was found. Those who removed his body from the water informed me they had also seen two small clefts on his head.

The suspicious nature of Jonas's death made it the subject of great consternation in Blind River. He died in a shallow pool, a place that Jonas knew well. He often fished there and was by all reports an excellent swimmer. He drowned, but he did not even have time to take off his diving mask or call for help from those who lived right in front of the pool. Nobody heard anything, and when they found him at dawn, he had already been dead for several hours. Nevertheless, the wounds found on his face and head left little doubt about the nature of his death: Jonas had been attacked by a *madre de agua*.

Water Mother

The dense network of rivers, streams, creeks, channels, floodplain lagoons, and marshes that exist in Bajo Atrato constitute an aquatic universe that, according to many elders, is inhabited by beings similar to those who populate the terrestrial and visible world in which humans live. According to some traditions shared by Indigenous and Afro-Colombian communities from the Pacific region, the universe consists of three different worlds: the world of the above, inhabited by God, the Virgin, the saints, and the souls that have accumulated sufficient merits to ascend to heaven; the world of the middle, in which humans live and where everyday life takes place; and the underworld, inhabited by the *sinculo*, people without anuses that feed on the smell that comes from cooked food (Escobar 2008; Losonczy 2006a; Sánchez 2002). This underworld is also inhabited by spirits and *visiones* that under exceptional circumstances make themselves visible to the world of the middle. *Visiones* are beings that scare people, induce misfortune, or even provoke illness. They are capable of adopting different forms in order to mislead people: a *visión* might be a human-like voice or a whistle that one hears in the depth of the forest and that causes one to lose one's way; it might also be a monstrous specter inhabiting the heart of a forest or swamp. Although *visiones* used to be associated with the wilderness, water bodies can also serve as portals for these beings, which are capable of causing real havoc. The *madre de agua* (water mother) is one of these aquatic beings.

Communities in Bajo Atrato consider the *madre de agua* to be a harmful entity that someone summons, generally through shamanistic means, in order to commit a mortal assault on another person. Among the Emberá, *jaibanas* are the only people who have the power to create a *madre de agua*, though some non-Indigenous peoples who are apprentices of shamanism, referred to as *chinangos* or *zánganos* by Afro-Colombian communities, are also capable of creating these beings. In any case, the *madre de agua* represents one of the most common dangers found in the rivers:

> *They are a kind of spirit that is used to cause harm by taking the form of animals—"There is a deer; there is a* paca*"—and if you approach to catch it, the* madre de agua *catches you; she takes you and drowns you. Then she takes you to the land to eat your nose and fingers, and then she leaves you there. (Josefina Arias, in conversation with the author)*
>
> Madre de agua *can also be a beast that comes from the water to take you. For example, you go down to the river for a dip or to defecate, and it's at that moment that the* madre de agua *catches you and drowns you. (Carlitos Blandon, in conversation with the author, Domingodó)*
>
> *The person who is going to be attacked by a* madre de agua *feels a heat, a high temperature, and is compelled to go to the water to refresh themselves. That is when the* madre de agua *attacks them. (Zurdo, in conversation with the author)*

For the Emberá, the *madre de agua* is but one of the beings that populate the aquatic world (Losonczy 2006b), whereas for the Afro-Colombians, the *madre de agua* is a strong demonstration of the power that they attribute to the Emberá. French anthropologist Anne-Marie Losonczy (2006a) describes the *madre de agua* as a primordial and powerful spirit, mobilized as a type of shamanic aggression capable of trespassing interethnic borders:

> The Emberá think that the interethnic aggression against Afro-Colombian people is transmitted by a primordial and very powerful spirit

that they call in Spanish "madreagua." This subaquatic jaï belongs to the underworld. They represent it as a hairy being of brilliant color. . . . They [*madres de agua*] may capture and eat indigenous children, unless a shaman captures these spirits. However, for their extra-ethnic victims, this cannibal jaï has the features of a naked indigenous man who captures Afro-Colombian adults and drowns them in the river or who, following the orders of a shaman, throws magic missiles that devour their insides. (Losonczy 2006a, 346)

These beings follow the orders of persons with shamanic knowledge who intend to cause harm or to take revenge for some perceived damage or offense. The assaults take place only in the water, and even though in principle they are created to target one person in particular, if for some reason their creator becomes hurt, the *madre de agua* can turn into a dangerous being unable to identify her victims:

> If an Emberá or any person suddenly wants to hurt or drown somebody, they can make a madre de agua *that is destined for one person only. If she is going to hurt you, she goes and drowns you, but only you; she does not do harm to anybody else. (Kempes, in conversation with the author)*
>
> A madre de agua *can be made of anything: a leaf of a* guarumo *tree, a corncob, a* balso *tree. But when the* madre de agua's *creator is killed, she remains disoriented, wandering from place to place. When she is confused, she can attack anyone. (Josefina Arias, in conversation with the author)*

Josefina's words convey the idea that a *madre de agua* can be created, but rather than being made out of nothing, *jaibanas* manage to bring a *madre de agua* from the underworld into this world by providing her the body of an entity that belongs to the world of the middle. Although summoned to target one specific victim, a *madre de agua* might lose her original purpose if her creator suffers some harm that impedes his ability to rule over her. In those cases the *madre de agua* will continue roaming the rivers in search of new victims. A *madre de agua* has no definite form. Rather, she is a force in constant mutation, capable of adopting the form of an animal, of a plant, or of an object that can drown her victims:

> There was once a man in Baudó named Manuel Gringo. One day, somebody sent him a madre de agua *in the form of a deer. He saw it and was going to kill it, but as soon as he approached, it took him into the water and drowned him. He was with his wife, who was pregnant, but nothing happened to her. He was found the next day in a creek. That is also why*

it is not recommended to bring a pregnant woman with you to the forest.
(Ramona, in conversation with the author, Domingodó)

It can be a sloth, a leaf of a guarumo *tree, or a person. For example,*
she paints herself as a sloth, her arms and her whole body. You approach
the madre de agua, *thinking it is a sloth, and you get close to touch it,*
but it is then that she catches you. If she is mad and attacks you, she
takes you underwater, and you will be found downstream, stranded on
a beach, all injured, with the nose, the top of the mouth, and the fingers
eaten up. (Martín, in conversation with the author)

Martín captures something very important about this being: her ability
to hide her true nature under the guise of an animal form. When Martín
describes the *madre de agua* painting her body as a sloth, he does not mean
that this being is imitating an animal but rather that she is inhabiting or ac-
tivating another kind of body. It is this ability to become a game animal—a
sloth or a deer—that allows her to get close to her victims and then invert
the relation between hunter and prey. In her account, Ramona also brings
up the risk of being in the forest with a pregnant woman. In the case that
Ramona describes, the attack was perpetrated by one of those wanderer
madres de agua that was somehow attracted by the presence of the woman.
According to many people in Bajo Atrato, the bodies of pregnant and men-
struating women exude a kind of heat that attracts sylvan beings, which are
often associated with the characteristic coldness of the forest. Attacks of a
madre de agua are identifiable by the marks she leaves on the victim's body:
the nose, ears, mouth, and/or fingers are devoured. The attacks can also be
distinguished by where they take place: while bathing by the riverbanks, at
common fishing spots, or in shallow pools where the chances of drowning
are very low. *Jaibanas* may also assault each other through *madres de agua*:

For instance, two jaibanas may wish to prove which one is the more power-
ful. To demonstrate his mastery, one might send a madre de agua *to the*
other. If the recipient has superior skills, he would return it back to the
sender. (Macario, in conversation with the author)

In those cases the *madre de agua* may get out of control and start attacking
anyone. Precisely because of these frequent *jaibana* battles so often mentioned by the Emberá people, I was warned in some places to avoid going
to the river at certain hours of the night. It is also because of the potential
presence of some mad, disoriented *madre de agua* that many people prefer
to always go bathing with company, for *madres de agua* do not attack their

victims unless they are alone or with pregnant women, according to what Ramona mentioned above.

The Uncertainty of a Coming Attack

Victor, the first one to see Jonas's body floating in the river, was so afraid that he did not dare to touch it. Instead, he called his older brothers. The news spread, and some neighbors quickly arrived. However, nobody wanted to enter the water to retrieve the dead body. It was not until later, when other Emberá neighbors arrived, that Jonas was removed from the water. Then people discussed the necessity of telling his widow what had happened; however, not only did nobody want to give such terrible news, but nobody was even willing to go because that meant traveling down the river. They were afraid that during that excursion they would find the being that attacked Jonas. After much discussion, they decided to form a committee of three people who would go to Jonas's home. When they arrived, they found his wife already awake. She told them she knew something wrong had happened because a few hours before they arrived, she had heard the footsteps of her husband taking off his boots and leaving the fish in the kitchen, just as he had done so many times before. The people in the committee confirmed from this account what the Emberá man that had taken Jonas out of the river had told them when they were deciding whether or not to inform the widow: that she was probably aware of the bad news already. This same Emberá said that while taking Jonas's body out of the water, he had felt something large and smooth rub against his leg. He believed the evil being that had killed Jonas was still out there. An old Emberá lady that was with them said that the victims of *madres de agua* are also identified by the bruises that appear on their bodies, the same ones that people saw the next morning on Jonas's arms and legs.

This knowledge of the cause of death nevertheless left two unresolved mysteries. First, locals did not know if the *madre de agua* had been sent specifically to Jonas or if she was one of those that had become disoriented after the death of her creator. The second question to be answered was about the form that the *madre de agua* had taken because it was important to be able to distinguish this being from an ordinary animal. Victor and his brothers, who were the first ones to find Jonas, mentioned that they had seen an enormous log next to the body. At the time they did not pay much attention to it because the river often carries a lot of fallen branches. After removing the body, however, they realized that the log was gone. Evaristo, Victor's oldest brother, told me that Jonas's feet were very close to this trunk and that although at first he thought they were entangled with it, he then realized that they were actually on the log, barely held above the surface. The next day they did not find any trace of this log, not even downriver, where it could have been taken by the stream. They speculated then that the trunk was actually a giant serpent, the same one that had grazed the leg of the Emberá who helped take Jonas's body out of the water. So the *madre de agua* was a snake, but the mystery of whether or not the attack had specifically targeted Jonas could only be solved in the coming days. In the meantime, Blind River inhabitants had to wait uncertainly and see whether there would be another victim.

On *Jaibanas*

"Water mother" is how I have roughly translated the Spanish term *madre de agua*, which is what this being is called in Bajo Atrato. In the Emberá language, the water mother is called *andomía*, a term that is also used to refer to evil spirits in general. This word is similar to that used to refer to a primordial being—Antumía—that has existed since the beginning of time and was banished, according to Emberá mythology, by the Creator to the underworld (Castrillón 1982; Losonczy 2006a, 2006b; Pinto García 1978; Vasco 1985). Antumía is a powerful entity, a fundamental spirit or *jaï* used by *jaibanas* to counteract attacks from other *jaibanas*. In the words *andomía* and *Antumía* the suffixes *do* and *tu* refer in the Emberá language to the word "river" in the same way as the suffixes that are found in the local toponymy: Truandó, river of the leaf-cutter ant; Domingodó, river of the fork-tailed flycatcher bird; Curvaradó, river of bats. When the Emberá translate the name of this entity into Spanish, they emphasize its feminine character: mother. In their use of the word "mother," Emberá also designate her as a primordial being because she is not only the origin but also the owner or master of the evil spirits that inhabit the underworld. The Spanish article *de* in *madre de agua* indicates that she is both made of and a part of water. The association with the aquatic universe, which is evident in its name, describes then not only the aquatic underworld where she lives but also rivers as the threshold she uses to emerge and convey her presence. In conclusion, a *madre de agua* is fundamentally a primordial, evil, feminine being that lives in water and that might be used by the *jaibanas* as a means of shamanic aggression.

The *jaibana*, literally "one who gathers a large number of jaïs" (Pinto García 1978; Vasco 1985), is a person of knowledge who serves as a traditional healer, a consultant, and an advisor—in short, a spiritual leader able to diagnose illnesses and heal them with the help of the *jaïs* (spirits) that he has learned to

FIGURE 3.2. *Jaibana* Carlitos and two of his staffs. Photo by author.

control. These *jaïs* are invoked through chants and through the use of staffs that *jaibanas* carve themselves. These staffs signify the type of spirits that the *jaibana* has as allies and the illnesses that he has the power to heal. The ceremonies in which the *jaïs* are invoked usually take place at night. The *jaibanas* gather people together in a house around a small altar, sharing food, drinks, and tobacco for several hours. Then they perform their chants while seated on a stool they have carved, keeping their staffs in one hand and branches of medicinal plants in the other (figure 3.2). *Jaibanas* drink large amounts of maize beer or *aguardiente*—a strong alcoholic beverage obtained by the distillation of sugarcane—that have been placed next to them on plantain leaves. They smoke almost uninterruptedly. Through their intoned chants, which are alternated with whistled melodies that seem to convey the shape, pattern, or energy of the summoned *jaïs*, *jaibanas* talk to and negotiate with these spirits, who finally agree to act under the *jaibanas'* guidance. This power makes *jaibanas* persons of ambiguous character: they are the ones who can detect and cure illness but also the ones who can inflict it.

Jaibanas can increase their power over time by attacking and weakening the *jaïs* that other *jaibanas* control. One of the *jaibanas* I interviewed explained to me that these battles happen in dreams, through chants, after the ingestion of certain plants. A *madre de agua* might then become one manifestation of these battles between *jaibanas*; probably the cruelest, because through this battle a *jaibana* seeks the rival's physical elimination and, with said rival's death, the control of all the *jaïs* that he had previously possessed. Controlling a *madre de agua* is extremely difficult, and even the most expert *jaibanas* struggle to make these spirits direct their attacks exclusively at their enemies. Furthermore, if for some reason the *jaibana* that controls a *madre de agua* is not able to submit her completely to his will, the *madre de agua* escapes, wandering the rivers and causing indiscriminate harm to anyone who stands in her way. The *madre de agua* is a powerful spirit used not only to attack but also to defend. There have been times at which the *jaibanas* have unleashed the *madres de agua*'s fury with the goal of defending their villages against the attacks of their enemies, whether those enemies be other Emberá, Afro-Colombians, or mestizo neighbors, and regardless of whether they be civilians or armed groups.

Becoming a *Mojano*

After the commotion that marked the first hours following the discovery of Jonas's body, the villagers started talking about certain omens that had anticipated the *madre de agua*'s attack. Because an omen is something that allows people to establish connections between things that apparently belong to different domains, Jonas's death became a kind of Rosetta stone that allowed the village residents to interpret the weird events that had happened previously. For example, the same evening Jonas was found, another pair of fishermen had tried unsuccessfully to catch fish but quit their mission after the nylon they were using for their nets had broken three times. One of the Emberá said that he had decided not to leave his house because he had felt something out of the ordinary in the river, something he described simply as a hint of bad energy. They even said that Jonas had heard the chant of a *jaï* the previous day and told his wife about it. Others who had seen Jonas in the hours before his death said that he had an unusual attitude: when they greeted him, he replied without looking at them. Someone else explained that the evil spirit that attacked him was probably already inside him exerting her power. In this sense a death caused by a *madre de agua* is not unlike any other death in Bajo Atrato: it does not occur in one instant, for there is often a sense of foreboding hanging over people and the places they visit. It is as if the attack itself is but the culmination of a process that had already started because in this region death is not a single, terminal event but rather a long-term transformation that announces itself with different kinds of auguries.

As if it were not enough to have to deal with the *madre de agua* and the possibility of a new attack, the Blind River community also had to decide what to do with Jonas's body. For them, mostly evangelical protestants, it was not a trivial matter. Although they knew the body had to be buried, for many people the local cemetery was not the best place for an Emberá that had presumably died by a *jaibana* attack. Given that Jonas was not originally from Blind River and that he had to be buried far from his homeland and far from what locals considered his own people, some inhabitants of Blind River feared he would become a *mojano*, a sort of monstrous man-eating were-jaguar that returns to life and starts devouring livestock, dogs, and people. Since nobody in Blind River wanted to take such a risk, people decided the best option would be to take the body to the town of Riosucio and give it to the Emberá regional organization.

In essence, a *mojano* is an Indigenous person that comes back from death as a cannibal with a feline aspect. However, such an extraordinary metamorphosis is performed only by a few powerful *jaibanas* who have accumulated a great deal of knowledge about a particular plant called *tonga* or *güibán* (Pinto García 1978). People in Blind River knew that this was not Jonas's situation, yet some fears prevailed and prevented them from allowing his body to be buried in the small local cemetery. According to some researchers (Cheucarama, Yabur, and Pineda 2006; Sánchez 2002), *tonga* is a psychotropic plant used by some Emberá traditional healers to diagnose and heal particular illnesses. But to many evangelicals, be they Afro-Colombian or mestizo peasants, the plant is but a means to enter into contact with demonic forces. It is through the ritual consumption of this plant that some are capable of turning into *mojanos* after they die. *Mojanos*, also called *aribamias* in the Indigenous Emberá-Katío language (Pinto García 1978), come bloodthirstily to life shortly after they have been buried, and the only way of killing them is by plunging stakes of the palm *chonta* or *caña flecha* into their chests.

When the people of Blind River delivered Jonas's body to the Emberá leaders living in the town of Riosucio, these leaders were reluctant to receive it because, according to them, even though Jonas was an Emberá, he was not from the region and had no relatives or close affiliations there. Moreover, according to the rules of the Emberá Regional Council, those who leave their community of origin lose their status of residency after one year. For the Indigenous organization, it was clear that Jonas belonged to the Blind River community and that it was this village which should take care of the burial. However, for the people of Blind River, Jonas was, above all else, an Indigenous person, and the time he had lived among them was less important than the fact that he was born and raised as an Emberá. Therefore, he should be buried by his people and according to their customs.

There were long discussions between the Emberá leaders and the people of Blind River because, in addition, no one had the resources to pay for the funeral. Together, the leaders of the Indigenous organization and some inhabitants of Blind River eventually arranged to have the mayor of Riosucio donate a coffin. The Indigenous organization decided then that Jonas should be buried in the Cliff, an Indigenous reserve located at the headwaters of the Salaquí River. According to one of the Indigenous leaders I interviewed, they chose that location for economic reasons: to bury Jonas in Riosucio's cemetery was too expensive, whereas in the Cliff they had to pay only for the transportation of the body. The people of Blind River were relieved by the idea that Jonas was going to be buried among his people, even though the truth was that he had never met anyone in the Cliff and that he could not even be buried following the traditional Emberá custom: with his most valuable belongings.

The Combination of All Forms of Resistance

In order to come to grips with Jonas's tragic fate, we need to go back in time to the period of the escalation of paramilitary violence in Bajo Atrato. In 1997, after the paramilitary offensive and the exile of a huge majority of Afro-Colombian and mestizo communities from the Cacarica, Salaquí, Truandó, Domingodó, and Curvaradó Rivers, the Indigenous regional authorities held several meetings with the intention of defining appropriate strategies for resisting both armed conflict and forced displacement. Despite the many threats against their leaders, the selective murders in their communities, the economic blockades that prevented people from traveling or going to work in their fields, and the pressure resulting from the presence of forest-dwelling armed men living in their territories, the regional Indigenous organizations agreed that they would not leave their lands under any circumstance. They stated that they were not going to leave their ancestral territories, thus putting themselves at the mercy of paramilitary interests, and that they would resist and defend themselves and their lands just as their ancestors had done since the time of the Spanish colonization of the Americas.

Indigenous communities planned their resistance on various levels: they strengthened their social organizations, ensured that the community would respect local rules and traditional justice mechanisms, denounced rights violations, demanded state intervention, and avoided any type of contact or transaction with the armed groups, including guerrillas and the official national army. It was also agreed that the *jaibanas* would use their ancestral knowledge to mobilize both forest and river spirits in order to protect their people and their territories. Accordingly, *jaibanas* who had the power to negotiate with the spiritual guardians or masters of animals released snakes, wasps, and venomous ants so that soldiers in the armed groups would experience difficulties in the forest. Others planned to send storms and winds to prevent the armed groups from reaching their villages. Some other *jaibanas* discussed the need to adopt more-active forms of resistance and some retaliatory actions against those who assaulted their communities. It was at this point during a meeting of Indigenous leaders that the idea of using thunder as a means of defense arose.

According to certain Emberá traditions, thunder is the noise produced by the drum of a very powerful *jaibana* who ascended into heaven in mythical times (Pinto García 1978, 216–18). Its sound precedes not only the arrival of the rains but also the arrival of great *jaibanas*, who are capable of using this element at their will. That said, in Bajo Atrato, its use against armed groups was unprecedented, and the *jaibanas* who were asked to produce the thunder did not really know how to perform such an attack. Dalila Conquista, a knowledgeable Emberá leader who worked for many years at the regional great council, told me about the day that *jaibanas* decided to use thunder as a means of defense. According to her, not many *jaibanas* have the knowledge to master the use of thunder because it must be invoked through a plant that is associated with this particular *jaï* and with the aid of very specific chants, which are restricted knowledge. Even though none of the *jaibanas* of Bajo Atrato had performed thunder attacks, they decided to at least give it a try to see if the chants and the invocation plants would work on this powerful *jaï*. One of them announced the day and place that they would do it: it would be in the town of Riosucio, directly over the police station. The police station was not a random target. Connivance between the police and paramilitary death squads was always flagrant in Riosucio: paramilitary boats traveled at their leisure without ever being stopped by the authorities, assassinations occurred with total impunity under the gaze of military officials, and paramilitary commandants often met with police officials. During many armed assaults conducted in the rural areas, people also observed that soldiers belonging to paramilitary armies and to the state's formal armed forces were often the same men, carrying the same weapons and wearing the same uniforms, although the men would be careful to remove the patches and insignias of one armed group and replace them with those of the other, depending on the context.

Dalila said that the afternoon of the day marked for the conjuring of thunder was particularly sunny and that she was skeptically watching from her house to see what would happen at the police station. Suddenly, at the agreed-upon time, she saw a bolt of black smoke descend fulminantly near the station. The thunder did not hurt anyone, and although it did not hit the exact place that the *jaibana* had intended, he had made it happen: he had successfully conjured the thunder *jaï*. Dalila thinks he did not hit the target because, as with any weapon, it takes practice to learn to use it properly. After this event and having confirmed its power, the *jaibanas* agreed to use thunder as a weapon but only when they were being attacked by the enemy and not under any other circumstance.

The *madre de agua* was also part of the repertoire of forces that *jaibanas* mobilized to protect themselves and their communities against the armed groups. Amaranto, a Riosucio inhabitant who worked for many years with the nongovernmental organizations that supported the Indigenous councils, told me the following story:

> We were once in a ravine called Chorrillo, in the headwaters of the Chogoroto River, and a madre de agua *was on a* pichindé *tree. It was around 6:00 p.m. I saw a mass, a mass that fell in the water and that almost fell in our boat. I asked one of the Emberá what had fallen, and he said it was a* madre de agua. *When he said that, I stood up and moved from the middle of the boat to the back where the driver sat because I was very afraid. When we arrived at the village, I asked the leaders why they had placed a* madre de agua *there, and they said that it was to support the people. It's a form of resistance: to use and invoke the things that they know. And that worked. I wished we the Afro-Colombians would do the same. (Amaranto, in conversation with the author)*

Amaranto emphasizes the tenacious willingness of the Indigenous peoples to resist the war without abandoning their territories, unlike most Afro-Colombian communities, who felt perhaps less equipped to fight this particular battle. His "I wished we would do the same" is also a statement recognizing the intimate relation of Indigenous peoples with the forest and their deep knowledge of the different kinds of beings dwelling in both this world and the underworld. That knowledge, in his eyes, represented a new way to counter the effects of the military presence. I heard similar stories about how some communities near the Domingodó River released *madres de agua* in order to prevent *kapunía*, literally "non-Indigenous people," from getting close to their villages. Reports abound about the effects that these and other spirits mobilized by the Emberá had on several paramilitary soldiers. Some were attacked at night while on guard by the riverside; others felt possessed by spirits that were controlling their will. In Riosucio, for instance, paramilitaries who settled by the canal close to the hospital used to see a huge alligator that transformed into a long-haired Emberá man as soon as it touched the land. The Emberá man would walk silently and calmly toward the soldiers, disobeying their orders to stop. When they would shoot, instead of hitting him with their bullets, they always ended up wounding one of their fellow combatants.

Another story I heard involved a local, young paramilitary soldier—forcibly recruited by a commandant—who was appointed to stand guard one night on the shores of the Salaquí River. There he saw a human-like presence wearing a camouflage uniform on the other side of the river. The soldier knew the man on the other side of the river was not one of his comrades in arms and, suspecting the person was a guerrilla soldier, he aimed his rifle. At the very moment he shot, he fainted and got seriously sick. He was hospitalized for several days, and his comrades never found any trace or sign of the presence that the young man swore he had seen. After that incident, the soldier started to be known as *Maraña*, literally "a thicket, a dense aggregation of entangled trees and tall shrubs." According to the people of Bajo Atrato, spending a lot of time in the wilderness, as paramilitary and guerrilla soldiers often do, can lead to a loss of discernment, as well as raucous, frantic, and savage behavior. This nickname encapsulates some of these traits.

The incidents of paramilitaries being affected by spirits, *visiones*, and other sylvan beings were so abundant and frequent in Bajo Atrato that they were not taken as the made-up stories of some superstitious soldiers. To fight back against these types of attacks, some paramilitary commandants decided to take two actions: the first was to threaten the *jaibanas* and anyone suspected of practicing anything they considered sorcery; secondly, paramilitaries planned to counteract the actions undertaken by *jaibanas* with another kind of sorcery.

A Latent Threat

In the days following Jonas's death, rumors started circulating in Blind River. This time they were not about the cause of his death but about the possible perpetrators. According to some beliefs, in the case of attacks committed through acts of sorcery, the first person to find the dead body is actually the perpetrator. Victor, the young man who found Jonas's body, considered these accusations outrageous and defended himself, demanding that the Emberá send a *jaibana* to determine who the real perpetrator was. He asked them to set in motion, and here I am using some of his own words, "their own kind of sorcery" and to send whatever "spirit they need to send" in order to determine who was behind Jonas's death. Victor insisted that he was just a witness and that he had nothing to do with what had happened.

It was also said that there was a warning circulating among the Emberá to avoid going to Blind River because that community was plagued by evangelical mestizos who certainly knew secret tricks of their own. In this way, Jonas's death accentuated some racial and religious prejudices: for the people of Blind River, mostly devoted evangelicals who place great importance on living a moral life and on rigorously adhering to what the Bible prescribes, the Emberá people's beliefs and rituals are nothing but a turn toward the devil. For the Emberá—suspicious of the strict religious observance of evangelicals and of their claims of being blessed by the Holy Spirit with gifts such as speaking in tongues, receiving direct revelations from God, and divine healing—what had happened to Jonas might have been linked to the summoning of spiritual forces taking place during the evangelicals' weekly worship services. In any case, the events reinforced existing prejudices in the region, especially among the non-Indigenous people who believe it is better to keep their distance from the Emberá because "they know too much" and because many of them apparently are envious sorcerers. At the same time, for the Emberá the event demonstrated the lack of solidarity of the mestizo peasants with a person who had lived in their village for a long time, as well as the existing discrimination toward Indigenous peoples since evangelicals perceive themselves as endowed with a kind of superior moral sense that all nonevangelicals lack.

In Blind River, everyone was wondering who would have wanted to kill Jonas because, despite some racial prejudices, they all remembered him as a hard worker who never had trouble with anyone. For them, the people behind his death were most likely some Emberá from Acandí, his hometown, who could have decided to take revenge on Jonas for having run away from his crime without punishment. It was later known that he had another wife in Acandí and that he had not treated her well, leading people to speculate that it may have been her who had ordered the attack in order to make Jonas suffer for his past offenses.

When the Indigenous people from the regional organization received Jonas's body in Riosucio and heard what had happened, they suspected that it was not an accident, and even though they assumed that it was an attack committed by a malevolent spirit, for them it was not a *madre de agua* that had been sent explicitly to Jonas. According to some of the people I interviewed,

Jonas had been drowned by one of the spirits of the underworld that inhabit the rivers and are disturbed from time to time. One of the Indigenous leaders said that they had consulted with their *jaibanas*, who said that there was an evil force loose in Blind River, the same one that had drowned four people in recent years. For the Blind River inhabitants, this explanation gained validity because all those who had drowned had died under strange circumstances: one was a very skilled swimmer who died from an epileptic seizure when he was crossing the river; another drowned when he was bringing some wood to sell in town.

The Indigenous authorities recommended that a *jaibana* go there to appease this being before there was a new victim. However, they said that inhabitants of Blind River had to pay the gas for the transportation of the *jaibana* and his delegation. They did not charge any money for their work but requested food, tobacco, and a*guardiente* in order to spend a few nights there and perform the *jaï* chants they needed to appease that loose presence. But people in Blind River were reluctant about that proposal because, as well-educated evangelicals, they did not want to pay from their own pocket for alcohol and cigarettes, even less so if they were going to be used in a ritual that they considered unholy.

Exorcisms

There are many stories about paramilitary soldiers who were frightened during the night, who felt sinister presences in their camps and when patrolling in the forest, who began talking nonsense, or who for some reason ended up shooting their own comrades. Dalila called these types of events *loquera* (madness), and even though some occurrences were related to the interventions of the *jaibanas*, some were simply the kind of ordinary, prewar appearances of the dangerous beings that live in the forest. According to her, these are spirits that manifest in the form of humans but that are not human, that confuse people's judgment, and that make people see things where there is, in fact, nothing.

There was once a group of Claretian priests and missionaries that, while visiting a rural community, helped treat a young paramilitary soldier who was very sick. This soldier was constantly spitting a thick, white slime and had not been able to sleep for several nights. One day, in his despair, he started shooting his rifle all over the place, injuring one of his fellow soldiers. One of the priests approached the soldier and uttered several prayers. When he showed the young man a scapular featuring holy images, the soldier destroyed it just by looking at it. The priest then bathed him with holy water and sprinkled more around the village, making crosses at certain places. After this intervention, the young man partially recovered his sanity, and the rest of his companions stopped feeling the spirit that had been tormenting them. Nevertheless, the events resulted in an escalation of threats against the *jaibanas*, to the extent that a paramilitary commander threatened to wipe out an Indigenous village if any more of his men got sick.

On another occasion a group of paramilitaries arrived at the parish in Riosucio and asked to see one of the priests. They were looking for him to perform some type of cleansing ritual because many of them were seeing and hearing strange things at their campsite in the forest. This request was actually an order, and the priest agreed to recite some prayers for them at the temple, as long as they disarmed before entering. They closed the temple's doors and windows, and the priest led some of the prayers that are commonly used to release evil spirits:

> Spirit of our God, Father, Son, and Holy Spirit, Most Holy Trinity, Immaculate Virgin Mary, angels, archangels, and saints of heaven, descend upon me. Please purify me, Lord, mold me, fill me with yourself, use me. Banish all the forces of evil from me, destroy them, vanish them, so that I can be healthy and do good deeds. Banish from me all spells, witchcraft, black magic, malefice, ties, maledictions, and the evil eye; diabolic infestations, oppressions, possessions; all that is evil and sinful, jealousy, perfidy, envy; physical, psychological, moral, spiritual, diabolical ailments. Burn all these evils in hell, that they may never again touch me or any other creature in the entire world. I command and bid all the powers who molest me—by the power of God all powerful, in the name of Jesus Christ our Savior, through the intercession of the Immaculate Virgin Mary—to leave me forever, and to be consigned into the everlasting hell, where they will be bound by Saint Michael the archangel, Saint Gabriel, Saint Raphael, our guardian angels, and where they will be crushed under the heel of the Immaculate Virgin Mary. Amen. (Amorth 1999, 200)

The Spanish version of this prayer, printed on a single sheet of a damp and wrinkled paper, was kept by one of the priests of Riosucio in a box, alongside his liturgical artifacts. The prayer was originally written in Italian by the Reverend Gabriele Amorth, a priest who belonged to the Diocese of Rome and who claimed to have performed hundreds of exorcisms. The priest who performed the cleansing ceremony for the paramilitaries at the church told me that when he was throwing holy water on them, a foul smell began emanating from their bodies and that at some point during the ritual the church's doors flung open violently.

I was intrigued by the powers a Catholic priest might have over a being such as a *madre de agua*. According to the *jaibanas* with whom I spoke, it is perfectly normal for a priest to have jurisdiction over evil *jaïs* because these spirits come from the underworld and priests have been trained for many years to summon the divine forces inhabiting heaven. That hard and long training, one of the *jaibanas* told me, is as good as the training of *jaibanas*, who are prepared since childhood to become men of knowledge. Moreover, the Catholic pantheon is not seen by the Emberá as being antagonistic to the Emberá gods: God, the Virgin, and the saints are mythically conceptualized as belonging to the domain of the primordial (Salomon and Schwartz 1999), to a time before time that is partaken of by all deities, including the Emberá ones. That domain, actualized through rituals, is also evoked whenever people decide to take actions against a present and current threat, such as the arrival of armed people. That Christian and Emberá divine forces are complementary and closely related was made clearer to me during a visit to the *jaibana* Carlitos, who asked me to buy a Bible and to bring it back to him so that he could learn the chants contained in that book. He used the word "chants"—as the ones *jaibanas* sing during their ceremonies—rather than "prayers" because after all a Catholic priest is like a *jaibana*: both know how to work with the divine forces that people the world.

It was known that the paramilitaries were hiring their own sorcerers to counteract the effects of the attacks against them and to strike back against the *jaibanas* and their *jaïs*. I once met one of these sorcerers. He called himself Salamancan Master, a name that comes from the Spanish city of Salamanca, home of the oldest university in the Hispanic world. He had a shop on Riosucio's main street, and in it he offered all kinds of herbs and procedures to bring back loved ones and stop infidelity; find jobs or lost objects; remove bad luck, black magic, curses, witchcraft, or the evil eye; and help to succeed in business or gambling. He also knew spells for mystical protection and how to reveal hidden enemies. During the short time his shop was open to the public, most of his clients were paramilitary soldiers. They arrived wearing civilian clothes, carrying bags full of new garments, canned food, or personal-care items. They were looking for protection against snakes, scorpions, and other venomous animals of the forest, but also for means to strengthen their bodies against bullets and protect themselves from the evil forces inhabiting forests and rivers.

Sometimes a boat would arrive and take Salamancan Master to the paramilitary camps in the forest, where he would spend several days doing his job

FIGURE 3.3. The place where Jonas died. Left: the tree in September 2015. Right: the same tree in July 2016. The shape of the roots changed considerably. Photos by author.

among the troops. The paramilitaries were hiring healers, clairvoyants, psychics, and sorcerers like Salamancan Master in order to better protect their soldiers, but in the end their work proved not to be good enough because the attacks from the beings summoned by the Emberá did not stop. Some commanders decided it would be better to face the root cause instead: they physically threatened *jaibanas* and anyone suspected of "sorcery."

Given the seriousness of the matter and because Indigenous peoples did not want to endanger their *jaibanas*, the regional Indigenous organization issued guidelines to stop the attacks against the armed groups. Following this, some paramilitary commanders and Indigenous leaders met a few times to establish a sort of nonaggression pact, and they established basic agreements to respect the communities' rights. However, at this point in the conflict the *jaibanas* had already unleashed furious sylvan forces and could no longer be entirely responsible for the damage these beings might cause.

The Emplacement of Death

I knew well the place where Jonas drowned (figure 3.3). I had bathed there many times, in the shade of an immense tree known locally as *bonga*. Doña Viviana, the lady whose house was facing this pool, had installed some boards that she used to wash clothes, pots, and other cooking utensils. Everyone in the house, including myself, used to frequent that place because it was a shallow pool in which anyone could dive and swim at ease. After the night of Jonas's death, Doña Viviana decided to remove the boards and install them a little farther down the river. She also stopped going to the river at night and began to always go with her daughter as a companion. A couple of times, her older sons challenged me to bathe there. I think they wanted to know whether I would dare or not and were curious to see if I, whom they described as a "well-educated" outsider, believed in the stories that were circulating. However, I felt that my secular education ill-equipped me to deal with the situation, so I chose to change my bathing spot, just as everyone else in the house did.

Victor told me that one of his brothers had been bitten by a snake that came out of the roots of that very *bonga* tree some months before Jonas's death. For him and his family, there was no doubt that this spot held some sort of malign force. A week after Jonas's death, the family noticed that the roots of the tree had started to dry up. It was as if the tree was retaining an imprint of that death. My inexpert gaze did not allow me to see anything unusual: it was a tree that had its roots partially exposed as a result of being in a ravine on the edge of the river. It is true that the water's reflection of the shape of its roots gave the place a peculiar look, but I could not see anything particularly frightening there. I decided to take some pictures in order to document the location's appearance and contrast these photos with some that I would take a few months later, when I returned to continue my field-work. When I compared the pictures, I realized that the tree actually was changing: some of the roots had rotted, and the trunk's base now had a red-dish color. That decay, according to Doña Viviana and her sons, was a result of the evil atmosphere of that place.

During the years I lived in Bajo Atrato, I visited many locations that had seen extreme, violent acts: places that had been bombarded by the army, old battlefields, abandoned villages, mass graves, destroyed cemeteries, houses of torture. They all contained some sort of material traces of those violent events—military waste, ruined houses, small shrines to the dead, and dis-appeared, long-forgotten objects—suggesting the comingling of the past with people's everyday surroundings. Some of these places are even haunted by the spirits of those who died there. In the same vein, that pool in front of Doña Viviana's house now contained traces left by Jonas's death: an event that not only lived on in the memories of Blind River's inhabitants but that also left a tactile trace in the landscape, in the form of that tree, slowly but uninterruptedly drying up and dying off. By virtue of some kind of mimetic faculty or contagion, the tree, and by extension the pool, bore witness to Jonas's death and its aftermath. The place was not just a silent background where everything happened. Rather, it reacted to the events; it gathered a certain hint of energy, a particular affective force that exceeded the memory people had of the event. This leads me to consider that through their affective materiality, places actively participate in the life of communities in Bajo Atrato, and they do so not as mere depositories of preexisting ideas but as agents with real effects on people and social relations (Tilley 2006). Let me discuss this from a phenomenological perspective.

Some phenomenologically minded scholars have pointed out that places actively participate in the generation of sense, adding a material emplacement to our modalities of experience. For example, philosopher Edward Casey contests the metaphysical neutrality of places—the view that they are an "empty substratum to which cultural predicates come to be attached" (1996, 46)—and he holds instead that places gather experiencing bodies and "unbodylike entities" (1996, 25) such as memories, thoughts, or modes of attunement. Casey states that "to gather placewise is to have a peculiar hold on what is presented (as well as represented) in a given place. Not just the contents but the very mode of containment is held by a place" (1996, 25). In other words, the hold of place, its power of gathering, is its capacity to bestow sense upon things. Here sense must be understood etymologically, as meaning ("the contents") and direction ("the mode of containment"). This capacity that places have for gathering leads me to consider that sense is not just the outcome of a human, volitional process of representation but that there is something "out there" beyond our human agency, something that invites us to experience the world as we do. The idea that places contain sense—meaning and telos—is an invitation to consider that there is not always arbitrariness between the particularities of a given place and the way that it is experienced and represented.

The idea of a place capable of conveying immanent sense undermines certain traditional philosophical approaches such as empiricism, rationalism, solipsism, and skepticism, which all maintain that meaning emerges only through the infusion of determinate epistemic processes—judgment, reason, logic. Within a phenomenological framework, anthropologists interpret the relationships between people and places as mutually co-constituted: as a holistic relation in which both people and places exist always together. This is their way of avoiding reducing the relationship between humans and the material world to either an idealist or realist perspective—in an idealist view the world is but a function of how people act on it, whereas in a realist perspective experiences are primarily constrained by what the world allows. The co-constitution between people and places entails the idea that there is a reciprocal, configurative process between contents or dwellers (things and people (and containers (places). The force of this configuration, the "holding" as Casey calls it, is such that "a given place takes on the qualities of its occupants, reflecting these qualities in its own constitution and description and expressing them in their occurrence as an event: places not only are, they happen" (1996, 27). The inverse argument, I hold, is also true: a place has its own "operative intentionality," as Merleau-Ponty claims ([1945] 2002, 208), extending its own influence back onto its subjects (Casey 1996, 22). Places can thus be seen to imprint their unique affective qualities onto people, whereas people in turn reflect the particularities of the places they inhabit. To put it differently, rather than resolute spaces containing objects with well-defined positions and directions, places need to be conceptualized as networks of emplaced associations in which human and other-than-human affective forces participate.

I take this little detour in an attempt to adequately explain two aspects of the transformation of the pool where Jonas died. First, through the decay of the tree the place was somehow participating if not in the fatal event itself at least in its aftermath—after all, death was toying with the roots. Second, the place, as I have already explained, was not just a screen onto which inhabitants of Blind River projected their own impressions of the event. Instead, this place discharged, so to speak, its own affective forces. Understanding how places may discharge particular moods or atmospheres upon people does not imply a return to some kind of new environmental determinism—such environmental determinism would just reify a subject-object dichotomy (i.e., places determine pathways of human agency). Consider the kind of fear that Doña Viviana and her sons experienced when forced to spend time at the place where Jonas died. Whatever we call that sensuous impression—atmosphere, hint of energy, affect—it is neither the product of the material world alone nor merely the reifications of people's inner ideas. Rather, such a mood or affect is coproduced; it is what results from the interactions between people and their surrounding worlds. When considered in this way, the impressions that people experience in places such as the pool in front of Doña Viviana's no longer need to be interpreted as either a fact or a belief: the fear hanging over that place is simultaneously located in and intertwined with both people's subjectivities and the materiality of said place.

Jonas's death is thus a double expression of place. It took place but also contributed to the creation of place. By "taking place" I do not merely mean that it happened but also that it was possible because of a particular arrangement of the constituents that make up place: it happened because of a being, such as the *madre de agua*, that has the power of becoming one with the living constituents of the pool (e.g., the snakes and logs that occupy said pool). It creates place because something of this violent death stays with people and the landscape, transforming the disposition of a given place (such as a tree that starts to wither gradually). This double bind (Jonas's death happens *in* and *to* place) is what gives this violent event an afterlife, albeit an elusive one, for in the aftermath of war you do not know beforehand what specific form that violence will adopt or the effects it will have (figure 3.4).

A Loose Spirit

Between December 2002 and September 2003 there was a streak of suicides among the Emberá youth: seven of them took their own lives, including five girls between the ages of twelve and fifteen who were found hanging from the beams that support the roofs of their houses. These deaths caused great distress, not only because of the victims' ages but also because suicide is very rare among the Emberá. According to some traditional authorities, the suicides were caused by evil spirits that inhabit the forest: some of these evil spirits were attracted by the violent actions of the armed groups, and others started to run amok because of the large quantity of unburied corpses produced by the war. The evil actions of the warring people provoked unexpected consequences, unleashing and strengthening the sylvan evil forces to the point that even the beings that had been mobilized for protection had acquired so much power that the *jaibanas* could not dominate them anymore. The victims of these spirits were not only Indigenous peoples—in Riosucio, some young, Afro-Colombian girls suffered episodes of possession, suddenly fainting, losing consciousness, and speaking in voices that were not theirs. One of those spirits even came very close to taking a girl out of her house through the window.

Following these terrible events, and in order to remedy the situation and ensure that such tragedy would never recur, the regional Indigenous authority brought to Riosucio all local *jaibanas* and even called on *jaibanas* from all over the country. For six nights the most powerful among them sang their chants, and after an intense battle with the *jaïs*, they managed to capture the evil spirit they considered the mother of all others. However, they warned that her children were still free and that in order to avoid future attacks by this offspring, it was necessary that there be no more fights or sorrow within the communities, that the youth respect their elders, that men respect their wives, that mothers not punish their children, and, of course, that the warring people stop bringing death and terror to the region.

During those long nights of chanting, the *jaibanas* also acknowledged that even though it was relatively easy to activate the forest spirits and ask them to defend their villages, it was also easy, because of the extremely violent nature of the war waged in the region, for these beings to acquire powers that the *jaibanas* could no longer control. It was then agreed that the two

FIGURE 3.4. **An evil look?** Photo by author.

most powerful *jaibanas* would ingest *tonga* with the purpose of examining the spirits owned by their colleagues in order to determine which *jaibanas* had sufficient power to control those unruly spirits. Those who did not have that power would have all of their *jaïs* revoked through a special ceremony involving baths and several special chants. Dalila Conquista told me that the *jaibanas* said: "If I cannot control the *jaïs* I have, then wash me." After several baths with medicinal plants and long nights of chanting to the *jaïs*, the power of certain *jaibanas* was removed, and the former *jaibanas* became, according to Dalila, "not *jaibanas* anymore, but civilians, just like us." By divesting many *jaibanas* of their authority and power to invoke *jaïs*, Indigenous regional authorities were able to guarantee that only *jaibanas* with sufficient power to control the *jaïs* they released remained, so there would be no more *jaïs* running amok because of war. No less importantly, by becoming "civilians" many of them were in effect saving their own lives, for guerrilla and paramilitary armies had already launched severe threats against all those that they considered sorcerers.

The baths given to the *jaibanas*, the nonaggression agreements they made with the sorcerers hired by the paramilitaries, and the decision to stop invoking these spirits in defense of their communities have helped to reduce the damage that these beings inflict. These measures have attenuated the attacks but not entirely eliminated them, as these beings remain an inherent part of the sylvan and aquatic universe. Their presence continues to be a risk, especially when the existence of armed groups, mass graves, and unburied bodies establish conditions that are favorable to their emergence and fury. In this way, many of these beings continue to manifest themselves occasionally in the region, wandering forests and rivers, causing havoc, and, of course, making fatal attacks on unguarded fishermen like Jonas.

Isn't It the Hill You Want to Die On?

Several months passed without any new victims being reported in Blind River. In one of the last visits I paid to this community, in 2020, the villagers discussed once again the advice given by Indigenous authorities that something should be done to expel the evil spirit from the river: even though it was not attacking at that time, there was no guarantee that it would not do so again in the future. The majority agreed because many of them had felt a strange presence moving up and down the river. Of Jonas I retain two images: the chirpy hat he was wearing the day I first met him, and the cadaverous color of his face in the picture I saw of the night he was found. His wife and children do not live in Blind River anymore, and the Indigenous council leaders from Riosucio are still waiting for his family in Acandí to repay the money that the organization had to spend for his burial in a foreign land.

Around Jonas's death, different worlds meet: the underworld and the primordial beings that inhabit it, the river as a way of life to people but also as a threshold used by *madres de agua* to emerge and act upon the world of the living, the realities engendered by the lasting consequences of a violence perpetrated by human and other-than-human creatures. Jonas's death also takes us to the worlds summoned by *jaibanas* to confront the kind of reality brought about by armed actors, and then it drives us to ordinary places where people and evil forces strive to compose a territory of mutual but asymmetrical arrangements. After showing how Jonas's tragic fate takes form and place at the intersection of all these worlds, I cannot help but feel sorrow for a dead person who, at the end, no one reclaimed or redeemed. All that we can see of these worlds and the beings that compose them was rendered visible to us through the death of a man who lost, in all possible ways, his place in the world.

4

AWAKENING FORESTS

The Smoke of Life

FIGURE 4.1. **The smoke of life. Photo by author.**

An abandoned house is doomed to fall into ruin because there are no people inhabiting it. It needs smoke; the smoke coming out of the kitchen is what keeps it up. That smoke drives off cockroaches and vermin. Without smoke, spiderwebs appear, the weeds surrounding the house grow higher, and, therefore, there is less sunlight lighting the house. Fallen leaves get stuck on the roof, and they deteriorate the roofing sheets. An abandoned house is also invaded by wasps. Wasps are always present, but when a house is inhabited, people keep them at bay: they burn their

FIGURE 4.2. Ruined houses. Photos by author.

nests down, and they do not let the wasps take over the house. Wasps are like burglars: what they find without a keeper, they take. But an inhabited house is kept from falling. The warmth of people helps houses to stay standing. (Egidio, in conversation with the author, Riosucio)

The Warmth of People

FIGURE 4.3. **The warmth of people.** Photos by author.

Where Do Fish Come from in New Ponds?

A very loud noise that made roofs budge and even the ground shake. This is how many people remember the impact of the bombs dropped by the army on the morning of February 19, 1997. Witnesses registered that clatter of bombs as a bodily form of angst and fear that, as they describe it in Spanish, made their heads expand: "*La cabeza se le pone a uno grande.*" This is the local expression for describing an atmosphere of nervous apprehension. The equivalent in English, perhaps, is something like having one's heart in one's mouth. But in Bajo Atrato, your head widens as a result of your becoming aware of something unexpected and stressful, in this case your own mortality. Though when the bombs fell, a head widening was also one possible literal effect of the earsplitting blast and resulting explosion that left a rough trace on the landscape (figure 4.4).

The explosion resulted in a crater in the pastures. After several years, the crater became a bowl-shaped pond in the forests along the Salaquí River (figure 4.5).

Twenty years after the air strike launched by the army there remains a heavily overgrown crater that becomes a pond during the rainy season. Although some of the best-documented ecological impacts of warfare include destruction of landscapes, plundering of natural resources, spreading of parasites and diseases, and violent transformations of land use (see, for example, Judith Bennett 2004; Le Billon 2001; Tucker 2004), in some cases, ironically, war has given a reprieve to forests from human pressures (Russell and Tucker 2004). In other cases, war has created vast zones of "no-man's-land" that, like the Korean demilitarized zone, have become wildlife sanctuaries (Brady 2008; Kim 2016). This suggests a somewhat counterintuitive aftermath to war: under certain circumstances war has enabled the recovery of some species and some environments. Through the images of this chapter I highlight how war might lead to a double process of negative transformation: first of all, the abandonment of places previously inhabited by people, and second, the flourishing of more-than-human presences that, as in the case of a resprouting forest in what used to be pastures for cattle, are not fully appreciated by people. This flourishing is often interpreted by local communities as a form of ruination. Consider the images in figures 4.4 and 4.5: the heliconia plants and the trees surrounding the pond are evidence of a forest claiming its dominion. This is a claim made in the absence of people. This recovering forest has covered the grass that a family previously sowed for their cattle (the same cattle that were raided by paramilitaries shortly after the attack). If the bombs

FIGURE 4.4. The explosion crater. Photo by Jesús Abad Colorado (1997). Source: Rueda 2016, 34.

FIGURE 4.5. The afterlives of an explosion. Photo by author.

started the process of undermining people's livelihood, the forest completed it. The pastures in figure 4.4 represent the work of those for whom the raising of cattle was a means of subsistence, an activity that required keeping the forest at bay in order to let other beings, like cattle, flourish. In figure 4.5 the forest, which before and during the conflict had been relegated to the background, has now come to the fore. This recovering forest points to a process of ruination; it epitomizes the abandonment to which some places were subjected. If the explosion crater and the military raids triggered the exodus of people, the growing forest represents the hardships that local communities have faced in their attempt to render their villages habitable again.

In the absence of people, the forest arrived with other beings, including fish. However, the new pond is not close to the river, and it dries up during the summer. Yet with the rains the fish arrive. During our journey to that place, one of the locals asked how fish managed to come to the pond. Someone else answered that some fish hatch from the eggs of frogs. I was intrigued and asked about it. It was explained that what really happens is that all are born frogs, but some may become fish in the process of growing up. It is a matter of behavior: some learn to behave as frogs and others as fish; in the process their bodies change. I told them I had heard about frogs that estivate: they bury themselves in the muddy ground and are capable of staying dormant to survive periods of drought. I also talked about fish that lay eggs capable of surviving long spells of drought. But my comment was in fact complementing and not contradicting what locals had been explaining: it described a very effective survival strategy, but it did not explain how fish had originally arrived in the pond, at least not to someone like me, who has interiorized that evolutionary principle according to which like begets like, meaning that fish cannot be born from frogs.

After some research, I learned that birds such as herons, which abound in Bajo Atrato, may incidentally transport eggs stuck to their feathers or feet. I also learned that the feet and fur of some terrestrial animals such as peccaries or tapirs might play host to fish eggs. To someone endorsing the idea that all members of any species always produce their own kind only and that fish, therefore, are a kind of unambiguous organism that can be differentiated from other life-forms, these explanations shed light on how fish had come to the pond. But such elaborations stem from a particular form of knowledge that defines fish and frogs as species whose clearly identified boundaries are prior to and transcend the specificities of space and time (Lien and Law 2011). Consequently, these explanations miss a beautiful component of that interspecies transformation described by locals: the form of some beings (fish in this case) is defined by the relations they undertake (they were born from frogs, but they learn how to be fish) and not the other way around.

The idea that fish hatched from the eggs of some frogs is compatible with the notion of *renacientes*, literally those who are to be reborn. Among Afro-Colombians, *renacientes* is a concept that entails a kind of succession, a continuity between the offspring of different beings (Escobar 2008; Losonczy 1993; E. Restrepo 1995). The concept means that beings are in eternal rebirth, each one an ontological extension or instantiation of a prior and continuous form of life. It therefore implies a constant flow where past, present, and future are tied together (Almario 2001) because the living beings, those that exist now, are but *renacientes* of former beings, those who were before. Under such a tenet, life becomes an incessant birth, and rather than a preordained world of pure actuality with well-demarcated species representing a fulfillment of possibility, one faces something akin to what Ingold describes as a world "on the verge of the actual" in which life "is not an emanation but a generation of being" (2006, 11–12). In other words, species are not already existent in the world but rather species have become what they are by virtue of the relations they sustain. In Bajo Atrato the aforementioned generation of being is possible not only as a transition from frogs to fish but also vice versa, as well as between species that a naturalist, for example, would tend to ascribe to different domains. That is the case of the *chitra* or *morrongoy*—the local name of some hematophagous insects that entomologists classify in the *Psychodidae* family—which are begotten from the fruit of the *higuerón* tree; of some bullet ants that become vines; of the larvae of some beetles that bloom as plants inside rotten trunks; of bats that transform into *chules*, a rat-like rodent; or of wasps that become fungi after death.

This constant generation of being presupposes the ongoing actualization of the properties that make up each individual. And this process bears similarities to the way in which Afro-Colombian communities define and experience their traditional territories. For them, rather than taking a physical setting for granted, they understand the territory as being produced or constantly enacted through daily practices of care. In other words, territory does not exist before the relations and practices that constitute it. This means that places like pastures or ponds are instantiations of specific processes in which human and other-than-human beings participate. Just as *chules*, *chitras*, fish, or frogs become what they are by virtue of their relations, places are an array of activities; they are brought into existence through the practices unfolded by certain presences. Accordingly, the ruination of villages, gardens, and houses, which one tends to think of in terms of physical destruction only, is in fact also what results from the transformation of the relations that these places enable.

Intrusive *Avichuchos*

Known in English as the red paper wasp and named by entomologists as *Polistes canadensis*, this *avichucho*—a local taxonomic category that includes flying insects, small lizards, and some arthropods such as spiders and scorpions—is an undesirable, recurrent visitor of people's houses. These wasps have the gift of turning wood into paper: females scrape wood fiber and break it down in their mouths with their own saliva. Wasps look for sheltered, dry spots to hang their nests. It is often the queen who starts the work by building a petiole—a tiny but powerful stalk from which the rest of the nest will hang (Giray, Gionanetti, and West-Eberhard 2005; Jeanne 2004; Polak 1993; West-Eberhard 1986). Once this pillar has been erected, the queen and other female wasps build an umbrella-shaped comb featuring hexagonal cells of identical size and shape in which eggs are laid and larvae develop. The egg takes about forty days to fully develop into an adult, a period during which the queen and their female kin enlarge the comb (Giray, Gionanetti, and West-Eberhard 2005; Polak 1993; Sumner, Kelstrup, and Fanelli 2010). A characteristic of these wasps is that only one generation uses a comb, so the brood is constantly moving and founding new combs. It has been argued that this is a strategy they follow to avoid their combs being infested by moths (Jeanne 2004). Moreover, as these wasps do not depend on any seasonal resource for their development (Polak 1993; Sumner, Kelstrup, and Fanelli 2010), they are building and abandoning nests throughout the year. Multiple-comb building and constant itinerancy are what make them "like burglars," as Egidio described them at the beginning of this chapter: they are always at work, going and coming, looking for the opportunity to seize a suitable spot to build their paper towns—the name that identifies their genus (*Polistes*) means "founder of a city" (figure 4.6).

These burglars are armed. Red paper wasp stings are very uncomfortable. Justin Schmidt, an entomologist who created a sting-pain index, describes the venom as caustic and burning: "Distinctly bitter aftertaste. Like spilling a beaker of hydrochloric acid on a paper cut" (2016, 229). I have not experienced the corrosive effects of an acid used in the production of batteries and

FIGURE 4.6. *Avichuchos.*
Photo by author.

flashbulbs, but I do know what it feels like to get stung by this wasp. Rather than addressing the pain itself, which Schmidt characterizes at a level of 3 out of 4, my own description would have focused on how much I regretted going into a place where I had not been invited: the presence of a wasp comb is actually the opposite of an invitation. Even if their colonies might not be big, wasps are dangerous, for they can sting more than once during a single attack. In Bajo Atrato people use the verb *clavar* (literally, "to nail") to describe the wasps' stings. Perhaps the wasps' nailing of people is part of their process of nailing down their paper towns because for their towns to run well, there must not be any people around.

If there is something that characterizes a deserted building in Bajo Atrato, it is the presence of these wasp nests. These *avichuchos* are indicative of how abandonment favors the proliferation of other presences. Another way of saying this is that wasps contribute to the creation of another kind of place: when building their combs inside people's houses they are not just manifesting their natural adaptive strategies; instead, through the very process of crafting these nests, they are contributing to the emergence of places of abandonment. Wasps are then participants in processes of ruination. I borrow the concept of ruination from Ann Stoler (2008, 2013), who objects to the traditional definition of ruins—sites that "condense alternative senses of history"—and emphasizes instead the idea of ruin as a verb rather than a noun. Stoler argues that ruination is an "ongoing corrosive process that weighs on the future" (2013, 9). The concept of ruin is also contested by authors such as Gastón Gordillo (2014) because it is so often used to depict alluring, romantic sites of the past. Drawing from his work, I prefer to see the durable, material traces created by violence as "rubble" rather than ruins. If within a modern tradition the concept of ruin establishes a kind of break of the present from the past, an object or situation that is not to be disturbed but rather to be preserved, rubble highlights instead the materialized ongoing outcomes of destruction and the effects that these instantiations produce on both the material environment and people's lives (Gordillo 2014, 6–11).

If the absence of people's warmth inspires wasps to settle in, we are not just bearing witness to how the destructive driving forces of war produce empty spaces like a vacuum. Instead, this is a process through which war materializes itself in the form of debris, rubble, abandoned objects, certain more-than-human presences, and, as I will proceed to describe, the changing shape of forests.

The Shape of Corrosion

Without the presence of people, things tend to rot and wear away faster than usual (figure 4.7). These are the kinds of effects provoked by the coldness of forests. If houses and villages materialize the warmth of people, forests, many people hold, exude a form of coldness that can even provoke illnesses. Abandoned settlements, with their rotten walls, collapsed roofs, broken floors, ruined courtyards, invasive weeds, filthy fields, and gray gardens, are cold because of the absence of the warmth of people and also the encroaching coldness of the forest. What first sprouts after abandonment is *rastrojo*. *Rastrojo* is the wild vegetation that precedes the growing of forests. *Rastrojos* are thick and invasive. In local parlance, the verb *enrastrojar* describes the process through which rot sets in, a process that, in tropical rain forests, occurs in an

FIGURE 4.7. The shape of corrosion. Photo by author.

extremely accelerated way. Many villages were overtaken by *rastrojo* after they were abandoned because of forced displacement. Those villagers who came back found their houses *enrastrojadas*: full of shrubs, weeds, stalks, brushes, scrubs, and brushwood (figure 4.8). But not everybody could or wanted to come back to their lands, and many houses—and in some cases entire villages—were swallowed, so to speak, by the forest. In Bajo Atrato one might be struck by the apparent absence of ruins, but in fact these ruins are there; it is just that their form is not always that of decaying buildings but of vigorous green *rastrojos*.

FIGURE 4.8. *Rastrojos.* Photo by author.

Green and Thick Absences

How to know when one is surrounded by rubble? I started to consider this question during a trip up the Arenal River. On our way, we passed through some small villages, including the abandoned hamlet where Melín, my friend who was driving the boat, was from. As the Arenal River began to narrow, I started to feel happily overwhelmed by the thick trees growing on the banks and by the shape of their canopy covering the river's course. It was as if the forest were closing in upon us. Then Melín pointed out a dense green spot behind some shrubs and told me that that used to be the very location of his *plataneras*, his plantain gardens (figure 4.9). While my gaze had been focused on an unrestrained forest, Melín was noticing the process through which his former swidden plots had disappeared at the hands of the *monte* or, to be more precise, through the advancement of branches, vines, lianas, foliage, and roots of the bush. Melín's gesture made me realize that the existence of that exuberant forest was in fact favored by the forced displacement brought about by armed conflict, bringing into focus the historical and social context of a landscape that I otherwise would have taken for granted. To put it in other terms, that particular forest stands to someone like Melín in some negative way: it materializes the abandonment of villages, crops, and animals.

FIGURE 4.9. Thick absences. Photo by author.

Some forests might then be interpreted as places of abandonment, as the materialization of the violent process that led people to forsake their livelihoods.

In many cases, war just accentuated the processes through which forests are constantly either disputing stewardship of the land or disrupting people's labor. In this context, disputing is simply the constant effort that people make in order to keep the forest from taking over their gardens and crops. Disruption is the dominant process of forest regeneration, which in tropical areas takes place at an incredibly quick pace and potentially disrupts the maintenance of houses, villages, and trails. An example will illustrate my point. During conversations I held in Bajo Atrato about the effects of forced displacement, one of the topics raised several times by my interlocutors was the loss of *caminos* (trails or forest tracks). These trails had been opened in order to connect villages, to allow people to go to work in their gardens and fields, and to make it possible to enter the forest in order to access game and timber. I use the verb form *to open* to describe the work of creating such trails not only because this is how people conceive of this task—*abrir caminos*—but also because it captures what this work entails in a place like a tropical rain forest, where the perpetual growing and quick sprouting of plants often obstructs said trails. To open trails is then to make the forest accessible to the circulation of people and their pack animals; it is to trace a thin

FIGURE 4.10. A request to the forest. Photo by author.

path on the ground that allows people to traverse the thick growth of trees and shrubs. "To open a trail," someone explained to me, "is to give warmth to the forest."

Trails actualize people's presence in the forest; they render possible their transit among the other beings and forces that also move there. Trails are not an attempt to occupy or transform forests but a request to safely move through them and let the warmth of people flow inside the coldness of the forest. A trail allows people to live next to and to travel through the forests. Trails are transitory, and transit is part of keeping them alive: when people use trails, they are cutting the vines and removing the fallen trunks and branches that impede passage. Without maintenance, trails will disappear. Trails, in short, are possible because of the transit of people; otherwise, the forest would easily cover that tenuous line made of footsteps. The importance of actualizing or renewing this kind of request to the forest is depicted in figure 4.10.

Like trails, a bridge without transit is doomed to ruination. Although it still works as a bridge, allowing us to cross the creek, its surface looks more like a lot full of weeds than a piece of human engineering. The presence of these plants is indicative of the absence of people transiting and therefore maintaining those trails. Where does the bridge start and the weeds end? This is not just an aesthetic question: these plants are helping decompose the bridge's wood and making it dangerous for crossing. In another setting, perhaps in Chinese or Japanese gardens, the aesthetics of the bridge would seem the masterpiece of a skillful gardener, for it would synthesize the spontaneity, roughness, and rusticity that Buddhist philosophy associates with nature. But here the presence of the plants, at least from the perspective of the people using the bridge, does not give life to the bridge but subtracts life from it. The weeds in the wood epitomize decay and the abandonment of trails that war had already made impassable.

The Loneliness of Marooned Beings

When the paramilitary violence began and compelled entire communities to leave their homes in 1997, most of these people left behind the material constituents of their rural ethos: "I lost a wooden house with all its goods and chattel, 12 hogs, 50 chickens, 60 ducks, 3 hunting dogs, 1 horse, 5 hectares of maize, 3 hectares of pineapples, 2 hectares of rice, 4 hectares of plantains." This is but one of the responses I collected while volunteering in a survey intended to gather information about the losses experienced by victims in order to formulate a plan for collective reparations. In their accounts of what people left behind, many included dogs, swine, pack animals, cattle, seeds, fruit trees, and cash crops such as sugarcane and manioc. Claudio, a traditional healer in his late sixties, told me that when he and his family had to flee from their village, they packed their dugout canoe with as much stuff as they could but that there was not enough space for their dog, an animal he had received as a gift from someone he had treated. The dog was such a good hunter that he felt very sorry for having no choice but to leave him, a decision that he still regrets.

While cattle were stolen and swine and poultry were slaughtered by the paramilitary armies, other animals were left to their own fate. They went to the forest and became marooned (*se encimarronaron*): they became feral animals. A couple of friends described to me their surprise at finding several of these animals alive when they returned to their villages after several months of forced displacement. Mules, horses, dogs, and some pigs managed to survive in the wilderness. When the first families returned, these animals gave up their feral lives and came back to the villages. Someone I interviewed said that they were attracted by the warmth of people.

Six years after the massive forced displacement, during a trip I made up the Quiparadó River I saw on the banks of the river one of these marooned animals: the most imposing cat I have ever seen. I was struck by the presence of such a magnificent cat in the middle of the forest and far from any human settlement. Not only his size was unusual. There was also a kind of nobility exceeding the usual dignity that only cats know how to haughtily display. Someone in the boat explained to me that the cat belonged to one of the families that used to inhabit one of the abandoned hamlets we passed and that he probably came to the riverbank attracted by the sound of our outboard motor. The cat's healthy coat of fur was proof that he was doing well in the forest, but his presence on the riverbank and the steady look he gave us while the canoe passed by was a reminder that he was, after all, a creature whose sociality was shaped by human presence.

This solitary feral cat shared a characteristic with the figure of the maroon: the runaway slave who retreated from the colonial world and immersed himself in the forest. Although the cat did not escape captivity but became marooned as a consequence of abandonment, its life in the forest, like the life of the maroon in the wilderness, set it apart from its kin and kind. Let me explain. In 1966 Cuban anthropologist Miguel Barnet published the testimony of Esteban Montejo, a runaway slave who spent several years in the forest before joining the army that fought in the Cuban war of independence (1895–98). Montejo describes how he lost all contact with people not only through the act of escaping from the sugar plantation but also during his time in the woods. Out of fear, he avoided encounters with both the officials of the colonial order and with other enslaved people—the former could bring him back to the plantations, and the latter could betray him and indicate his location: "I didn't even allow other *cimarrones* to spot me: *cimarrón* with *cimarrón* sells a *cimarrón*" (quoted in Barnet 1968, 47). A true *cimarrón* learns to live in the wild in the absence of his own kin and kind, as the individual experience of Esteban Montejo demonstrates. Similarly, without human caretakers the cat learned to survive in the wild, but once in the forest he did not have the chance of finding kin or any other creature of his kind. The cat was then a unique creature of the forest, the only one of his kind, which makes me think that the forced displacement led him to the loss of his kin too, by which I mean the people with whom he had previously coexisted.

The mutual relations between humans and other kinds of beings are somehow depicted in figure 4.11, a map drawn by some women from a village on

FIGURE 4.11. The inhabitants of a village in the Salaquí basin. Source: personal archive.

the Salaquí River. It represents how their village looked before the forced displacement. Besides a soccer field, several houses, and some gardens, the map includes two different kinds of forests and the names of some trees used for timber. Along with some fruit trees (mangos, guavas, lemons, and coconuts) and some medicinal plants found in the gardens that women used to keep (*siteamañas*, *llantén*), the map also shows horses, poultry, cats, and dogs—the typical companion species of peasant life. Plants and animals are included because they are constituents of the village and, to some extent, part of the community. Through this map and the stories of marooned animals, I realized that because of war, people lost many of their nonhuman companions just as many of these beings had to learn to reconstruct their lives in the absence of people.

The Resilience of Plantains

Plantains are the quintessential staple in the diet of Bajo Atrato: roasted, fried, steamed, braised, dried, baked, smashed; green or ripe; for breakfast, dinner, and supper. Their multiple varieties—*hartón*, *dominico*, *popocho*, *primitivo*, *muslo de mujer*, *felipita*, *manzano*, *guineo*, *quinientos*, *salahonda*, *boa*, *caleño*, *dos racimos*, *coco*—serve different purposes, from compotes for babies to feed for pigs (figure 4.12). Plantains are so prevalent in the local culinary arts

FIGURE 4.12. Plantains ready for shipment. Photo by author.

that a meal without plantains is not fully considered a meal. It lacks texture and even taste. Plantain is a synecdochical figure. If someone says she has eaten plantain, she means she has had a meal. Similarly, a plantain field (*platanera*) has come to mean a crop garden even if plantain is not the only planted crop. In the process of clearing new lands, plantains are always used as pioneer crops. *Plataneras* epitomize the time and efforts required to transform patches of forests into crop gardens. Their semi-perennial nature means that once plantains have been established, a field may be productive for many years (Price 1995). Compared with other staples like maize or rice, plantains require little land preparation, care, and maintenance. This and the relatively high yields that might be obtained from a single harvest make plantains one of the cheapest and most efficient food staples to produce (Price 1995, 9).

Plantains also help create and maintain a certain version of the territory. The existence of a village or a house is often first noticed by the presence of a nearby *platanera*. Plantain fields determine different kinds of boundaries: between the lands of neighbors, between gardens and forests, between land that has been occupied and land that remains unworked. *Plataneras* make evident a certain sense of place too. If, etymologically, to have a culture means, as suggested by Casey, to inhabit a place sufficiently intensively to cultivate it, "to be responsible for it, to respond to it, to attend to it caringly" (1996, 34), then to plant plantain is one of the best ways communities have found to take care of, and be responsible for, their territories. For example, during the time communities spent away from their villages because of forced displacement, they often organized teams of workers who traveled to clean and maintain the abandoned *plataneras*. Even in the absence of people, plantain fields kept growing and producing, not as much as when they are appropriately maintained but enough to invite people to travel regularly between their native villages and the towns where they were living in conditions of forced displacement. Even during the worst peaks of violence and displacement, plantains were the reason behind the journeys that allowed people to stay in touch with their lands and hamlets, nurturing in this way their presence in their traditional territories.

Plataneras participate thus in the coming into being and maintenance of territory. The power of plantains became evident to me during my first travels to Bajo Atrato. In 2003, when many communities in Riosucio were planning the progressive return to their lands in the Salaquí and Truandó basins, some humanitarian aid organizations offered tools and seeds, including plantain suckers, to help communities recover their crops. At that time, many villages were occupied by paramilitary armies, but there were other villages to which people felt they could go back in security. Communities from these villages welcomed many families that could not return to their own territories but who urgently needed to work the land in order to overcome the precarious situation they were facing while living banished from their own lands. Although most of the families appreciated the tools and seeds that would help them regain their food sovereignty, the offer of plantain suckers was not well received by everybody, in particular by the families who were welcoming the others who could not cultivate in their own villages. They feared that by allowing these guest families to sow plantain, these guests could later claim compensation for agricultural land amelioration. At the same time, some of the families who were being welcomed found it pointless to plant plantain on land that was not their own. In both cases, the reluctance to accept the humanitarian aid in the form of suckers shows to what extent plantain is so important in the creation of a sense of place and in the material maintenance of territories. *Plataneras*, to put it in other words, are deeply constitutive of the practices of care of the territory.

Plataneras are incredibly long lasting, and part of the reason is that plantains are seedless. This means they do not reproduce sexually but propagate by vegetative means: new plants grow from corms—underground bulbs known as rhizomes that are the plant's true stem (figure 4.13). The rhizomes send out roots from multiple nodes and produce shoots that are, in fact, clonal plants. These clones or suckers might be considered baby plants, and they grow at the bottom of each mature plant and are used to start new plantain plants (Price 1995). *Plataneras* therefore may remain in production for many years, the only necessary care being the removal of weeds—which in Bajo Atrato is usually done manually rather than via herbicides. *Plataneras* expire only after a very long absence of humans, and their resilience is captured in figure 4.14.

The photo shows an abandoned *platanera* we found during a journey in search of some fine timber trees. It has not been adequately maintained, as evidenced by the size of the trees and other herbs growing around them. And yet it is still productive. During this journey I remembered the stories I had heard about the state in which people found their villages when they returned after their forced displacement: looted houses, ruined buildings, lost trails, weedy gardens. But the *plataneras* were always there, surrounded by the shrubs and brushes of a resprouting forest yet still yielding fruit. They eased the return of people to their territories; but also, it must be said, during the absence of these communities they were an important source of food for the armies that occupied said territories. Plantain has made the prospect of returning home not only possible but even desirable in Bajo Atrato. Many times, I heard men expressing their willingness to go back to their abandoned villages because they wanted to recover their gardens and crops, to take care of their *plataneras*. Unlike other species of plants that destroy bridges, erase forest trails, and make human presence difficult, *plataneras* attract people and their warmth: the warmth of their stoves and houses, the fervor of their labor.

Witness Trees

Trees respond to inflicted damage in an incredible way: they wall off the affected tissue (figure 4.15). Agroforestry experts say that, at least technically, trees do not heal. Rather, they seal (Clatterbuck 2011; Shigo 1984). Unlike many other living creatures that heal by repairing or replacing the damaged tissue, tree cells seal off the wound in an attempt to impede decay or the spread of disease. This process, known as compartmentalization of decay (Shigo 1984), is how they respond to the impossibility of reinvigorating a wounded part of their bodies. Trees literally embrace the wound; they seize it eagerly and enclose it by building healthy tissue around it. This is exactly what the trees in figures 4.15 and 4.16 have done with the bullets lodged inside it.

FIGURE 4.13. The forms of plantain. Photos by author.

FIGURE 4.14. An *enmontada* plantain plantation. Photo by author.

FIGURE 4.15. Witness trees. Photo by author.

FIGURE 4.16. **Trees do not heal but seal. Photo by author.**

The trees were heavily pocked from gunfire. The calluses in the trunks are the scars of past violent encounters between guerrilla and paramilitary armies. Each bullet provoked a wound that opened the tree up to bugs and decay. But tree cells halted the spread of damage by forming a strong tissue that encapsulated the bullets. Yet the immediate surroundings of each embedded bullet are dead. But it is just that tiny zone encircling the metal that these iron pellets succeeded in killing. The bulgy forms emerging from the trunk are made of new layers of wood and bark. They bear witness to a story of military violence, death, and resilience, but also of the coexistence of the living and the dead.

In land surveying a witness tree is a tree used as a reference point to define a boundary. Historians, for their part, call witnesses those trees located on former battlefields and that often hide within their trunks the bullets of such battles. In both cases, trees are considered witnesses because their presence establishes and bears out some kind of truth. US poet Robert Frost dedicated some verses to a "deeply wounded" beech that "has been impressed as Witness Tree and made commit to memory" (Frost 1942). But it is not just memory that is encapsulated in these trees. They are not just tenacious, wooden symbols of the past; instead, they retain, expose, and even amplify the material traces of war. The ordnance embedded within these trees' bodies discharges some emotional effects of war: it retells tales of suffering and woe, and it reminds us that armed violence can happen again. When the forms of trees emerge as a result of mortal encounters between enemies, perhaps some of that violence remains alive. Attention to these emergent forms may shed light on how the presence of military debris sustains a certain state of vulnerability and uncertainty. As noticed by other anthropologists documenting the material left behind after war, to people who live amid the rubble and waste that remains after conflicts, these traces actualize distress and fear (Henig 2012) or even emit other forms of material melancholy (Navaro-Yashin 2009). Wartime does not cease because bullets are not ripping through the air anymore. Military waste, including exploded ordnance embedded in trees, is a constant reminder that even if armed confrontation has stopped, violence is a state of things not fully overcome: it is, after all, part of the very material form of trees planted in the front of a village (figure 4.17).

Quiebrapatas and the Suspicion of Their Existence

If stories of military conflicts can remain preserved as rubble inside vegetal forms, the ground may hide dangerous war debris: land mines. These mines are illustratively called *quiebrapatas*, literally "leg breakers": the perfect name for an artifact designed to rip off toes, feet, and legs. *Quiebrapatas* are uncertain but potent presences because no one knows for sure where they are. Facing the impossibility of asserting whether they are or are not in a particular place, people are forced to assume their potential presence and to act accordingly: to avoid transiting or working in suspected areas. This entails a nega-

FIGURE 4.17. Scars. Photo by author.

tive transformation of places because the presumptive existence of mines ultimately restricts movement and land use (Pardo Pedraza 2022; Tucker 2004; Unruh, Heynen, and Hossler 2003). But at the same time, such presumptions produce unintentional new environments: resprouting forests that might render places "safe for non-human flourishing" (Kim 2016, 173; Russell and Tucker

2004; Unruh, Heynen, and Hossler 2003). In this way, more than merely disrupting or degrading nature, war—and its material remnants—forces different relations between local communities and land resources (Unruh, Heynen, and Hossler 2003, 845), becoming co-constitutive elements of the environment (Kim 2016, 182; Pardo Pedraza 2022) or even, as Simo Laakkonen (2004, 175) ironically puts it, "an ecological alternative to peace."

In an essay on minefields in the Korean demilitarized zone, Eleana Kim (2016) suggests that the understanding of land mines should go beyond the humanitarian approaches that depict them as dangerous remnants of war threatening defenseless civilians, as well as beyond the postcolonial critiques that interpret them as imperial debris actualizing colonial forms of violence. Instead, she suggests that a relational ontological approach may be useful to understand how local communities deal with the presence of mines and how these artifacts, along with their potential victims, partake in a kind of distributed agency. For example, by virtue of having sometimes unexpectedly long life spans and being embedded in shifting ecologies that render their activation unpredictable, land mines often exceed "expected technological and political determinations" (2016, 166) while stubbornly retaining their long-term perilousness (Russell and Tucker 2004). In other words, land mines may acquire a life of their own, and often it is up to people living among them to decipher under what conditions they will or will not explode. Therefore, the unpredictability of land mines accentuates people's vulnerability: land mines take some agency from local communities because their presence forecloses the social, economic, affective, and even aesthetic possibilities afforded by forests (Kim 2016, 171). The way that this war debris—or the suspicion of its existence—becomes part of everyday life is illustrated in figure 4.18.

The blue poster dominating the wall behind the domino players is pedagogical material distributed by the Colombian Red Cross, and it is a reminder of how the lives of these people are constantly plagued by danger and uncertainty (Henig 2012). The poster describes some basic measures to be taken in case one finds land mines or other explosive remnants of war: one is to stop and remain still if one finds suspicious material, to retrace one's footsteps to avoid the danger, to mark dangerous areas, and to inform authorities and warn other people. The poster also depicts the most commonly mined areas: military camps; battle positions; bridges, dams, and surrounding areas; abandoned houses. Perhaps the size of this poster, when compared with the others hung on the wall, reflects how big and dangerous military waste can be. Perhaps it is not by chance that the whitish, torn poster next to it is about Decree 4635, the law recognizing the rights of Afro-Colombian victims. The

FIGURE 4.18. Playing dominoes after work. Photo by author.

wall might be seen as a micro-version of the reality in Bajo Atrato: just as the land mines poster is bigger than the poster about the laws to protect victims' rights, the threats against these communities (figure 4.19) are always bigger than the existing measures to protect them.

The Warp and Woof of Others' Lives

Danielito holds in his hands the stone he inherited and uses to treat snakebites (figure 4.20). Kept preciously in a box full of sawdust, the stone is nourished monthly with some milk and a cup of brandy. The feeding is usually done at night during the crescent moon, when the stone is placed in a small bowl containing the mixed liquor. In the morning, after verifying it drank all the content, the stone is returned to the box, where it will remain until needed again. The power of the stone resides in its capacity to suck up the venom contained in a snakebite wound. Therefore, it is used only during the hours immediately following a viper's attack, when it is placed on the area of skin where the snake sank its fangs. In Bajo Atrato, healing these types of dangerous wounds entails various procedures carefully undertaken by both healer and patient.

Healers like Danielito use certain prayers (*secretos*) and a homemade bitter balm known as *botella* or *toma*. *Secretos* might be described as fervent

FIGURE 4.19. *Quiebrapatas* and ordnance. Photo by author.

FIGURE 4.20. Danielito. Photo by author.

prayers requesting divine intervention in bringing about the patient's healing and recovery. I hesitate to use the word "prayer," for it is not only a plea to a deity but also a powerful series of exact words, like an incantation, that both activates divine forces and strengthens the healer, allowing him to perform his healing. *Secretos* do not merely evoke forces but also activate them, channeling and applying the flow of divine energies that are somehow present in the world but that are also contained within the healer himself. As *secretos* are capable of triggering powerful forces, they need to be used with great care. This is probably why they are secret, for they might lose their power if they are used improperly. No one has the ability to create *secretos*; they are learned from someone who usually passes them down as a gift or an act of indirect reciprocity. Those who know *secretos* have learned them from someone else and cannot keep them for themselves indefinitely. There are *secretos* for numerous purposes: to protect oneself when walking in the forest; to alleviate toothache; to become invisible or invulnerable to bullets; to prevent bleedings; to make money always return to one's pocket; to treat sprains, strains, and broken bones; and, of course, to treat snakebites.

Tomas (balms)—often referred to as *botellas curadas* ("cured bottles")—are viscous beverages made with *aguardiente*, a distilled spirit derived from sugarcane. The beverage contains a mix of several medicinal leaves and vines that turn the otherwise sweet liquor into a bitter drink. Each of the herbs used has unique properties associated with its place of origin. For instance, vines and tree barks collected in the forest are associated with the power of the wilderness; because these plants are not grown by humans, they possess a strength that cultivated plants lack. But the balm balances this potency of the forest by including other kinds of herbs that are cultivated in gardens. The nurturing provided to cultivated medicinal herbs is perceived to instill in them certain sociable traits that help counteract the untamed properties of forest plants.

In general, plants are classified as belonging to a particular thermal category: warm plants and cold plants. Plants are used to treat diseases, which are associated with a particular thermal classification: cold plants are used to treat warm diseases, and cold diseases are treated with warm plants. Accordingly, healing in Bajo Atrato might be described as the work necessary to bring a patient's body temperature into equilibrium. However, plants are not always unequivocally classified within a specific thermal domain: the leaves of a given plant might be considered warm, whereas its roots or fruits are cold. Besides this, as plants are collected or prepared for use in *secretos*, their thermal properties may change according to the healer's aims. Some *secretos* may maximize certain properties of a plant, whereas others render these same properties inoperable. In any case, healers seek to establish a connection with the plants they use in their cured bottles. They talk with them, they ask their permission, they ask them for advice, and they give them instructions, such as "You're going to be used to do so and so," "I need you in order to treat this or this," or "I summon you in order to heal this particular person." In this way, *secretos* are also a key component in the creation of *tomas*, whose power is not dissociated from the capabilities of, or the prestige attained by, a given healer. But *tomas* are not only tools for healing—they can also be used for prevention. There are also balms that shield bodies against spiders and vipers, others that increase sexual desire or treat issues of fertility, and even some that are capable of poisoning people. To some extent, *tomas* and *botellas curadas* synthesize the powers of plants; moreover, they come to epitomize accumulated knowledge about the healing properties of the forest.

The use of stones, *secretos*, and *tomas* for treating snakebites is not completely incompatible with other medical treatments used as venom antiserums. However, the latter treatments are available only in certain hospitals, which are not always accessible to those living in rural areas. Sometimes *secretos* and *tomas* help prepare the patient to receive care in a hospital, although in most cases traditional medicine proves to be sufficient. Any help for treating snakebites is very welcome in the tropical rain forest of a region that is home to about 5 percent of all reptiles worldwide (Proyecto Biopacífico 1998; Rangel 2015). Venomous snakes are not a trivial concern. *Mapanas (Bothrops atrox), corales (Micrurus dissoleucus), patocas (Porthidium nasutum), bejuquillos (Oxybelis fulgidus), verrugosas (Lachesis acrochorda), equis* or *pudridoras (Bothrops asper), cornudas (Bothriechis schlegelii), tallas (Bothriopsis pulchra), bocaé sapos (Bothrocophias campbelli), jergones (Bothrocophias hyoprora), cabezas de lanza (Bothrocophias myersi), cascabeles (Bothriechis muta), corales (Micrurus clarki), rabos de ají (Micrurus mipartitus), cazadoras, candelillas,* and *matabogas* are some of the many species that pullulate the forest and are often found creeping around gardens and houses. I was told that there are snakes that attract their prey by whistling, others that prefer to drink breast milk and are capable of doing so while mothers sleep, snakes that give birth, snakes that lay eggs, snakes that produce cancer, snakes with a head at each end. They are the most feared creature of the forest and considered to be, as told to me by an elder, the principal threat to humans:

> *The most dangerous things in this region are snakes. Not the jaguars, not the panthers, but snakes. Not even the paramilitary nor the guerrilla*

soldiers. We have learned to not be afraid of those people because if they are in a fight, at least you know where to hide, how to protect yourself from their bullets. But with snakes, you never know where you'll encounter them. (Egidio, in conversation with the author, Riosucio)

You never know. They might be found in the mornings in the *balsas*, traveling with some *palizadas*, sneaking around houses and gardens, hiding in the stacked firewood, sharing burrows with game animals, creeping along the forest ground, climbing trees, or mimicking the shapes of small branches. Some people maintain that even if deforestation has forced certain animals to retreat, this has not been the case for snakes: the quintessential wicked being. As a matter of fact, in places like the Curvaradó River the clearing and ruination of forests that preceded the development of oil-palm plantations led to an increase in the snake population. These snakes, according to the communities that returned to these lands after several years of forced displacement, represent a major danger because their bites have become more lethal than ever.

Under certain circumstances, a snakebite might become an even more delicate matter than usual. For instance, for those who had sexual intercourse the night before being bitten, the venom might prove lethal, or at the very least the recovery might be more difficult. Or if one has been bitten and needs to cross a river, the venom will act faster. Or if you managed to kill the snake that bit you, but it dies face up, your treatment will be more complicated. All of these types of events are considered a *trama*: something that renders one's recovery more difficult. The word *trama* might simultaneously be translated as both woven thread and plot, in the sense of a storyline. In the context of a snakebite a *trama* is then an event or a behavior—performed either voluntarily or involuntarily—that might render a snakebite fatal. It amplifies the effects of the venom, making any healing treatment more difficult by somehow twisting, deviating, or transforming a snakebite's possible outcomes. A *trama* might also be conceived of as a weft that has not been appropriately woven over and under the warp yarns—it is then a knot, a tangled thread capable of altering the warp and woof of one's life. This is why the best healers are those capable of untying or undoing *tramas*.

A snakebite can be *tramada* on account of one's behavior, such as having sexual relations before going to the forest or wearing clothes inside out. But a *trama* can also originate from someone else's witchcraft. In that case, the *trama* is conspired during the patient's treatment, making the healer's work more challenging. One can also *tramar* herself by not following the dietary and sexual restrictions prescribed by a healer. Some older snakes may have a venom

FIGURE 4.21. Former oil-palm plantations dismantled by families from the Curvaradó basin once they returned to their lands. Photo by author.

that proves to be stronger than usual, whereas others may become more venomous because they have bitten several dogs or persons. In those cases, their bites easily become *tramadas*, so the *trama* is not necessarily the consequence of one's actions but is instead a feature acquired by particular snakes.

Since 2005, people who have returned to the hamlets of the Curvaradó River following several years of forced displacement have noticed an increase in the snake population and in the bites being *tramadas*, which has rendered these snakebites more difficult to heal with the treatments normally used by traditional healers. The increase of snakes is associated with the ruination of their lands and the presence of large swaths of oil-palm plantations developed by companies that formed criminal alliances with paramilitary groups (figure 4.21). In the Curvaradó basin, thousands of families were expelled and their lands turned into vast fields of palm extending beyond the reach of the eye. Some inhabitants of the region assert that palm ruined and poisoned the land, and that this poison is now, through the snakes, polluting people's bodies. What do these *tramas* say about the effects of war? Are they illustrating some kind of cultural representation of suffering and dispossession? Or do they express the way in which an experience of violence shared by humans and other-than-humans materializes in the places and beings that constitute Indigenous and Afro-Colombian territories? In order to address these questions, it is better to say something further about the kind of ruination brought about by oil-palm plantations.

Industrial oil-palm plantations require the remaking of landscapes, the configuration of a *terra nullius* through both the felling of huge patches of natural forests and the violent displacement of inhabitants. Plantations severely transform a forest's native entanglements, both human and other-than-human. Based on the work of Anna Tsing, I understand oil-palm plantations as a model for scalability: a design intended to maintain its immutable structural composition regardless of changes in size or scale. A scalable project is one that expands or grows without allowing for any change in the relationships between its constituent parts. Scalability may be understood as a feature through which elements of a given project do not form "relationships that might change the project as elements are added" (Tsing 2012, 507). In other words, scalability is the ability to move components across different sizes or dimensions without changing their form. Under normal conditions, any change in scale or size requires a minimum of qualitative transformation in the form and composition of things, in the kind of associations of which elements are capable. But that is not the case with scalable projects such as oil-palm plantations and many other industrial monocultures.

Designed as scalable projects, palm plantations must remain uniform, autonomous, and separated from other organisms and from relationships that might modify their intended outcomes. Such a goal is possible only through the exclusion of beings that might enter into transformative relations with the palms. In the Curvaradó basin, paramilitary armies did not leave this task to chance, and they took away both biological and cultural diversity so that neither people nor forests could transform palm plantations. This kind of occupation, Escobar argues (2015, 2016), not only replaces the diverse, heterogeneous, and entangled world of forests and communities but also entails an ontological occupation of territories: palm erases relationality as a condition of possibility for human and other-than-human beings, creating instead a domain of relations in which nature is but an assortment of resources to be exploited by people who see themselves as autonomous and external subjects. However, in a location like the tropical rain forest, where transformative relationships between species are the very foundation of their diversity, the violent ruination of forests and the replication of controlled landscapes do not function without consequences. Snakes might explain part of this story.

Research conducted in Guatemala (Escalón 2014) and various regions of Colombia, including Meta, Santander, Nariño, and Bolivar (Lynch 2015), demonstrates that snakes are adopting the oil-palm plantations as their new habitat. For example, herpetologist John Lynch (2015) has reported up to thirty-eight different species of snakes, of which about 33 percent are venomous. He believes that palm leaves retain higher levels of humidity when cut and gathered into piles, attracting lizards, frogs, and their natural predators: snakes. Evidence suggests that oil-palm plantations augment the densities of snakes well beyond the densities found in natural or minimally transformed habitats (2015, 169). Therefore, it seems that oil-palm plantations have not fully succeeded in removing diversity; they have just transformed it into a different kind of diversity—that of snake species. Palm monocultures have not fully destroyed forests but have instead created new kinds of relationships between their various amphibian and reptile inhabitants.

There is no doubt that the violent transformation of the forests of this region has provoked irreversible environmental damage. Deforestation, the clearing of huge patches of one of the most biodiverse hot spots in the world, the demise of critically endangered species, the diversion of rivers, declining water quality and quantity, and pollution and soil erosion are only some of the consequences associated with the conversion of natural forests into oil-palm plantations. But the snakes now teeming in these territories are more than environmental disturbances brought on by war. Consider this. People in Curvaradó are well aware of the existing correlation between the presence of the *Elais guineensis* monoculture and the abundance of snakes. However, when these communities describe the effects of this correlation in terms of an increased number of snakebites now being *tramadas*, it is not simply that they are using a variation of cultural language to come to the same conclusion already reached by biologists and agronomists: because snakes are so abundant on palm plantations, they are more likely to bite people. Changes in the ruined landscape have led to significant transformations in the potential associations that people, snakes, and other animals may make, a shift that is more than a metaphor. *Tramas* not only describe the evils of the paramilitary and capitalist forces that stole and ravaged the lands of communities from the Curvaradó basin; they also describe a poisonous moment in the associations that humans and other-than-humans may forge in these ravaged landscapes. *Tramas* are evidence of the fact that there remains a lethal poison stealthily and slowly affecting these territories.

To conclude, when examining the ways that local communities experience the violent ecological transformation of their territories, it is important to bear in mind that these communities are addressing a different phenomenon than the one environmentalists might describe: according to local inhab-

FIGURE 4.22. One of the billboards installed by the families who returned to their stolen lands along the Curvaradó River. Maize and plantain have replaced oil palms. The billboard says, "Zone of Biodiversity. For the defense of life and the territory. Area of protection, conservation, and recovery of native ecosystems and for the affirmation of the right to food." Photo by author.

itants, a poison was planted by the palm growers and now invades their bodies through the snakes. That such a phenomenon materializes in a way that coincides with what scientists have observed—primarily, an overpopulation of venomous snakes—is quite another matter. The new *tramas* are symptomatic of a violent shift in the relationships among people, their territories, and the other beings that live there, which is not limited to the kind of environmental transformations that a biologist, for example, may describe. The difference between examining war in terms of its environmental impacts versus as a process of ruination that brings about new forms of ontological occupation stems from the fact that people describe the damage provoked by the palm as not just the violent transformation of their lands and their rights to their territories but as the ominous presence of a poison capable of polluting their bodies. Therefore, people's major concern is not only the control of snakes through the eradication of palm but rather finding methods to properly deal with this poison and heal both the territory and their own bodies (figure 4.22).

5

THE SHARED WORLD OF THE LIVING AND THE DEAD

Many of the beings that live in the forest leave subtle traces in their wake. A cut branch or footprints on the muddy ground, for example. Other traces, like the scent that follows a herd of peccaries, are even more ephemeral. There are other kinds of beings that leave even less palpable marks, yet their presence may provoke more-lasting effects, as when someone walks in the forest and without particular reason feels her hair standing on end or when the cornucopia of plants and shrubs that characterizes the rain forest of Bajo Atrato simply stops growing in a particular spot. This chapter is about emplaced incidents of suffering and violence that may produce such lasting effects. I show that in the wake of such incidents, traces are not only engraved upon people's memories but also come to inhabit places and transform their qualities. The affective remains contained in a given place are not always reducible to the stories and beliefs that people create about places. Although it is true that memories of events can influence how people perceive places, intangible features such as impressions and atmospheres might also be contained within places and discharge their affects upon people. A short example may illustrate my point.

At the beginning of the 2000s, there was a skirmish between paramilitary and guerrilla armies near a small village on the shores of the Salaquí River. After hours of combat, the surviving paramilitary soldiers arrived at the village, shouting and swearing at the villagers, blaming them for what had happened, and accusing them of hiding information about the guerrillas' presence. Then they went from house to house, breaking down doors and pulling out men in order to force them into the forest to retrieve the corpses of the dead paramilitary soldiers. Adults and teenagers alike were forced to carry several corpses, which were then stacked like cordwood in the shadow of a tree that was right in the middle of the village. "That very spot is now a haunted place," recounted the young man who told me the story. "One can hear noises and footsteps at night. You can hear things, and you cannot explain where they come from." Places may become connected with the memory of particular events and thereafter trigger associated feelings and thoughts. But phenomena like those uncanny footsteps or quiet wails heard near this tree are made of more than the stories people tell. Rather, these incidents are embedded in the places they occur, and said places acquire the ability to affect and to dispense their unique imprints upon people.

In this chapter I explore a variety of interactions between people and a place that has been deeply scarred by war. This is a place inhabited by ghostly presences with which people, upon returning to their lands after years of forced displacement, have had to learn to deal. It is located at the mouth of Caño Claro, a small river of the Curvaradó basin. What happens in this place is central to my analysis because the way its human and ghostly inhabitants intermingle epitomizes the ability that some places have to orchestrate the living and the dead into what Edward Casey (1996, 26) calls "an arena of common engagement." I see this engagement as a deeply political endeavor in which secular and religious aims are not easily discernible or mutually exclusive. I call this engagement *ecumene*, a Greek word (οἰκουμένη, *oikoumenê*) meaning the inhabited world, the known world, or, as I prefer, the habitable world (Oxford Dictionary of English Etymology 1966). *Oikoumenê* comes from *oikeô*, the same Greek prefix one finds in "ecology" and "economy," meaning simultaneously the family and the household. According to Augustin Berque, *ecumene*—the inhabited world—was considered by ancient Greeks to have come about via a dual process of habitation through which the Earth is humanized and by which humanity is rendered earthly (1987, 16). A similar ecumenic process takes place in Caño Claro, for to render their abandoned territories habitable again, people there pursue the double aim of healing their lands through various forms of labor and occupation (rehumanizing their former territories) and helping these spirits retrieve their path to the afterlife (allowing some former human beings to find their place on Earth). I then describe the existing associations between certain places and armed violence in order to illustrate the fact that the people who live in these places must relate with the death that pollutes there and that interaction between the partially connected worlds of the living and the dead is a precondition for creating an acceptably habitable world—or what I later describe as an ecumenic peace.

The chapter is divided into five sections. First, I describe the nature of the encounters people in Caño Claro have with the spirits that haunt this place. In the next section I briefly depict the violent sociohistorical context that led to the proliferation of these uncanny presences. Later I present the particular relations that people keep with the ghostly presences of Caño Claro, which are but the souls in pain of those who experienced a violent death. Next, I describe the rituals and mourning practices with which local communities honor their dead. Finally, I detail the conditions that some communities have identified as crucial for healing their territories, which are also essential for attaining an ecumenic peace: an entente between the living and the dead.

Rusty Metal Mugs and Wretched Skulls

In Caño Claro the fallout from an act of violence carried out by guerrilla and paramilitary soldiers is still palpable despite the return of the forest and the flourishing of the myriad vines, shrubs, palms, and trees that now grow in this place. The desolation that resulted from this devastation continues reverberating even though many families succeeded in returning to their lands after an eight-year period of forced displacement. Since their return, these families have been working hard to restore their ruined houses and replant their gardens and crops. Yet traces of annihilation are still present, and the echoes of the deaths of dozens of soldiers can still be heard. I walked around this spot with Petronio and Pontus, two leaders from the Curvaradó basin, but I could not see anything out of place. All I identified was the stubble of some maize fields, a couple of old coconut palms, and a rusty but still red oil drum in the undergrowth (see figure 5.1).

Before this visit with Petronio and Pontus, I had heard various accounts of what had happened in Caño Claro, and I also collected many stories of what still happens to the people living there now. While we walked, I stopped close to a roofless shack. It was there that Pontus began to share his memories of the event: "There would have been about sixty paramilitary soldiers killed," he said. The paramilitaries were ambushed one night during a sudden and violent guerrilla raid that left no chance for them to react. Some people say that more than one hundred paramilitary soldiers were killed. No one knows for sure. But they do know that the corpses of those who died were either left there to

FIGURE 5.1. **Entangled ruins. Photo by author.**

be eaten by vultures or simply thrown into the river. According to Pontus, those who survived had to cross the river, swimming and leaving behind all their gear. We followed the muddy track leading to the mouth of Caño Claro in the Curvaradó River, the place where the paramilitaries built their camp. Seeing how wide the Curvaradó River is, I tried to imagine how hard it must have been to cross its swift current amid the hail of bullets unleashed by the guerrilla soldiers. This confrontation between guerrilla and paramilitary armies took place in early 2002. In vain I have searched for written records of this event. I believe the reason for the lack of any official report is that the combat involved illegal armies and there were no civilian casualties. Moreover, it happened during a period of terror when very few people dared to travel by the Curvaradó River and everybody was afraid to speak out. The raid, conducted by a squad of guerrilla soldiers, destroyed a camp used as a checkpoint for controlling the transit of local boats and people who were, according to the twisted logic of paramilitary forces, supplying the guerrilla armies. Besides being a base for the monitoring of goods and the disciplining of people, the location at Caño Claro's mouth allowed paramilitaries to seize control of an area that was fundamental to their economic interests: a huge plantation of oil palm that had been planted along the Curvaradó River shortly after hundreds of communities were expelled from their lands by these same paramilitary armies.

FIGURE 5.2. A roofless hut. Photo by author.

Although the fields we were crossing with Petronio and Pontus originally seemed to be just another empty plot of land used for crop rotation, after a closer examination of the site I noticed that the occupant of that land had deliberately decided not to use it. It was odd because these kinds of fields are usually appreciated because of the fertility associated with floodplains such as this, where plantains or bananas are often cultivated along the stream banks. But this was not the case here. The hut where we stopped to chat had no roof, which I had initially assumed was because it was under construction, but I later realized that the aluminum roof-tile panels had been removed to be used elsewhere. In other words, the place had been deliberately abandoned because of the afterlife of that mortal confrontation between guerrilla and paramilitary armies (figure 5.2).

Later that day, just after Petronio started the motor of our small boat for our departure, Pontus pointed to an object stuck into the steep riverbank. As we got closer, Pontus stepped onto the bow of our rather unstable boat and began to dig into the bank with his bare hands. He pulled out a small, dirty piece of green fabric. This ripped fabric turned out to be a mosquito net, and its olive-green color left no doubt that it had once belonged to a soldier. Dusting off this fabric and thinking about the stories I had heard, I realized that this place was not only ravaged by the effects of paramilitary

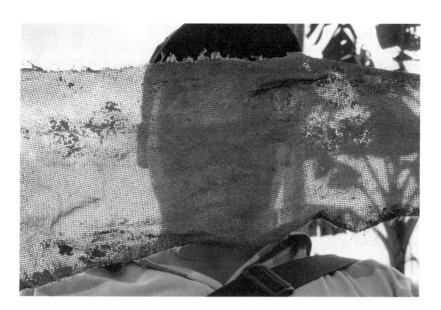

FIGURE 5.3. **A piece of mosquito net. Photo by author.**

and guerrilla violence but full of remnants of an incident of long-lasting proportions. Through that piece of mosquito net, I gained a glimpse into the process of that place's ruination. The net reminded me of the importance of such objects in the daily lives of people living in Bajo Atrato, where a large diversity of mosquitoes and flies swarm like a horde of desperate blood-thirsty devotees at night as well as during the day. In places like the Cur-varadó basin, a mosquito net becomes a frontier between those who enjoy a calm and restful night and those who will eventually get sick with malaria, yellow fever, chikungunya virus, dengue fever, or zika virus (figure 5.3). Having to live in the forest, as irregular armies usually do, a mosquito net is not an accessory but an indispensable item that can be the difference between life and death. In the context of what happened in Caño Claro, the abandonment of such an important object suggests either the desperation of a sudden flight or the unexpected arrival of death surrounded by one's belongings.

During my interviews with people living in the Curvaradó basin, I also learned about other traces of past violence that are still discovered in Caño Claro. Doña Liliana, a widow in her late fifties who lives near the river's mouth, told me about something she found as she was digging for fishing worms. It was a *cédula*, the official Colombian ID card:

That guy, I remember, his name was Ovidio, I think. His family name was Monterrosa. The owner of that cédula came from Necoclí [a municipality located 200 kilometers (124 miles) north of the place we were]. I kept that cédula because I wanted to preserve it, but someone at home ended up throwing it away. I told myself that with the identification number of that man I could have the chance of picking a good lottery number. (Doña Liliana, in conversation with the author, Carmen del Darién)

Rusty military cooking sets, empty bullet cases, and even a Galil rifle are some of the objects that have been found in this area. People have also found the skulls and bones of those who died there. Pontus remembers that some years ago he found a couple of small mounds: landmarks of two improperly buried corpses. Someone else found a skull after plowing and decided to play a joke on Doña Liliana by placing it on top of a stick and telling her there was someone waiting for her on the path. She was not afraid upon seeing the skull; instead, she offered to the prankster a lower jawbone she had found earlier that day: "Here you are, take it and make that skull smile," she told him. "And he did, that miscreant!"

However, encounters with death are sometimes gloomier than a smiling skull hung on a stick. Some people have heard wails during the nights or felt sudden cold breezes while crossing those fields. I was once told the story of a girl who found an enamel iron mug at that place—like the ones the military use—hanging over a pile of rotting logs. At the very moment she took it, she heard in the woods the sounds of a heavy presence breaking branches and running toward her at full speed. Scared, she ran and dove into the river, trying to swim without losing the mug. That proved difficult, so she dropped it and reached the shore as fast as she could. The next day, the person who eventually told me the story decided to return to that place, and there he found the iron mug suspended over the very same logs where it had previously hung. These kinds of encounters are examples of the ghostly presences that still remain in Caño Claro and that have not only disrupted the lives of people but have also altered the distinguishing features of that place (figure 5.4). The uncanny nature of these experiences might be better understood by taking a brief detour through the history of paramilitary presence in the region.

Patterns of Armed Violence

In 2012 former Colombian Army general Rito Alejo Del Río was sentenced to twenty-five years in prison. Some of the charges included murder, reliance on death squads, and complicity with paramilitary crimes. Del Río, a graduate

FIGURE 5.4. Vestiges of violent encounters. Photo by author.

of the infamous US Army School of the Americas, was the commander of the Seventeenth Brigade, the military unit in charge of the Bajo Atrato region. The former US ambassador to Colombia had reported to the Department of State that since 1998, Del Río's "systematic arming and equipping of aggressive regional paramilitaries was pivotal to his military success" (National Security Archive 2010). Under Del Río's orders, Operación Génesis was executed: a huge military campaign led by the official army that was intended to capture members of the guerrilla armies. This campaign, conducted in collaboration with paramilitary forces, involved multiple cases of killing, torture, disappearances, and forced displacement of Afro-Colombian and Indigenous communities. The Inter-American Court of Human Rights condemned Colombia for that military operation in 2013. Del Río's case became emblematic because it showed not only how some military commanders turned a blind eye to the paramilitaries' crimes but also how in Bajo Atrato some officers in the highest ranks systematically armed, equipped, and assisted these criminal groups.

Operación Génesis is a milestone in the history of political violence in Bajo Atrato. In December 1996, several paramilitary squads from the ACCU (Peasant Self-Defense Forces of Córdoba and Urabá) took control of the town of Riosucio using economic blockades, abduction, torture, and systematic killings. The paramilitary commanders have always maintained that their aim was to undermine the presence of the 57th Front of the FARC (Revolutionary Armed Forces of Colombia), but the course of events revealed that the ACCU was not just weaving a counterinsurgency war but was also preparing the ground to deprive local communities of their lands and for the subsequent incursion of large extractive industries. Given the fact that Bajo Atrato is situated at a crucial point for accessing oceangoing drug and weapon routes, guerrilla groups have always had a presence in the region. Moreover, the vast forests and extreme inaccessibility made the region a sort of haven where guerrillas could take respite from army offensives. Guerrilla armies also used to hold many of their kidnapped civilians in this region. On February 24, 1997, the army launched a vast air attack on multiple villages along the Cacarica, Salaquí, and Truandó Rivers. Peasants fled as soon as they could: some took refuge in the forest, hiding in trees and spending several nights in the wilderness; others undertook a long march across forests, swamps, and rivers to reach a safer place (Chica Jiménez, Gómez Nadal, and Ramírez Flórez 2017). The air strikes lasted three days. No one knows for sure how many people died during the bombardments, but multiple accounts describe the hardships faced by those who fled: "There were people who died in the forest because they fainted, they were hit, or they got sick. No one could help them because when you run with fear nobody looks behind" (quoted in Valencia 2013, 61). Someone else recalls: "We had to cross several rivers and follow paths in the forest. Everyone carried the few belongings they could, and we just tried to go ahead. I had never seen in my entire life so many people wounded by barbed wires" (quoted in Valencia 2013, 61). People also remember seeing soldiers from both the army and the paramilitary forces patrolling together and sharing transportation. The attacks, which extended to other basins such as Domingodó, Curvaradó, and Jiguamiandó, succeeded in forcing the guerrillas away from main towns and villages, but it also drove, according to the UN Commission on Human Rights, between twelve thousand and fifteen thousand people from their traditional lands (UNCHR 1998, ¶103).

The indiscriminate air strike and attack on Riosucio were just the beginning of a campaign of terror launched by the paramilitaries in collusion with Colombian military forces. From February to March 1997, the paramilitaries went from village to village pillaging houses, stealing cattle, burning crops, threatening people, and killing leaders. The death of Marino López Mena, an Afro-Colombian leader from the Cacarica River, epitomizes the atrocities committed against civilians: he was beheaded in front of his community, and the perpetrators played soccer using his head (IAHCR 2013, 44). People from the different basins organized themselves in order to leave their lands and march toward towns where their situation would not be ignored by regional and national authorities. More than 3,000 people arrived at the town of Turbo, in Antioquia; in Paya, a small town of 565 inhabitants located in Panama's Darién Province (there were about 450 displaced people); at least 6,000 more arrived at Pavarandó, also in Antioquia (Valencia 2013). According to several sources (Arbeláez 2001; Chica Jiménez, Gómez Nadal, and Ramírez Flórez 2017; Giraldo 1997; Hernández 2008; IAHCR 1999; Valencia 2013), the town of Pavarandó became the largest camp of displaced people in Colombian history, with rows and rows of tents bearing insignias of humanitarian organizations that provided food and some medical care to the thousands of families refuged there. But not everyone left their communities. Some peasants— about 2,500 according to some figures (Valencia 2013, 62)—managed to hide for many months in the forest, especially in the Jiguamiandó basin, living under the cover of the dense roots of immense trees, using plastic or large-leafed plants that could be easily installed and taken down in order to flee when necessary (Comisión Intereclesial de Justicia y Paz 2005).

Massive displacement was not just a collateral effect of the war waged against communist guerrillas. Instead, forced displacement was instrumental to the interests of a large group of entrepreneurs who aimed to illegally seize Afro-Colombian collective lands and forest resources. For example, Maderas del Darién, one of Colombia's biggest timber companies, established itself at a paramilitary base and systematically exploited and depleted native forests in the Cacarica, Truandó, and Salaquí basins (Defensoría del Pueblo 2002, 2014). Other companies—some of them even receiving government subsidies (Internal Displacement Monitoring Centre 2007)—implemented oil-palm plantations on huge tracts of Afro-Colombian collective lands, especially near the Jiguamiandó and Curvaradó Rivers. In these areas more than 14,000 hectares (34,600 acres) of land were illegally seized for palm cultivators, who made criminal alliances with paramilitaries, businessmen, security forces, and governmental agencies (Chica Jiménez, Gómez Nadal, and Ramírez Flórez 2017; Comisión Intereclesial de Justicia y Paz 2005; Franco and Restrepo 2011; Internal Displacement Monitoring Centre 2007; Mingorance, Minelli, and Le Du 2004; Ruiz-Serna 2005). As a matter of fact, the paramilitary armies played an important role in the consolidation of these huge oil-palm plantations. This was not just an open secret but a blatant admission, as one paramilitary top commandant declared in 2005: "We have been developing some entrepreneurial models that we would like to set in motion at a national level. In Urabá [and the Curvaradó basin] we have plantations of oil palm. I myself searched for entrepreneurs that could support that project. Our idea is to get the wealthy there and in other zones throughout the country since once they arrive, state institutions arrive as well" (*Semana* 2005).

In order to implement the oil-palm projects, corrupt officials from the former Colombian Institute of Agrarian Reform (INCORA), public notaries, and governmental funding agencies allowed entrepreneurs to legally take over lands seized by the paramilitaries (Chica Jiménez, Gómez Nadal, and Ramírez Flórez 2017; Comisión Intereclesial de Justicia y Paz 2005; Franco and Restrepo 2011; Mingorance, Minelli, and Le Du 2004). Some of these entrepreneurs have been sentenced for crimes of conspiracy, forced displacement, and the invasion of protected areas, but the majority of the oil-palm companies that took the lands from the Curvaradó River are still awaiting trial.

From the very beginning of their banishment, communities set in motion different organizational strategies to return to their lands and regain their rights. They declared their neutrality with respect to all armed groups and organized a gradual return process to different provisional settlements (Arbeláez 2001). In 2001, after a long legal struggle for the recognition of their rights to land ownership, Afro-Colombian communities received title deeds from the Colombian president supporting their collective property ownership. But things did not necessarily improve once people managed to go back to their lands. Between 1999—when the first return process started—and 2002, at least 130 homicides and 19 forced disappearances were documented (Observatorio del Programa Presidencial de Derechos Humanos 2003, 14). Attacks against Indigenous and Afro-Colombian communities included looting, burning of crops and houses, arbitrary detentions, death threats, and economic blockades. Between 1999 and 2006, when the paramilitaries from the ACCU were finally demobilized, there were at least 119 killings, 41 disappearances, and 32 people tortured (CINEP 2016). In the Curvaradó and Jiguamiandó basins alone, the cradle of the oil-palm project, more than one hundred crimes against their inhabitants were reported between 1999 and 2005, all committed by paramilitary groups that worked, if not in collusion with, then at least with the assent of the Seventeenth Brigade (Comisión Intereclesial de Justicia y Paz 2005, 57–77).

Not only did the paramilitary armies lead the counterinsurgency fight; they have been instrumental in helping the interests of regional politicians, powerful cattlemen and landowners, traditional wealthy families, and drug traffickers (Mauricio Romero 2002). According to some scholars, in regions where the paramilitaries from the ACCU actively waged war (those regions include the departments of Chocó, Antioquia, Bolívar, Sucre, and Córdoba), about 3 million hectares (7.4 million acres) of land were abandoned (Salinas and Zarama 2012). Most of these lands were illegally seized, and the peasant economy in these territories was severely damaged. Food-crop plantations were replaced by biofuel-crop operations or cattle ranches. Revealingly, the zones from which people were forcibly displaced overlapped with areas of strategic interest for mining, industrial forestry, or mega-infrastructure, such as dams, highways, and cargo ports (Espinosa 2012; Salinas and Zarama 2012).

The paramilitary actions in Bajo Atrato demonstrated a pattern of violence that repeated itself throughout the country. First, the primary targets of their military actions were mostly civilians, not guerrilla combatants; second, the forced displacement of local populations clearly helped the economic interests of local warlords and regional wealthy elites; third, systematic killings, threats, and dispossession of lands were designed not only to discipline local populations but also to establish political and economic regimes that were useful to the paramilitary agenda; and fourth, regions under paramilitary influence progressively became the focus of economic models linked to national and international neoliberal agendas (Dufort 2014; Duncan 2007; Espinosa 2012; Mauricio Romero 2002; Salinas and Zarama 2012).

Paramilitaries set in motion a vast and violent agrarian and land counter-reform in Colombia. Paramilitaries have been historically allied with right-wing politicians defending the property rights of an elitist minority. Paramilitaries even presumed their political power by taking control of 35 percent of the elected Congress in 2002 (Álvaro 2009; López 2005). In 2007, during the second presidential period of Álvaro Uribe, at least sixty-six politicians, including congressmen, governors, mayors, and even one of his ministers, were indicted for colluding with these paramilitary forces (*Semana* 2007). Between 2003 and 2006, Uribe led a heavily criticized demobilization process with these paramilitary armies. A law approved by Congress made broad concessions to combatants and commanders, limiting sentences to a maximum of eight years and raising serious concerns about the legal framework under which members involved in violations of human rights and international humanitarian law were brought to trial (IAHCR 2004). Although the law provided reduced sentences to paramilitaries in return for honest disclosures, reparation to victims, and promises to not return to lawlessness, fewer than 10 percent of those demobilized applied for benefits, and those who actually did "offered no significant information on illegal acts or crimes committed by the paramilitary units to which they belonged" (IAHCR 2008, ¶34). Most paramilitary members enjoyed relative impunity, including those commanders accused of such crimes as massacres of defenseless civilians, forced displacement, and selective assassinations of social leaders, trade unionists, human rights defenders, judicial officers, journalists, and members of LGBT communities. For example, the commander of the ACCU, Freddy Rendón Herrera, alias "El Alemán," never took full responsibility for the crimes committed by his armed group in Chocó during his free confessions. One of these offenses was the Bojayá massacre, a horrendous crime where more than 119 Afro-Colombian civilians were killed inside a church during the combat that the ACCU waged against the FARC guerrillas in May 2002. El Alemán was released in 2015 after being imprisoned less than nine years for crimes related to drug trafficking and homicide. He was never condemned for other crimes directly related to the armed conflict, such as forced displacement, forced disappearances, or military use of children.

Paramilitary groups remain active in many regions of the country, with Bajo Atrato remaining the site of some of the bloodiest confrontations between new illegal armed groups and guerrillas. In 2008 the Inter-American Commission on Human Rights reported that paramilitary armies, often under new names, continued operating and committing violations in supposedly demobilized areas (IAHCR 2004). Human Rights Watch reported in 2010 that these successor groups "have taken on many of the same roles, often with some of the same personnel, in some cases with the same counter-insurgency objectives" of former paramilitary forces (2010, 18). That report also produced substantial evidence that portions of paramilitary groups have remained active, describing how members of the groups who had supposedly demobilized were still engaged in illegal activities (Human Rights Watch 2010, 19). As of 2020 in Bajo Atrato, paramilitary armies are still present, although they have adopted different names (Autodefensas Gaitanistas de Colombia, Aguilas Negras, Los Urabeños, Clan Úsuga). All these armies have their roots in the former ACCU, and they are still engaged in drug trafficking, mining, forced displacement, selective assassination, and the threatening of Indigenous and Afro-Colombian collective-life projects.

Uncanny Encounters

As a part of their war strategy and in an attempt to cut off the guerrillas' supply lines, paramilitaries blockaded the Curvaradó River between 1999 and 2003. Paramilitaries stated that supplies were carried by locals in the boats that people usually used for their own transportation. At the checkpoint at Caño Claro, paramilitaries inspected all these boats and set limits on the amounts of food and items such as candles or batteries that people could transport. The blockade not only affected the movement of boats but essentially removed the people's access to subsistence goods. As in other places occupied by paramilitaries, in Caño Claro the soldiers took abandoned houses and built their own shelters by helping themselves to the community's roofs, walls, and floors. Over several months, Caño Claro's checkpoint became a paramilitary camp, hosting dozens of combatants. Although the paramilitaries experienced some military success at the beginning of their campaign in expelling guerrillas from certain areas, the return of the FARC was only a matter of time. One night, during the first rainy months of 2002, the paramilitary camp was heavily attacked by guerrilla squads. The ambush, according to some testimonies, was a well-planned and lethal attack, leaving no chance for the paramilitaries to react. After a few hours, the paramilitaries who were not killed were forced to flee. As mentioned earlier, no one knows for sure how many people died. According to some testimonies, the guerrillas took their own dead comrades and left behind the corpses of the paramilitary soldiers. Many of these corpses were simply left on the ground to be eaten by vultures, and others floated downstream on the Curvaradó River. Fearing a new attack, no other paramilitary squad dared to look for the corpses. Peasants also dared not bury or even touch any of these corpses, as doing so would have been interpreted by the guerrillas as exhibiting some sort of empathy or political allegiance to the paramilitaries.

At the time of that attack, people like Pontus and Petronio, who were living away from their lands in temporary settlements established by international humanitarian organizations, started to organize the definitive return to their lands. When Pontus decided to return to his family's land, he found it full of oil-palm plantations. To be exact, his entire village had been converted into a vast field of palms that extended farther than the eye could see. The plantation owners had left no stone unturned, and even the cemetery had been brutally razed. When Petronio came back to his land, he had to rebuild the house and once again plant his staple foods. The return to places like Curvaradó was the result of the displaced communities' tireless efforts to go back to their traditional livelihoods. During 2002 hundreds of families managed to take back most of their stolen lands. Sometimes they just came back and hastily built makeshift shelters amid the oil-palm plantations. Other times they organized demonstrations and marches to reclaim their lands. With the support of nongovernmental organizations, they also brought lawsuits before national and international courts. After several months of tenacious hard work, the families that returned were able to *sanear* (literally, "to heal") their fields and to make their lands suitable again for their own crops. In Colombian law, *saneamiento* corresponds to the process through which authorities establish the legality of title deeds and confer rights to ownership of property. During these years in Bajo Atrato, *sanear* signified acknowledgment of the illegality of violent land-grabbing perpetrated by entrepreneurs and warlords, but, more profoundly, it was also the process undertaken by local communities to take care of their lands—that is, healing them by making them habitable and productive once again—bringing them into the form and order required for the maintenance of their traditional livelihoods.

What followed the guerrillas' raid at Caño Claro's mouth only worsened the already harsh situation that the returning families were experiencing. The paramilitaries chose to retaliate, and many peasants were individually targeted. Many were threatened for supposedly being part of guerrilla armies. New pillages, economic blockades, and selective assassinations affected all returning people. As is often the case in an irregular war, what resulted from the attack at Caño Claro was a retaliation against civilians rather than against combatants. Paramilitary presence and power have persisted since 2006, the year when the official demobilization of the ACCU took place. Leaders such as Petronio and Pontus have received multiple death threats, and during our time together in 2015 they were even under the protection of a government program designed to prevent harm against human rights activists. The situation for the communities living in the Curvaradó basin is so delicate that since 2003, the Inter-American Court of Human Rights has granted precautionary measures of injunction to protect families returning to their lands. These measures, granted to those in grave and imminent danger, were ratified in 2009 and once again in 2013.

On the Caño Claro River, the paramilitary presence did not go away after the guerrilla ambush. Rather, this presence changed because those who had died during the guerrilla raid became spirits which haunted that place. Encounters with these ghostly presences are deeply emplaced, meaning that these encounters take place around the area where the killing happened. For example, Doña Liliana told me that one day, when she was fishing near that location, she heard human-like voices coming from the riverbank. She saw nothing, and because she thought it was one of her neighbors trying to scare her, she remained concentrated on her task. Then a lump of earth fell into her dugout canoe, close to the place where she was seated. She looked again toward the riverbank, and still she saw nothing. She was not scared, but after returning home and asking her neighbor why he was being so annoying, he told her he had not gone to the river that day. She then realized that what she had experienced was something uncanny. When I asked her if she thought it was the spirit of one of the dead soldiers, she expressed no doubts about it: "That is a place that scares you. Someone is in pain."

Another encounter with these dead happened to someone who was walking through the former paramilitary camp. He heard steps coming from the opposite direction, like someone who was forcing his way through the bushes. He could not see anything, but he heard this presence suddenly stop some meters in front of him. Others have described how they have heard loud movements of invisible presences, noises of something like a big animal forcing its way through the forest and diving hastily into the river. Doña Liliana told me that she had had these kinds of encounters not once but three times and that during the last one she decided to confront those invisible presences: "The day they scared me, I started to insult them, to tell them a lot of things like 'Because of you we have had such a hard life; you are the ones to be blamed for everything we have lost.'" Like many other inhabitants of Caño Claro, Doña Liliana was a victim of paramilitary violence, having to endure forced displacement and the many losses that eviction implies. Her insults were the iteration of a grievance against the perpetrators of her suffering. She explained to me the situation she faced after returning to her land with her family:

> Look at me. I'm an old, tired woman, and when we came back to our land we had to start over again to cut down the forest surrounding our house. That day [when I confronted the spirits] I said a lot of nonsense, and I must have looked like a crazy woman: "It was because of you that our soup stock became cloudy; you never worked, and you never let us work." Now that I've come back to my land, they don't want to let us work again. (*Doña Liliana, in conversation with the author, Carmen del Darién*)

Although these ghostly presences are causing a lot of trouble, people have found ways to deal with them. One way is to never demonstrate fear. Although these spirits may scare people, their primary intention is not to hurt anyone but rather to call people's attention to their unresolved situation: these spirits are, as Doña Liliana described them, souls in pain, *ánimas penando*. Even if she had been frightened during her last encounter with them, she nevertheless felt the need to reproach these paramilitaries—or what remains of them—for all she has suffered because of them. The spirits did seem to hear her reproaches, for they stopped assaulting her. Doña Liliana's reaction does not mean that she was not listening to these spirits in pain but rather that she, like the hundreds of people who have suffered paramilitary violence, has trouble empathizing with these restless souls.

The image of an *ánima en pena* is a frequently recurring subject in various cultural traditions, as documented by Robert Hertz in his celebrated essay on the collective representation of death ([1909] 1960). At least in Bajo Atrato, where the Christian tradition plays an important role in the spiritual life of local communities, the image of a soul in pain is associated with the restless spirit of someone who died but cannot reach the afterlife. Therefore, these spirits in pain seek help from the living to alleviate their suffering and be assisted in their entrenched incapacity for leaving the world of the living. This is precisely the fate of the paramilitary soldiers that died in Caño Claro: rather than receiving proper funerary rituals, their bodies were simply abandoned in the forest. Unable to make their journey to the afterlife, these spirits were condemned to linger in the place where they violently died.

Ghostly presences associated with unnatural death in contexts of political violence are common. For example, after the Indonesian occupation (1975–99), many families in Timor-Leste redoubled their efforts to recover the remains of their loved ones in order to conduct appropriate mortuary rituals and in this way avoid the spirits of the deceased continuing to wander as ghosts, tormenting the lives of both their descendants and those responsible for their death (Kent 2016). Those rituals, explains Lia Kent, aim to, on one hand, "release the spirit of the deceased from the pain and suffering they experienced" and, on the other, "render them spiritually harmless and restore the balance between the worlds of the living and the dead" (2016, 43). Sasanka Perera (2001) describes how in Sri Lanka, after the harsh clash between the communist guerrillas from the People's Liberation Front (Janatha Vimukthi Peramuna) and the counterinsurgency forces of the state, many villagers from the southern regions of the country have encountered the ghosts of those who died during the war years (1988–91). As in Caño Claro, these ghostly encounters occur in places that have been specifically demarcated by violent death: sites where the corpses of young men were set on fire, buildings where people were tortured, waters where people drowned in their attempts to hide (Perera 2001, 171–73). Perera sees in the nature of these encounters a "symbolic reference to the problem of conscience and guilt among both survivors of terror and the perpetrators" (2001, 162). According to him, the guilty conscience results from the people's feelings of powerlessness in being unable to prevent, in any way, the violent murders that occurred. Perera suggests that these experiences with ghosts and the ensuing narratives "are mechanisms by which a community remembers the people it has lost, a mechanism that helps place in perspective the community's collective losses and memories of the violent past. Such memories are also constructed as expressions of the guilt of the living over the dead, a desire for justice and revenge, and the need to alleviate the otherworldly suffering of those who died unnatural deaths" (2001, 197).

From this perspective, ghosts and haunted places are epiphenomenal manifestations of collective and individual trauma, cultural processes through which a tormented and unhealed collective conscience expresses its suffering and its aspirations for justice and preservation of memory. Although I agree that ghosts and haunted places are manifestations of violent experiences and difficulties with coping, I believe that Perera's approach tends to pathologize this "supernatural activity" (2001, 197) by situating encounters with spirits and experiences of haunted places exclusively within people's inner worlds. Thus, according to him, once provided with the adequate means "to come to grips with the experiences of the past" (2001, 170), people will stop seeing the spirits of the dead and places will stop being haunted. However, describing the haunting attributed to some places as the result of trauma or psychological damage goes against one of the tenets of this chapter: places are not only endowed with the meanings and memories that people create for them but are also active agents in the creation of a certain affective sensibility, especially when people have to deal with experiences of violence, terror, and social suffering. Therefore, I see spirits and haunted places as attributes embedded within the world and not as the outcome of disturbed people trying to reconcile themselves with an overwhelming reality. Let me explain. When dealing with suffering and pain, Veena Das argues that a statement like "I am in pain" is not only a statement of fact but also "an expression of the fact" (1998, 191), meaning that experiences of pain are not just expressed but are shaped by the very means one uses to convey them. In the same vein, local experiences with spirits and haunted places are not just cultural expressions of social suffering, but they shape the very possibilities of how people experience suffering and envisage reconciliation and peace.

The ghostly experiences recounted in southern Sri Lanka and Timor-Leste and those of Caño Claro might be contrasted in another crucial way: in Caño Claro people are not witnessing ghosts of people of their own communities and kin. Quite the opposite: people are seeing the unquiet spirits of the perpetrators of violence against their kin, of those who, recalling Doña Liliana's words, were responsible for everything they have lost. This is why I do not think these haunted presences can be interpreted as "reflections of the distraught conscience of the community" (Perera 2001, 170), for it would understandably be hard for Caño Claro's residents to feel guilty about the fate of those paramilitaries who threatened their lives and expelled them from their lands. The difficulty of empathizing with such spirits can be seen in the treatment given to the remains of the bodies found in Caño Claro. Remember the man who found a skull and decided to play a joke on Doña Liliana, as well as how she used the lower jawbone to make the skull smile. Perhaps under other circumstances those human remains would have been treated differently, but in this case the playing with these bones was proof of the contempt felt toward those who had caused so much harm. But the little empathy toward the dead themselves does not mean that people like Doña Liliana are unaware of the needs that the spirits manifest. People understand that unless these dead receive appropriate burials, their spirits will continue inhabiting Caño Claro. In this sense the experiences that people in Caño Claro have with these spirits may be more comparable with the relations that anthropologist Heonik Kwon (2008) describes between people, spiritual ancestors, and ghosts of war in Vietnam.

Deeply embedded within the Buddhist tradition of ancestor worship, ghosts in Vietnam are considered to be the products of violent deaths that occurred far from home. According to Kwon, ghosts of war have a double liminal identity: on one hand, they are neither severed from the living world nor fully integrated in the world of the dead; on the other, they are not completely separated from the place where they died or assimilated to the positive and transcendental space that people confer to other dead people, such as their ancestors. More than reflecting a traumatic engagement with reality, these ghosts are objects of care and are of ontological concern because people understand that proper respect for the dead is a primary condition for the well-being of the living (Kwon 2008, 16). This is why to appease the suffering of these ghosts, people build graves and shrines, address prayers, and offer oblations in the places associated with their presence. In many cases, people succeed in identifying the lost families of these ghosts, and reburial rituals are then performed. But when that is not possible, people may create a fictional kinship tie with these ghosts in order to incorporate them into the ambit of familial, local ancestors. In such cases, ghosts become ascending spirits that are treated by families as both kin and deity. According to Kwon, these spirits aspire to demonstrate to their adoptive families and communities that their membership is productive: they are therefore attentive to the social affairs and material conditions of the living world, they intercede before deities on behalf of their adoptive families, and they even mediate between deities and other ghosts.

This manner of treating ghosts in Vietnam shares similarities with how people in Caño Claro aspire to interact with the spirits of those who experienced a bad death. In both places, it is understood that these apparitions are associated with demands for adequate burial. The violent circumstances of their deaths not only confine these spirits to the places where their tragedies occurred but also bind them to a particular flow of time, dooming them to appear over and over again and to repeat their vicious demise. The principal aim of appropriate burials and prayers, or of oblations and rituals as in

Vietnam and Timor-Leste, is thus to liberate these ghosts from this dismal situation, to insert them in the proper flow of time. In one way or another, people are interested in alleviating the suffering of these spirits because the absence of remembrance or other action from the living will aggravate the condition of the dead. However, unlike in Vietnam, the people of Caño Claro would rather not be responsible for performing these essential duties toward the dead, primarily because these ghostly presences are still associated with a recent, painful past. On the contrary, in Vietnam the identities of these ghosts, who died in a war that concluded almost fifty years ago, are no longer relevant because people give little importance to which side of the war the combatants sacrificed their lives for.

Those who violently died in Bajo Atrato may have actually improved the material conditions of the living. This was a possibility insinuated by Doña Liliana through her intention of playing the lottery with the number of the ID card she found. Because this number belonged to someone who had not yet left this world or entered into the realm of the dead, it was believed that it could offer good luck. These spirits embody then an ambiguous message of suffering and release from suffering: they wander in pain, but their fate may always be redeemed. The connection between these *ánimas en pena* and magic practices has been pointed out elsewhere by Michael Taussig. According to him, the haunting that results from those who suffered violent deaths also contains "a quotient of magical force" (1992, 27). Belief in these magical forces of the dead can be seen in several regions throughout Colombia when people often make earnest requests to these spirits for help in matters of employment, love, health, or poverty. In some cemeteries in Bogotá, for example, people visit the tombs of the unknown dead on Mondays, carrying flowers, candles, and even music in order to ask for some kind of miraculous intercession on their behalf (Trujillo Molano 2012). Similarly, but in a context of political violence, inhabitants of Puerto Berrío, a town where violence between paramilitary groups, drug gangs, and guerrilla forces reached inordinate heights, began rescuing the hundreds of unknown bodies that floated on the Magdalena River. The villagers adopted these anonymous dead, giving them names, headstones, and adequate burials. They continue to take care of these lost souls by offering masses and prayers, always with the aim of obtaining some kind of divine intervention because these dead in their penitential and reverent condition are believed to accomplish miracles (Echevarría 2013; Nieto 2012). In Caño Claro these dead are far from considered objects of veneration; however, their presence, or in Doña Liliana's case the number found in their belongings, may lead to good fortune. In the relationship between people and spirits there is the possibility of a mutually beneficial arrangement: through rituals of remembrance the suffering of these wandering spirits may be appeased, and in exchange, these spirits may intervene in the divine sphere to improve people's fortunes.

Death Doesn't Occur in One Instant

Among Afro-Colombian peoples, death is considered a continuous process rather than a single, clear-cut event. One's death is often preceded by omens: the plaintive howls of dogs in the middle of the night, the song of a *guaco* (laughing falcon) (Serrano 1994), ants walking around the kitchen (Velásquez [1961] 2000), the sudden movements of *palma de Cristo* leaves. Even before any sign of illness or bodily decay, one's soul may start venturing about on its own, visiting friends, family, or cherished places in dreams. Life is not simply something that one has or does not have but something that one may have in certain quantities. For example, life decreases a little when the soul wanders in dreams. Similarly, death may occur little by little, not because one gradually loses one's physical or mental faculties but because there are parts of the self that may fall away before one actually dies. Similarly, even after the body ceases to be the depository of life, there are parts of oneself that do not completely leave the world unless people carry out appropriate funeral rites.

Along with reinforcing collective bonds and shared social values, these rites constitute indispensable ways of taking care of the dead and their souls. Death does not imply the extinction or nonexistence of the self but rather a severe transformation of it. People, like trees, plants, game animals, or fish, are considered *renacientes*, literally reborn, and as such they are subjects of rebirth (de Friedemann 1974; Escobar 2008). However, as I explained in the previous chapters, this rebirth has nothing to do with any sort of metempsychotic event in which a person's soul is reincarnated in a new body. Instead, the concept is one of a permanent resprouting of life for the constant emergence of new forms of being. Death is then considered an inexorable transformation of the state of the self, which must be accompanied by a series of ritual procedures conducted by the living in order to help the soul transit from one state to another. Failure to observe these rites may cause the soul of the dead to lose its path toward the afterlife and perhaps remain wandering in its favorite place or in places that, like forests and cemeteries, are considered not properly human.

There are good and bad deaths. A good death in Bajo Atrato is one that happens surrounded by kin, at home or close to your homeland, and when the departure has been accompanied by appropriate funerary rituals (Quiceno 2016; Serrano 1994; Velásquez [1961] 2000). A bad death, on the contrary, is one that happens suddenly or violently, or one that has not received proper burial. Without these rituals an ordinary death may turn into a bad one. Closely tied to Christian cosmology, traditional Afro-Colombian funeral rites involve a period of wake, a mass, a procession of mourners, and a burial. Although its form may resemble that of the Catholic tradition, the Afro-Colombian funeral has its own particularities. The wake is one of them. It is a huge social gathering that takes place over the course of nine nights following the burial—the ritualistic disposition of a corpse to a consecrated place. While the burial represents the completion of ceremonies dealing with a dead body, it does not mark the complete departure of the dead because the soul, in the form of an ethereal presence wandering among the living, will leave this world only at the end of the nine-day wake (*novena*).

Until recent years, *novenas* used to be huge, well-attended gatherings in which people sang and prayed around an altar built in the living room of the deceased's house. Abundant food, coffee, *aguardiente*, and cigarettes helped people stay awake until dawn. Today, only a few can afford to bear the costs of a *novena*, but the essence of this important ritual is still present. A sober but solemn altar is usually built in the house of the deceased or in that of one of their closest relatives. The altar is dedicated to their soul and may contain images of the Virgin Mary and the saints to whom the deceased expressed devotion. It is also adorned with candles, a glass of water, and a vase of flowers or *palma de Cristo* leaves. It is believed that the soul comes to this altar every night until it finishes the process of collecting its own steps. People gather around this altar to pray or sing their dirges and *alabaos*. Outside the house, people play dominoes or cards, listening to music and drinking coffee and *aguardiente* in order to stay awake and combat the cold expelled by the dead. One of the most significant moments of this *novena* takes place during the last night, when the soul of the deceased makes its last visit to the realm of the living. That night, just before dawn, the soul leaves this world, and it is only then that the dead really die. It is a solemn moment at which people cry, mourn, and say their last good-byes. The altar is then fully dismantled, marking the full departure of the soul (Losonczy 2006b; Serrano 1994; Velásquez [1961] 2000; Whitten 1974).

Even for those who in Bajo Atrato profess other religious creeds, death involves an elaborate set of ritual procedures whose object is to ensure the journey of the soul to the afterlife. Failure to follow these procedures may compromise that journey. To be buried, mourned by loved ones, and accompanied during the time the soul collects its steps are all factors contributing to a good death. The souls of those who die suddenly, violently or away from their homeland, do not have the chance to collect their footsteps and so will wander mournfully in this world, which is precisely what happened in Caño Claro: the dead soldiers were not given any type of the aforementioned care.

Violent death, as highlighted by some of the anthropological literature dealing with memory, mourning, coping, and trauma in contexts of political violence, violates the cultural norms that govern ordinary deaths, leaving a deep mark that usually transcends the nature of the death itself (Das 1998; Hertz 1960; Kent 2016; Perera 2001). In Bajo Atrato, wandering spirits are the outcomes of such violent deaths. They are considered part and parcel of the world, which makes them an ontological concern: for the living, they represent an undesirable state of being. These spirits represent some sort of failure, an anomaly that rudely disrupts the proper flow of life and time. They interrupt the flow of life because they stand at the threshold between the realm of the living and the realm of the dead, becoming liminal beings that, besides wandering unwittingly between worlds, blur boundaries between life and death. These spirits disrupt time because they juxtapose temporalities: they are obstinate apparitions that interrupt the present time of the living by enacting the suffering of their past death. They are like a fixity, like "a tragedy condemned to repeat itself time and again" (del Toro 2001). I borrow Guillermo del Toro's words from one of the characters in his movie *The Devil's Backbone*, who speculates that a ghost is "an instant of pain . . . something dead which still seems to be alive. An emotion suspended in time. Like a blurred photograph. Like an insect trapped in amber." Ghostly presences like the ones of Caño Claro are stagnant both in time and place because they appear time and again where they died; they are ambivalent beings that contain, but from which also emanate, the sorrowful affects of violent death.

The spirits of those who experienced a bad death cannot help but relate to the world through similarly disruptive, violent means. However, the violence with which these spirits manifest themselves is of a different order because it is not inherently intentional or agentive. Rather, their violence is no more than a consequence triggered by their mere presence: when these spirits manifest themselves, they produce a sort of disturbance, a bump in the flow of time, a distortion in the consistency of a place. The apparition of these spirits is like a wake, a turbulence caused by a body moving in water. In the same way the waves caused by a boat ripple the river's surface, the ghostly presences of Caño Claro create a kind of crack in the disposition of things as they normally manifest themselves. Like the waves provoked by boats, ghosts' trajectories are violent simply because they disturb something that would otherwise remain still.

The wandering spirits of Caño Claro also represent an existential failure. They are the opposite of *andar*, which means "to move, to walk, to embark, and to travel." Life is movement: rivers, animals, clouds, trees, the wind, and the sun are all alive. The lack of motion is associated with death: stagnant waters, rocks, *palizadas*, decayed tree trunks (Velásquez [1961] 2000). Living beings travel, but other beings, like the spirits of those who experienced violent death, are stagnant. These spirits therefore stand in contradiction to the positive values associated with traveling and embarking. As I showed in chapter 1, traveling in Bajo Atrato is associated with the cultivation of values, ties, skills, and modes of being that are essential to navigate both social and natural worlds. But the spirits of Caño Claro are no longer capable of traveling; therefore, they do not really know or learn about the world. In this sense these spirits are not fully agentive. *Andar* is to live and to exert one's will: "The living walk, the dead wander" (Whitten 1974, 125). The uncanny means through which these wandering spirits relate with the world are neither evil nor good. Rather, the spirits do only what they are condemned to do: stagnate in the places where they violently died in order to look for help to redeem their tragic fate.

An apparent contradiction of these spirits is that they are suspended in time and space but their spatial stagnation has little to do with a positive value like dwelling: the sense of belonging to a place. By dwelling in their territories, people nurture and build a particular sense of place that ghostly presences cannot. Building and nurturing imply a back-and-forth relationship between people and their vital places—the attributes of each are mutually constituted— whereas spirits do not participate in this co-constituted circuit and only take but do not reciprocate. Therefore, these spirits do not belong to places, but instead they are trapped within a place's contours because what their suffering ultimately signifies is the impossibility of finding a place to rest, of having a territory to care for and from which be nurtured. As the people of Bajo Atrato who experienced forced displacement are well aware, the suffering of having to be away from one's homeland can doom any existence. This is why in order to effectively heal their territories and fully regain their lands, people must insert these spiteful spirits into the appropriate flow of time and space.

An Ecumenic Peace

Invisible frontiers and disputed sovereignties: that is what the presence of antagonistic armed groups create when they converge in the same region. Sometimes implicitly, sometimes explicitly, they make arrangements to demarcate the areas under their influence: a river, a road, a village. The presence of an armed group in a given zone attaches a certain stigma to that zone's inhabitants, as if during their travels they were carrying in their bodies a sign revealing their supposed political and moral allegiances. During the hardest years of the war in Bajo Atrato, villagers inhabiting a zone under the control of paramilitary forces could not go to zones where guerrilla forces were present, and vice versa. To do so meant becoming a military target. These stigmas did not disappear once the groups demobilized or left these zones, making it important for people to be aware of which group controlled which zone when moving between places. Doña Lucía, a woman in her early forties who occasionally hires workers to help her harvest her crops, told me of the difficulties she sometimes experiences when she goes to the town: "If you need a laborer, they always ask where you live. Then they say: 'At the mouth of Caño Claro? There? I'll not go to that place. That's full of guerrilla armies.' You always receive a resounding 'No.'"

The permanent and long-lasting presence of antagonistic armed groups may end up blurring the political allegiances of the civil population. Although grassroots local organizations have done hard work in distinguishing communities and their interests from those of armed groups, advocating for the protection of civilians who do not participate in the hostilities, in Bajo Atrato many individuals and families have willingly provided services to these armed groups, like transportation, food, information, and even health care. In most cases this kind of support reveals a sort of pragmatic rather than ideological allegiance: besides representing a source of income, these groups might indeed provide security. That being said, communities are not always simply caught in the crossfire, and armed groups have been capable of co-opting some locals in order to mobilize their own political and economic agendas. This is why in the polarized climate of mistrust created by years of war it is easy to stigmatize the communities where the presence or effects of armed groups are notorious. In the case of Caño Claro, Pontus explained to me that the idea of this place being a guerrilla bastion came from the massacre that took place there, even though guerrillas never managed to establish a permanent presence in this zone: "As they were the ones who won that terrain, then that idea of their presence is still present." Others add that they struggle against that mark of infamy every time they go to the town, that what happened in Caño Claro has created a terrible reputation for the place and, of course, its inhabitants. Some people I talked to during my visits to the Curvaradó region told me that the stigma has discouraged some families from returning to their lands and that a few, such as the owner of an abandoned shelter located at the mouth of the river, have even preferred to leave permanently.

It is as if the aftermath of that infamous military raid had centripetal and centrifugal effects. Centrifugal because of the negative ways that inhabitants are perceived by some outsiders, extending the aftermath beyond Caño Claro's boundaries. Centripetal because of the aforementioned relations between the residents of Caño Claro and the dead, which means that the aftermath remains inside this place. Although these two registers are qualitatively distinct, they do not belong to two independent realms, but rather, like the Möbius strip, both belong to a single political domain of undistinguishable surfaces and blurred boundaries. Both are public, knowable arenas with particular obligations, values, relations, and modes of representation. Both compel people to action. Both deal with memory and its worldly consequences. Both are concerned with how to appropriately connect beings to the world: on one hand, the relations of villagers from Caño Claro with their neighbors, and on the other, the relationship between people and spirits. In other words, both are part of the same way of conceiving of politics: a politics in which what is at stake is not only power relations but also the creation and maintenance of relations among different forms of beings and the worlds they enact.

One of the main problems in Caño Claro is the unbearable amount of uncertainty about what happened and what should happen to these spirits. Nobody knows how many people died there, much less their identities. Nobody cared for them: locals could not care for them and weren't interested in doing so, and the families of these dead soldiers do not know for sure if their loved ones are alive or dead. Away from their loved ones, away from their homelands, and entangled within a thick forest that harbors everything people do not consider properly human, these dead combatants became souls in torment, *ánimas en pena*. Their inconsolable state of abandonment is epitomized by the phrase that people often use to describe the lamentable fate of dying alone in the forest: they became carrion for the vultures. Human beings, regardless of the role they played during their lives, do not deserve such a tragic end. To be abandoned in the forest and not receive appropriate burial has compromised their souls.

During my conversations with Petronio, Pontus, and Doña Liliana, a crucial point emerged: if the corpses of those who died in Caño Claro are identified and their remains given back to their mothers or relatives, their ghostly presences will disappear. This opinion was also shared by other leaders of the Curvaradó basin I later met. "What we need," Petronio told me, "is some sort of act to publicly dignify what happened there. Only then will our land be consecrated again." Then Pontus gave me a more in-depth explanation. According to some elders, the forest is inhabited by *encantos*, some of which are haunting spirits that are attached to the places where treasures were buried. For example, in the old times Spanish conquistadors used to hide their fortunes in the forest, but they would first kill one of their slaves in the place of burial, in order to keep his spirit as guard. In this case the act of burying a treasure with the dead prevents the soul from going to the afterworld. But when these treasures are removed, Pontus explained, the haunting disappears. As long as the treasure remains buried, the spiritual custodians will be attached to these places. According to Petronio, something similar happens in Caño Claro: as long as all the military gear and human remains are kept in this place, the souls of the dead will not be capable of departing. "This is why," insisted Petronio, "we think and believe that by moving these corpses to another place, by taking them away, the land and its people will heal. Moreover, if it is the Colombian state that does this, it would help us change these misunderstandings that the guerrillas live here."

What prompted my interlocutors to request state intervention was not only their desire to lessen the stigma associated with Caño Claro and its inhabitants. There was also a need to come to terms with those ghostly presences and deal with that ruined place. And there was something else too. The word *dignity* caught my attention when Petronio explained his point: digging into the ground where dozens of bodies are concealed within the soil and identifying those remains will help both the living and the dead regain some of their dignity. To the inhabitants of Caño Claro, an official exhumation will shed some light on the events that occurred there, demonstrating that locals had and have nothing to do with the guerrillas and their business, and eventually changing the way that locals are perceived by some outsiders. But the dignity of the dead and of their loved ones is also at stake: the former would finally be found, identified, and buried; the latter would finally find some relief from the profound grief that engulfs people when faced with the unknown whereabouts of their kin.

I was astonished that Petronio placed such an emphasis on dignity with regard to unburied paramilitary soldiers, particularly because he is a man who had received several death threats from the paramilitaries and had even been banished from his land by them. At the time of our last encounter, he lived under the protection of a governmental agency because he was still considered a paramilitary target. I felt that Petronio's words were, if I may borrow these lines, "like I was shot with a diamond, a diamond bullet right through my forehead" (Coppola 1979). I realized that these paramilitary soldiers, despite the unspeakable crimes they had committed in the region, were not seen as monsters. Petronio made his point crystal clear with the following words:

This war is not about poor people fighting against poor people. There are no children of the rich in the army, and there are no children of the rich in the guerrilla armies; there is not a single child of the rich in the paramilitary armies. There are but the children of us, the peasants. We are the ones who were banished from our lands by them [the rich], and later they took advantage of us and of our children who were in need. That is exactly the guilty conscience that inhabits Caño Claro. How many mothers are looking for those dead? One hundred mothers? Eighty? We don't know, but we do know there are hopeful mothers out there. (Petronio, in discussion with the author, Curvaradó River)

Petronio's words were a gift, particularly his consideration that these soldiers were surely sons of peasants like him and that these peasants are also no doubt in search of their loved ones, just as some people from Caño Claro are seeking their own disappeared kin. The way he used the expression "guilty conscience," *cargo de conciencia,* to describe what dwells at Caño Claro's mouth, caught my attention. That guilty conscience is a force embedded in the place, not a feeling coming from the people. This guilty conscience should not be confused with remorse—after all, locals do not feel guilty for what happened to the paramilitaries who violated their lands and threatened their lives—nor with any kind of moral judgment about the perpetrators of that deadly ambush. Rather, *cargo de conciencia* is a kind of burden entangled in that place, a collection of impressions, of affects (Thrift 2008), "the hints of energy" (Stewart 2007, 70), "the forces and intensities" (Seigworth and Gregg 2010, 2), and "the exuded feelings" (Navaro-Yashin 2009, 11) discharged upon Caño Claro's inhabitants by the place itself. The expression *cargo de conciencia* captures something about the state of helplessness that most local communities experience—the multiple interests that linger over them and their lands, the state politics of abandonment, the power of the wealthy who invested their money in palm cultivation, the state of terror imposed by armed groups—but in essence a guilty conscience is not just an expression of their inner worlds, for, as Petronio points out, guilty conscience inhabits that place. In this sense it is like something hovering over people, something lying, floating, stalking the people who dwell in that place. It is something through which, to use Kirsten Hastrup's words, the "place makes *itself* felt" (2010, 194).

The kind of guilt that Petronio describes no doubt stems from the suffering and injustice that took place in Bajo Atrato: the injustice committed against the families who were persecuted and murdered by those that violently occupied that place, injustice against the place itself because it was corrupted and diverted from its proper use, and the suffering of those souls whose bodies were abandoned. This is what makes Petronio's proposal—to remove the bodies of these perpetrators of violence in order to return them to their families—a proposal of ecumenic peace, a proposal that binds together the different people, spirits, and places that have suffered violence. But I do not want to overemphasize a kind of empathy toward the paramilitary soldiers. Pontus and the other leaders do not necessarily express sorrow for or solidarity with what happened in life to these combatants. It is rather an empathy toward their souls, which is something that transcends political allegiances. More than anything else, it is empathy toward the potential mourners: the mothers and relatives of these soldiers who, like many others in Bajo Atrato, still carry the suffering of having lost their loved ones without knowing their whereabouts.

I witnessed what that kind of suffering might mean. It was in a completely different setting, among a group of victims of the armed conflict participating in a reconciliation program run by volunteers, many of whom identified themselves as former victims. Some of the victims taking part in this program had created short autobiographical plays or what various authors call autobiographical performances (Heddon 2008), documentary theater (Sotelo 2010), or even docudrama (Spence, Frohlich, and Andrews 2013). More than conventional scripts, these performances use the actual memories and words of the victims, who are simultaneously presenting and representing their own experiences. In the case of those participating in the reconciliation program, these autobiographical performances have become a means to give testimony of their own suffering, raise awareness about the situation of many other victims, and, of course, heal their own wounds. One of these performances, called *Anunciando la Ausencia* (Announcing the Absence), is enacted by a group of women who are in search of their disappeared relatives: sons, daughters, and husbands who were all victims of forced disappearance and whose whereabouts remain unknown after many years. They were abducted, kidnapped, or forcibly recruited by guerrilla, paramilitary, or even official armies. These women, all of rural origin, perform their dramas starting with what seems an invitation to a nice getaway: "Let's go, women; let's look for them in the creeks," one says. "Let's look for them in the rivers. Let's look for them in the lakes, in the savannahs. Let's look for them under the rocks," the others answer. Then they start walking in circles around small mounds of leaves and red flowers. They repeat: "Let's look for them on the riverbanks, in the forest, under some tree they might be." One by one, without stopping walking, they list the towns and cemeteries where they have searched for their loved ones: "Let's keep searching, women; let's not falter." Then one of them kneels in front of one of the mounds: "Here, I found a shirt. Whom does this shirt belong to?" One of the women answers: "It belonged to my son. He wore it the last New Year's Day he was with me. I remember we danced a lot that day. I remember the saddest day of my life too: it was on March 31 at 5:30 a.m. when they took him from his bed." She hugs the shirt, and she speaks haltingly: "Here the dreams of my son end. Also his father's dreams, as he died five years ago without knowing our son's final fate." She stands up, catches her breath, and says: "Let's keep searching." The women resume their march, always walking in circles, like evoking the eternal return of their own search. One by one they go and kneel on the mounds, finding different clothes: a blouse, some pants, a poncho. Each woman describes the owner of the clothes, the circumstances under which they disappeared, the effects of such a crime on their families. Each story is as sorrowful as any of the others: "I have been eleven years, nine months, and five days looking for my daughter"; "My sons ask for their father's whereabouts, and I don't know what to answer"; "As long as I don't find his remains, the suffering that consumes my soul will not stop." After enacting and sharing their suffering, they again resume their march while uttering in the saddest tone: "Let's not stop searching. Let's search in the rivers since surely they were thrown in one of those rivers." I cannot write these lines without feeling grief. A final T-shirt is found: it had belonged to Rosita's son, and they explain that she died of cancer without having found her son's remains. Then they stop walking and take the clothes, put them on the ground, and fold them. They kneel beside them now wearing mourning veils. In a bowing posture they express their last laments: "They tore my son from my house, but they will not tear him from my heart"; "My dear husband, I will not falter until I give you the burial you deserve." They stand up once again, take one another's hands, and speak in unison: "We want no more forced disappearances; we want no more false positives.* Death to all these things that hurt us." Someone else adds: "Mother Earth is tired of this bloodshed; the land is stained."

Where to seek their family members who have disappeared? The women look for them unsuccessfully in different cemeteries, in mass graves. They have

---

* The so-called false positives refer to civilians murdered by members of the official Colombian Army and presented as guerrilla soldiers killed in combat. These killings were used to justify foreign-aid military packages and allowed the officers responsible for these extrajudicial killings to be rewarded with promotions and time off. According to the transitional justice body known as the Special Jurisdiction for Peace (JEP 2021), at least 6,402 civilians were executed by the army between 2002 and 2008.

to turn to where the war is taking place: the forests, the savannahs, the rivers. Their loved ones might be in other regions, in other departments. They might be under a rock, in the shade of a tree, in a lake. Those places might say something about their whereabouts; after all, their remains are entangled within their surroundings. Those dead, as described by one of the women, stain the land as the sort of guilty conscience described by Petronio: a hint of energy inhabiting not only Caño Claro but also those other haunted places where the dead cannot rest. The stain pollutes the Earth, harms the land, and haunts places. To remove that stain, to appease the haunted voice that echoes through these places, to get rid of that guilty conscience, is what Petronio and the other leaders aim for when they call for procedures that restore the dignity of the dead and their families. In a context of transitional justice, this is a win-win strategy in which humans, places, and other-than-humans can heal.

The dignifying act that leaders like Petronio and Pontus have in mind has nothing to do with performing the mourning rituals usually employed when there is a death in the community or with supporting a healing process related to local people's traumatic experiences. Rather, the dignifying act aims to alleviate the torments that spirits and places are capable of feeling, easing the transition of the spirits of the dead to the afterlife. By calling for state presence, locals are pointing out how this should be done: exhuming human remains and giving them back to their families. As can be seen, the mediation of people is vital in the transition process of these spirits. It was human agency that triggered the massacre in the first place. Therefore, human agency will be needed to restore these spirits to the flow of time and space. However, this centrality of human agency does not mean that these ghostly presences affect only people. Instead, both spirits and the places they haunt become objects of care because both of their fates have been compromised by the effects of violent death. Through their ecumenic proposal, people in Caño Claro expect to reestablish broken connections with their lands and let their lands heal. They also expect that these ghostly presences will establish adequate relations with the world of the living. At stake then is the alleviation of suffering: the suffering of the territory, the misery of the wandering souls in pain, and the distress of their living relatives, who are still looking for their missing loved ones. The dignifying act will help people from Caño Claro recover and heal their territory by letting others retrieve their dead relatives. In this sense the act will help reverse the incompleteness, suddenness, and lack of closure associated with the effects that violent death produces among both the living and the dead.

An Intimate Space

This chapter has brought to the fore the dilemmas that people in Caño Claro face when confronting the ghostly presences of the paramilitaries who were responsible for the violence that expelled entire communities from their traditional territories. To some extent, these obstinate presences represent an extension of the paramilitary violence that these communities have endured. After all, as Doña Liliana expresses it, the spirits of these soldiers continue making things difficult for the families who returned to their lands. People in Caño Claro are vulnerable to the presence of these spirits, but overall, they empathize with the suffering of the families of said spirits because locals, themselves victims of paramilitary violence and the disappearance of their loved ones, understand too well the suffering of not knowing the whereabouts of the missing. That local communities need to come to terms with these haunting presences is not a need for reconciliation with their former perpetrators or the need to overcome a painful past. Rather, the families of Caño Claro need to heal their territories and fulfill a broader existential goal: to let those souls achieve eternal rest.

The haunting spirits of Caño Claro represent a kind of collective failure: of their comrades in arms, of course, who lost at the hands of their enemies; of the local communities that lack the means, and sometimes the will, to take care of these human remains; of their mourning families, who lack the resources to locate their whereabouts; of the state, which has showed little willingness to respond to the exhumation demands requested by communities; and perhaps, as Petronio pointed out, of the whole society, which has enabled an unjust system that led poor young peasants to fight a war that favored the interests of powerful elites and warlords. That collective failure haunts Caño Claro and makes it difficult for both local communities and their territories to heal. In the end it seems that the political allegiances of these dead soldiers are not as important as the shared class identity and suffering that people in Bajo Atrato and other neighboring regions have endured on account of the armed conflict.

The place of wandering spirits is an existential concern for the people of Caño Claro: it is important to allocate a proper physical space to the human remains associated with these spirits, which is what will liberate them from the painful condition that keeps them trapped within the contours of the place where their violent deaths occurred. Until this happens, the dead will continue haunting a place that the living want to *sanear*: to heal and retrieve.

People in Caño Claro know that it is the lack of care for these spirits in pain that perpetuates their haunting of this place, but it is difficult for these families to help such spirits find their way. Locals have understandable objections to cultivating mercy, compassion, and empathy toward these dead, particularly because the aftermath of their violent acts is still a strong influence in the daily life of local communities. The presence of these spirits will then continue to be strongly attached to that place, where these spirits are visible and almost palpable, where their existence is not always reducible to the beliefs or collective cultural representations of people. Without the funerary rituals provided by their mourning families, these spirits will remain in the world of the living, where they will do only what they know best: express their pain time and again.

6

A JAGUAR AND A HALF

Seated behind his desk in a room with bare walls, the municipal secretary of the town of Turbo looks at the camera and describes the events: "We are facing a very alarming situation indeed. On two separate occasions, two different persons were killed by a jaguar that has been attacking civilians" (*Noticias Urabá* 2013). He explains that the last victim was an elderly fisherman whose body was found by his companions on a riverbank, close to the mouth of the Atrato River. "His name was Matías Escarpeta and the people of his village, when they noticed his lengthy absence, went to the forest to verify what was going on. In the place where they found his dugout canoe, they also saw a jaguar that was at that very moment devouring his body" (*Noticias Urabá* 2013). In the same coverage the reporter interviews the doctor responsible for the autopsy performed on a beheaded and eviscerated corpse in the bloating stage of decomposition. He confirms that the man was attacked by a jaguar but does not have enough evidence to state that it was the same animal that had been blamed for killing another man some weeks before. Asked about that previous attack, the doctor replies that all they received was a head and a hand that were then sent elsewhere for a more detailed forensic identification. At the end of the coverage the municipal secretary explains that although he understands that people are afraid and willing to hunt the feline, he must enforce the laws that protect endangered species such as jaguars. Accordingly, the municipality, along with the Colombian Navy and regional environmental authorities, will set in motion a plan to capture the animal and take it to another place where it cannot cause more damage.

Almost a year later, another TV news report announces that the regional environmental authority, Corpourabá, has forbidden the hunting of a jaguar blamed for killing five people and attacking at least three marines. The jaguar, explains the Corpourabá spokesperson, is protected by international and national laws: "Actually, it is people who are invading the jaguar's territory," she says. "Those are protected areas. People are not supposed to go and log there because it is strictly forbidden by law" (*Teleantioquia Noticias* 2014). The last attack caused the death of a lumberjack who was working in the forest with a comrade. I met a friend of the man who saw this attack and he told me how the witness described the incident: the jaguar caught the lumberjack by the head, and after having thrown his prey onto the ground, planted his sharp teeth directly behind the ears. The witness tried by all means to force the jaguar to release his friend but had only an ax as a weapon. Then the jaguar tried to flee, pulling the lumberjack with his jaws, but was followed by the witness who, shouting loudly and brandishing his ax, managed to get the jaguar to drop his friend—or what was left of him. I try to visualize this raw scene: a powerful hunter running into the forest with an adult man in his jaws, a prey releasing its last breath and becoming a piece of meat, and a desperate person pursuing them in an attempt to reestablish that illusory premise that we humans are more than edible beings (Plumwood 2000).

Despite Corpourabá's ban, people in Bajo Atrato wanted to kill that jaguar because those living near the mouth of the Atrato River repeatedly observed the animal stalking prey in the forest in the company of another jaguar and a cub. The fear increased because there was now an entire family of man-eating jaguars wandering freely. It also happened that one of these jaguars attacked three marines who were patrolling the area during one of their counterguerrilla operations in the region. The colonel responsible for the military unit explained that the marines received considerable injuries and were hospitalized (*Noticias Uno* 2014). To avoid another lethal assault, officials of the Colombian Navy decided to hunt down the jaguar themselves. In this coverage, the reporter uses warfare metaphors to describe that hunt: "A tactical tracking and persecution operation which aimed to ambush the enemy" (*Noticias Uno* 2014). The military then set a trap using a sheep as bait. To confirm the efficacy of their tactic, a marine hid in a nearby tree. Not only did the trap not work at all, but the marine almost became the prey himself. According to some local people, the marine committed a major mistake: he wanted to attack the jaguar from the left side. "A jaguar," explains the lumberjack who tried to save the man that was killed, "must be attacked from the right side. Everybody here knows that" (*Noticias Uno* 2014).

The controversy revolved around whether or not the jaguar should have been hunted. To the environmental authorities, the jaguar had to be protected no matter what—his ferocity was but a response to the threat that humans and their activities represented to his natural environment. Jaguars do not attack: they defend themselves because humans, according to that narrative, are somehow outside and above the food chain. To try to hunt the jaguar was therefore proof of local ignorance: locals did not know that jaguars are an endangered species and that they attack only when people infringe on their territories (Martínez Arango 2013; *Noticias Urabá* 2013). For my interlocutors in Bajo Atrato, these two ideas—namely, that jaguars might one day become extinct and that they seldom go after humans—were hard to grasp. They saw that particular jaguar as a dangerous threat, one that was jeopardizing their very livelihood because they were now afraid of going into the forest in order to earn their living. There was an ethical tension at stake here, captured by the municipal secretary when he admitted that he had to take into consideration both the lives of the citizens and the laws protecting jaguars. If cohabitation between people and an endangered species seemed implausible, someone needed to be taken out of the equation. It seemed like a matter of pondering what existence deserved to live at ease in the forest and what presence was disposable. However, the Corpourabá spokesperson made it clear: jaguars do belong to the forest, whereas local communities are just trespassing and disrespecting natural borders.

The diplomatic response of local authorities—that the jaguar had to be captured and taken elsewhere—aimed to put as much distance as possible between the jaguar and people. The goal was to take the jaguar to the heart of the neighboring Los Katíos National Park, a nearby protected area of about 72,000 hectares (178,000 acres) listed as a World Heritage Site by UNESCO in 1994. However, a relocation operation of this nature had never been performed in the region, and the few that had been done in the Americas failed (Kelly and Silver 2009; Rabinowitz 2000). Ordinary people in Bajo Atrato were more reluctant: to relocate a jaguar to a nearby forest whose only difference is the status of a protected area will not ensure people's security, for the jaguar could come back at any time. Did the experts from Corpourabá and the Ministry of the Environment not know that jaguars are dangerous animals? Why take the risk and make such an effort to track and capture a jaguar, only to leave him alive and set him free? These were some of the concerns raised by the people in the town of Riosucio. I remember how indignant my friend Marieta was when we listened on the radio to a forestry expert working for Corpourabá. He made it clear that jaguars should not be hunted—they are not natural enemies of man, and if they sometimes appear to be, it is only because people have become a hindrance to their having a free run of everything the forest has to offer. "I would like to see one of these professionals leaving their little kids playing or running their errands near these forests," Marieta said. "I would like to see if they will not feel afraid for their kids." Marieta, and here I prefer to paraphrase Marisol de la Cadena (2015, xxii), made a good point: those professionals probably knew a lot, but they did not know best.

One thing got me thinking. The municipal secretary said that the jaguar had killed some civilians, but why did he use the term "civilians"? Was the jaguar violating the rules of war—that is, international humanitarian law and the protection of people who are not participating in hostilities? Do jaguars differentiate between civilians and combatants? Or was this a slip of the tongue, one of those verbal mistakes that according to Sigmund Freud ([1901] 2003) reveals some sort of subdued wish, restrained impulse, or repressed conflict? Perhaps the secretary did not find the appropriate word and was just using some sort of metaphor, like the journalist who described the jaguar hunt in military terms: "A tactical operation to ambush the enemy." Actually, in that case the words described the very way the military unit conceived of the hunt—and perhaps this was the reason that the operation failed: hunting, at least in the tropical forest, is more an act of mimicry than of persecution, a capacity of inhabiting another point of view rather than a rampant chase, the ability of becoming like the prey because, as another hunter describes it, "jaguars can read in the eyes what one will do, he sees what the eyes send, what one thinks. . . . The good hunter must learn to see what the beast thinks" (quoted in Manuel Romero 2005, 47). Besides turning the jaguar into an enemy rather than a prey, and hunting it into eradication, the language and practice of warfare reveal the kind of lethal possibilities that might arise when violence is so deeply entangled with the forest and the beings that inhabit it. But again, what did the municipal secretary mean by "civilians"? In this chapter I explore if, after all, the slip did reveal something about the nature of that particular jaguar and his involvement in matters of armed conflict.

Jaguars and Their Enactment

In the following pages I describe the "more than one" but "less than many" jaguars brought into existence through the practices and interactions of diverse kinds of actors. Following Annemarie Mol's (2002) work on atherosclerosis, the "more than one" refers to the way this disease emerges as a different entity under the expert gaze of the radiologist, the pain of the patient, the interpretation of the physician, and the microscope of the pathologist, yet these partial, different versions of atherosclerosis overlap in the patient's body and are rendered somehow singular by virtue of heterogeneous health-care practices. Similarly, the figure of the man-eating jaguar emerges not as a single, coherent jaguar roaming around and stalking in the forests of Bajo Atrato. Instead, paraphrasing Maurice Merleau-Ponty ([1945] 2002), the man-eating jaguar is a fabric onto which different jaguars are woven. In this jaguar we meet the endangered species that biologists and environmental managers want to protect at all costs, the wild enemy ambushing military troops, the habitual *tigre* that local communities want to avoid when they enter the forest, the animal as a matter of political concern for authorities who want to protect people's livelihoods without contravening natural resources laws, the feline raising cubs, the animal whose existence must be assessed through the forensic examination of some alleged victims, and the wicked beast discharging all its fury upon unarmed fishermen. Each jaguar has some sort of world-making power because each one demands different kinds of obligations, values, attachments, and rules of engagement from its practitioners: scientists, politicians, local communities, and military officials. Each one encounters not a jaguar as such but a jaguar emerging in relation to their own material and conceptual apparatuses (Metcalf 2008): some encounter jaguars in zoological literature, some in environmentalist legislation, some in oral stories, and a few on the trail. It is by virtue of these encounters that each actor defines what information about the jaguar may be accepted as relevant. Each of them allocates different sets of properties to jaguars, defining what matters most and deciding, in the last instance, the kind of relations that a jaguar entails and therefore the course of action to be taken.

Yet these "more than one" jaguars become "less than many" in the actual figure of the man-eating jaguar—that is to say, by virtue of its very presence, its thereness or nearness to people's lives, and its inherent capacity to shape different social relations. A jaguar transforms social relations when, for example, it behaves in one way rather than another: a jaguar stalking livestock invokes different kinds of responses from people than a jaguar wandering free in the forest. That difference is not just the outcome of people's actions but rather what shapes people's responses. In this sense jaguars are emergent via their own actions and the relations they sustain with people and other beings (Ogden, Hall, and Tanita 2013). Moreover, as with most animals in Bajo Atrato, locals conceptualize jaguars as conscious subjects capable of decision making and intentional action. Therefore, rather than having a kind of pre-discursive existence, jaguars are defined by the interactions of which they are capable, becoming a particular kind of being through their contingent relations with people. Jaguars are such because they tend to behave like jaguars: they live in the forest and hunt the prey this place has to offer, occasionally going after poultry, swine, and dogs; sometimes crossing people's paths when they are performing their work in the bush; and eventually going after human prey. However, when the intensity of these activities changes, some ontological distinctions between jaguars and other-than-jaguars start to blur: what presents itself in the disguise of an animal might be a *mojano*, a monstrous were-jaguar that devours people; what seems to be an endangered species from the forest becomes a being attacking "civilians." In other words, the jaguar is a "being-in-relation" (Benjamin 2015) that is defined by virtue of its actions and its engagement with the constituents of its world, people being one of these constituents.

Following the story of this man-eating jaguar, in this chapter I explore another afterlife of war, one in which armed conflict simultaneously reverberates in human and other-than-human socialities in ways that are not always determined by human agents. To show this I describe how around this animal different kinds of jaguars converge: the greedy and gullible *tigre* of local oral traditions, the quintessential but wary predator of zoologists, the daring hunter of livestock that the locals complain about, the endangered species of environmental managers, the feared man-eater of loggers and fishermen, and the pet of some warlords. The events involving this man-eating jaguar are instances in which hybridization of all kinds emerges because the contours among ecological, evolutionary, historical, and cultural aspects of the jaguar dissolve, resulting in a being of many natures, simultaneously cherished and feared, an animal to be controlled but also in need of protection, capable of great feats as well as of mean forcefulness. My attempt is thus to show how all these jaguars are not only possible but are produced by determined political, historical, and material conditions, including the violence of war. This armed violence, so often reaching sylvan beings and shaping their subjectivities, exacerbates interspecies asymmetrical relations of power, rendering the forests of Bajo Atrato akin to what Donna Haraway characterizes as contact zones: places for "mortal world-making entanglements" between species that are constituted in and by their relations to each other (2008, 4). It is then in these forests where jaguars meet and are met; where each actor unfolds their own contingent, learned, and historical rules of engagement with the world; and where recognition and response between humans and other-than-humans are at stake.

I start this chapter describing the place jaguars occupy in the oral traditions from Bajo Atrato in order to show, on the one hand, the ambivalent ways locals relate with this animal and, on the other, how in the face of the rampant effects of armed conflict the figure of the jaguar has been mobilized as a symbol to conceptualize war. Later, I contrast the jaguar that locals find in their forests and oral traditions with the animal species that zoologists describe. I explore the kind of ethos or "natural" disposition that scientists ascribe to this animal in order to examine the conditions under which a jaguar might actually become a human predator. I finally return to the case of the man-eating jaguar in order to show the way this animal embodies a form of excess that renders him a hybrid figure capable of dislocating multiple borders: between human and other-than-human forces, between environmental and social processes, between predation and warfare. Ethnographic attention to this excess, I hold, sheds light on the instances of hybridization and multiplicity that render war an experience extending beyond the human.

The Duped Uncle

Jaguars are one of the most frequent symbols presented in the art and mythology of Indigenous peoples throughout the Americas. Often associated with warfare, hunting, shamanism, and preeminent social status, jaguar imagery— including a large array of humans with feline attributes and jaguar-like creatures—is found in a significant number of spatially and chronologically separated societies (Benson 1998; Saunders 1998). Because they are the ultimate, unbeatable predator, jaguars are the quintessential model of both physical and spiritual power: their fierceness and strength have been equally mobilized as symbols of courage in hunting and warfare but also as spiritual protectors and custodians of shamanic knowledge (Benson 1998). Jaguar-warriors, jaguar-rulers, jaguar-hunters, jaguar-shamans, jaguar-lords: all these figures conjure up a particular conception of sociopolitical power in which master-ownership relations and the maintenance of the positions between hunters and prey, chiefs and followers, or subjects and objects are always at stake (Costa and Fausto 2010). But if in Mesoamerican and Amazonian Indigenous societies jaguars are endowed with powerful characteristics that situate them at the pinnacle of sociopolitical relations, these very same traits become a matter of derision in the oral literature of Afro-Colombian communities.

In Afro-Colombian traditional tales, the jaguar is called Uncle Tiger and is the protagonist of different misadventures in which his antagonist, Uncle Rabbit, takes advantage of his supposed avidity, lack of self-restraint, and even naïveté. The first time I heard about these characters, I was with my friend Ives. It was during one of my first visits to the villages of the Truandó River, and one night, to pass the time while we were both engaged in swatting mosquitoes that had managed to penetrate our mosquito nets, he told me about the incredible stratagem used by Uncle Rabbit to convince Uncle Tiger to "shell" his own testicles. Taking different versions into account (CAMAWA 2005; Castrillón 2010; Centro Cultural Mama-U 2002; de Friedemann and Vanín 1994; Pineda 2002; Velásquez 1959), the story goes that Uncle Tiger wanted to hunt Uncle Rabbit and that he found him eating some nuts with great pleasure. As the rabbit noticed the tiger's presence and the tiger felt ashamed of catching his prey via an easy, head-on approach, the tiger only dared to ask where he had found such appetizing nuts. The rabbit answered that he got them from his own body after shelling his own scrotum with two rocks. The rabbit persuaded the tiger by saying that if he had gotten so many and such tempting nuts from his own tiny testicles, the tiger would obtain greater and better nuts from his own genitalia. The tiger agreed, reasoning that as he had been raised eating so much meat, he would have tastier nuts. Then he took two rocks and proceeded with such strength and vigor that he immediately fainted after the impact. The rabbit ran away, leaving the tiger crying out for revenge.

In another tale, Uncle Rabbit challenged Uncle Tiger to a contest of strength. After having been chased and caught, the rabbit asked for the tiger's mercy, saying that he would accept being eaten if the tiger could defeat him in a tug-of-war. Confident of his own strength, the tiger accepted, and both agreed to meet the next day at the seashore. Before the appointed time, the rabbit went to the beach and asked a whale if it was true that she was as strong as everybody said and if she would accept to demonstrate it by engaging in a tug-of-war with him. She acquiesced. Then the rabbit gave her one end of the rope and told her he would take the other end, which he had left behind some shrubberies. There, the rabbit met Uncle Tiger and asked him to take the rope's end and to wait for his signal once he took the opposite end, which was supposedly on the beach. The rabbit hid in the bushes, pulled the rope, and tiger and whale engaged in a fierce contest in which neither succeeded in taking any significant advantage over the other. Whale and tiger realized that rabbit was not as weak as they had initially thought, and when Uncle Rabbit saw they were tired enough, he came out and made fun of them both (Centro Cultural Mama-U 2002; de Friedemann and Vanín 1994; Pineda 2002; Velásquez 1959).

Another story goes that Uncle Rabbit saw Uncle Tiger going home carrying bundles full of food. As many animals were facing famine, the rabbit decided to trick the tiger. He lay down on the path, playing dead, but the first time the tiger saw the rabbit, he ignored the "gift" and preferred to keep going with his heavy bundles. The rabbit got up, took a shortcut, and played dead again farther along the tiger's route. The tiger wondered if there were some kind of plague in the forest and said to himself that if he had not been carrying such a load, he would have taken this and the other rabbit he had previously found. The tiger continued on his way, and the rabbit played his trick for a third time. This time, the tiger decided to take the rabbit and the previous prey, leaving all his bundles on the ground and going back, first of all, to where he had found the other dead rabbits. Meanwhile, Uncle Rabbit stole all of Uncle Tiger's packages (de Friedemann and Vanín 1994, Velásquez 1959).

Uncle Tiger and Uncle Rabbit are important symbolic characters in Bajo Atrato, although strictly speaking there are neither tigers nor rabbits in this region. Tiger (*tigre*) is the common name that people assign to the jaguar, and rabbit (*conejo*) is the name used in tales and oral traditions when referring to other rodents that do exist in the region and belong to the *Dasyproctidae* genus: *ñeques*, *tinajas*, and *guatines*, all known in English as agoutis. If in most Amazonian and Mesoamerican societies hunting and the phenomenological context of predator-prey relations constitute the essential source for the conceptualization of jaguars as the archetype of power, on the Pacific coast, Afro-Colombian societies seem instead to privilege the figure of the prey as a means for conceptualizing autonomy and resistance in the face of an overwhelming power. Uncle Rabbit, as evidenced by the aforementioned tales, is the archetypal trickster: a smart, cunning character that playfully deceives conventional authoritative figures and undermines established societal rules. The trickster, argues essayist and poet Lewis Hyde (1998, 7), is "a boundary-crosser" but also a creator of new boundaries because he often "brings to the surface a distinction previously hidden from the sight." According to David Leeming (1991, 154), the trickster is "at once wise and foolish . . . promiscuous and amoral; he is outrageous in his actions." Joseph Campbell (Campbell and Toms 1990, 39) states that the trickster's actions are driven by an inability to conform to some norm, revealing "someone who is beyond the system" and therefore someone who represents new possibilities of life. Trickery, deceitfulness, amorality, humor, and extreme inventiveness are the traits of a figure that, like Uncle Rabbit, succeeds through his cleverness rather than through his strength.

Uncle Tiger and Uncle Rabbit's stories are important in Bajo Atrato because they make the world intelligible by expressing assumptions about what kinds of things and relations do or might exist, validating and supporting existing values, and awakening a sense of awe about some animals and their possibilities of becoming. Uncles Tiger and Rabbit also make evident the relational ontological constitution between predator and prey: one is what it is by virtue of the strategies the other unfolds or because of the capacity of one for interfering in the plans of the other. In this sense the trickeries of Uncle Rabbit tell us as much about him as about the forces he wants to overcome. These stories are not only important to Afro-Colombian communities: Indigenous peoples in Chocó have incorporated these tales into their own oral literary traditions. They are often told and enacted by storytellers during social meetings, in informal gatherings, or even simply at home. What is important here is that these stories do circulate in the region and play a key role in the creation and maintenance of a particular sensibility about jaguars: they are strong but gluttonous, and they care little about the means they employ to get what they want.

Some other values attributed to jaguars are exemplified in the following story. Aunt Tiger was looking for someone who could help her to babysit her cubs because she was very busy harvesting rice and maize. After asking Uncle Paca, Uncle Deer, and Uncle Otter, who were also busy with their own housework, Aunt Tiger went to Uncle Rabbit's place. The rabbit accepted the job but only after negotiating an advantageous wage. When Aunt Tiger returned home after the first day, Uncle Rabbit welcomed her with a succulent meat soup. Tiger was surprised because she had not left any meat in her provisions. Rabbit told her he had set some traps while the cubs were sleeping and had been lucky to catch a small prey. But what really happened was that Rabbit had killed one of the seven cubs. Tiger thanked him and asked for her cubs because it was nursing time. Rabbit told her he would get them and give them to her one at a time. Aunt Tiger agreed, and after she finished nursing the first, the rabbit gave her the cubs one by one, presenting the last one twice. The next day Uncle Rabbit killed another cub, cooked a soup, and offered it to Aunt Tiger, who again found the meat delicious. When it came time to feed the cubs, the rabbit did as he had the previous night, but this time giving her the last cub three times. The situation repeated itself during the following days until there was only one cub left. When the tiger was nursing the same cub for the sixth time, she noticed that he was overfull and did not want more. She asked Uncle Rabbit about it, and he said that the cubs were probably gorged because of the food he himself had given them earlier that day. On the eighth day after finishing her soup, Aunt Tiger asked for the cubs, and Uncle Rabbit revealed the terrible truth: she had already eaten all of them. Then the rabbit fled at full speed.

Tiger and Rabbit embody different possibilities of being. Whereas Uncle Tiger is the archetype of strength—big, powerful, and capable of killing— Uncle Rabbit is the archetypical trickster: small but agile, able to make good decisions and act creatively in an array of different contexts. Part of long-standing oral traditions, these stories contribute to preserving local knowledge, transmitting norms and moral values, and even promoting a particular sense of belonging. Some scholars (Losonczy 2006a; Oslender 2003; E. Restrepo 1995, 1996) see in these Afro-Colombian traditions everyday cultural manifestations that challenge some mainstream moral assumptions and resist hegemonic representations of nature. Cultural geographer Ulrich Oslender (2003) calls these oral traditions "hidden instances of resistance," for although they do not openly challenge the dominant powers behind the misappropriation of Afro-Colombian traditional lands, they are mobilized by Afro-Colombian social actors as a part of their political action in their efforts to guarantee differential rights based on their cultural singularities. I found this kind of mobilization in one of the few existing written versions of these tales. In a special issue of a magazine published by the Mama-U Cultural Centre, a local institution that promotes art, music, and dance with the aim of valorizing the Afro-Colombian cultural identity, the aforementioned tales are examined in light of the violent and destructive changes resulting from both the armed conflict and extractivist development projects in Chocó. The tales are considered "experiences of resistance in war times" (Centro Cultural Mama-U 2002, 15). According to the editors of this issue, Afro-Colombian communities may draw on teachings found in these stories in order to face the threats of the armed conflict and the violent extractive economies. For example, Uncle Rabbit always avoids direct confrontation and is very resourceful when finding ways to be safe and sound—he demonstrates a profound knowledge of the territory by always being one step ahead of Uncle Tiger (he arrived first at the beach in the strength contest; he knew the path used by the tiger very well and was able to repeatedly get ahead of him in order to play dead). Most importantly, Uncle Rabbit not only looks for a deception or evasion but in some instances intelligently fights against Uncle Tiger. He does not do so directly, but through ruses that jeopardize the very possibilities that tigers have for accomplishing their own future existence, like when Uncle Tiger destroys his own testicles or when Aunt Tiger devours her own children (Centro Cultural Mama-U 2002, 17–18).

In the violent context faced by the communities of Chocó, the two characters embody radically different values. On the one hand, the editors argue, Uncle Tiger represents brute force, as well as lack of intelligence and imagination. In present times he represents the jaws of private capital, wanting to raze land, steal natural resources, and destroy the lives that Afro-Colombian communities have patiently created in their territories (Centro Cultural Mama-U 2002, 18). In contrast, Uncle Rabbit represents archness, and his mischievous character is proof of his ability to be creative and convince his enemies that his lies are true—he represents the capacity to dream and resist even in the most unfavorable situations (Centro Cultural Mama-U 2002, 19). In sum, the editors argue that these tales re-create the historical situation of Afro-Colombian communities in Chocó, where war and annihilation have been the raison d'être of slaveholders and masters, and now of armed groups and greedy capitalists: "Uncle Tiger and Uncle Rabbit's tales are the best synthesis of the means and experiences of resistance cultivated by communities that have learned to survive in their own territories" (Centro Cultural Mama-U 2002, 17).

The trickeries of Uncle Rabbit are then mobilized within the framework of a large oppressive power. He disrupts and even reverses an overwhelming system: a subjugation first associated with slavery and colonial domination, and now with war and extractivism. In the same way some literary critics (Gates 1988; Levine 1977; Savoy 1995) have found in the figure of Brer Rabbit in African American literature a trope of identification that allowed enslaved communities to create their "own symbols in defiance of the perverted logic of the oppressor" (Earl 1993, 131), the fragile but resourceful character of Uncle Rabbit represents the possibility of overthrowing the violent programs represented by the devourer figure of the jaguar. Uncle Tiger, in oral literature, embodies a fool to be deceived, a greedy opponent to be taunted. However, the place that jaguars hold in these traditions does not mean that people in Bajo Atrato simply deride them. Actually, just as the armed conflict and rapacious capitalist development represent a danger in people's daily lives, jaguars embody a permanent risk, one of those inherent perils stalking the forests that make up *Bajoatrateño* territories.

A Mind That Attained Complete Composure

Jaguars (*Panthera onca*) are the largest cats in the Americas, and although they occupy different habitats, ranging from tropical moist and dry forests to savannahs and grasslands, jaguars require forest cover to live and stalk prey (Novack and Main 2012; Zeller 2007). As a matter of fact, their bodies are so well-adapted to the thickness and temperature of tropical forests—short limbs, short tail, deep chest, and stocky bone structure—that they are considered dwarves among the other felines from the *Panthera* genus, such as lions, leopards, and tigers (Rabinowitz 2000). Jaguars depend exclusively on meat for food, and more than eighty-nine species of animals have been recorded as their prey—including large mammals like peccaries, tapirs, and calves; canopy species like birds and monkeys; and snakes and turtles (Mejía 1995; Novack and Main 2012). Unlike other felines, jaguars are incredibly good swimmers—they travel frequently via watercourses, and they prefer areas near water where they often bathe, play, and hunt for fish, sometimes using their tails (Rabinowitz and Nottingham 1986). It is known that jaguars tend to live alone and that they come together only during mating periods. Mothers care for their young for 1.5 years after birth, and although some researchers say that males play no part in raising cubs (Novack and Main 2012), others hold that both parents form a temporary association for rearing the young, at least until they have been weaned or are old enough to travel (Mahler 2009; Rabinowitz 2014).

Jaguars are beautiful yet lethal creatures. They have robust skulls, massive muscularity, oversized paws, powerful jaws, and structurally reinforced canines, which make their bite more powerful than that of a tiger or lion (Rabinowitz 2014). Having almost no stored fat, they are lean but muscular and agile. When stalking prey, they rely more on stealth and surprise than on speed, being able to get extremely close to their prey without being detected (Guynup 2009; Rabinowitz and Nottingham 1986). As naturalist and wildlife photographer Richard Mahler explains, "The jaguar has evolved a two-pronged approach to fetching dinner—stay virtually invisible to the last possible moment and then deliver an overwhelming blow" (2009, 36). Able to overcome their prey in a single bound, jaguars are the quintessentially strong hunter. In Bajo Atrato, people are well aware of this set of traits, to the extent that there is a kind of revered fear for jaguars. Conceptualized as definitive human predators, jaguars, along with venomous snakes, are considered the most dangerous animal that one may face in the forest. According to many of my interlocutors, jaguars are menacing, avid hunters lacking any restraint. Stories abound about hunters encountering jaguars face-to-face, as well as jaguars killing hunting dogs, being able to smell people's fear, taking chickens from henhouses, climbing trees with preys in their jaws, and fishing in the rivers. According to locals, whenever jaguars rely on anthropogenic food sources, they do so because they are motivated by a kind of wicked will, for they have countless prey available to them in the forest. I learned also that jaguars become infinitely more dangerous under three circumstances:

when a female has given birth, when they stalk prey around the hamlets, or when a jaguar has already dared to attack a dog or a human. All these conditions were fulfilled in the case of the recent attacks against people.

However, zoologists recognize jaguars as strangely mild-mannered creatures, not showing strong aggression or territorial defense against other jaguars and other cats. Jaguars, says wild-cat scientist and conservationist Alan Rabinowitz (2000, 2014), rarely engage in fights against human hunters and their dogs. According to him, this reluctance to directly confront adverse situations is an attribute, a fundamental trait of their "jaguarness." Rabinowitz argues that jaguars are remarkable warriors and that "like all great warriors, their success and longevity comes not from the number of fights fought, but the number of fights avoided" (2014, 185). This means that during the classic "fight-or-flight" response—that reaction occurring when animals face a perceived harmful event—jaguars commonly choose not to engage in a fight. From an evolutionary point of view, this propensity to flee from danger is a sound survival strategy: in the warm and moist climates that characterize tropical rain forests, any damaged muscle, deep cut, or broken tooth may easily get infected, become a serious injury, or simply cause severe impairment that solitary hunters in particular cannot afford.

"Jaguars," adds Rabinowitz, "never rush into something. The jaguar watches, waits and evaluates" (quoted in Niiler 2014, ¶4). Jaguarness then has to do with the fact that these animals are more alert and cautious than other felines; that they are always stealthy, extremely vigilant, and persistently wary; that they are confident, tenacious, and efficient, "like a long-distance athlete. If a jaguar moves, something is going on and he is going to get what he wants. . . . The term *fudōshin* is used to describe the state of mind of only the most advanced practitioners of Japanese martial arts. It denotes a determined, immovable spirit, a state of imperturbability. This immovable spirit is part of what has made up the audacity of this species, the jaguarness" (Rabinowitz 2014, 177, 179).

But for people in Bajo Atrato, jaguars' strength and determination are the traits of an avid hunter rather than those of an impeccable warrior. Moreover, the vile attacks of the man-eating jaguar revealed something extending beyond what local environmental authorities and zoologists described as the natural reaction of these animals when feeling threatened. Although jaguars have occasionally attacked people, never before had five different men been killed in such an incredibly short lapse of time. And with a family of man-eating jaguars stalking at ease in the forests where people earn their living, locals saw the recent attacks as a dangerous threat jeopardizing their very livelihood. I was told that if those jaguars dared to attack people in the daytime, it was either because they had lost their fear or were experiencing an eagerness for something different. The attacks revealed then a kind of ferocious appetite that was not easily satiated even after the jaguars took several dogs from different houses. No, those jaguars needed more—they wanted to go after humans, and they did not stop once they devoured the first one. There were no doubts that these particular jaguars were showing some kind of perverse fervor that exceeded what locals have customarily known about these hunters.

According to most zoologists, jaguars tend to favor their natural prey, and humans and dogs are not among them. To these specialists, attacks on domestic cattle or poultry reveal a kind of desperate last resort launched by jaguars in order to survive: for these animals, crossing large open areas, hunting in an open field, or going close to dwellings represents an unjustified risk (Azevedo and Murray 2007; Polisar et al. 2003). After some surveys conducted in Belize, Venezuela, and Brazil, researchers found that most of the jaguars killed while preying on cattle had previous shotgun wounds in their bodies that caused either ossified wounds in their heads, damaged limbs, or broken canines (Rabinowitz 2014). In other words, jaguars causing problems to domestic animals were impaired jaguars: animals experiencing some kind of chronic pain or new physical disability (Kelly and Silver 2009; Mahler 2009; Rabinowitz 2000, 2014). Attacks on people, though unusual, do happen, but the reasons that jaguars may go after humans remain a point of dispute. As stated by some scholars (Rabinowitz and Nottingham 1986; Shepherd, Mills, and Shoff 2014; Zeller 2007), jaguars strike back or respond aggressively only when they have been provoked or when they feel threatened or trapped. For example, during his work in Mexico philosopher and ecologist Aldo Leopold (1972, 469) was not able to confirm any reports of people-eating jaguars: "Men undoubtedly have been killed by cornered or wounded jaguars, but unprovoked attacks are rare. In this respect, the jaguar differs from its relatives in the Old World. Lions, tigers, and leopards may all become man-eaters under certain conditions; the American cats fortunately do not." Rabinowitz (2000, 201) asserts that, out of all the big cats, jaguars are "the least known to attack humans unprovoked and they are virtually undocumented as man-eaters." Mahler (2009, 84) reports that during the last hundred years, he documented only three verified cases of jaguars killing humans in the wilderness and that all other cases involved careless zookeepers. Shepherd and colleagues (2014, 223) claim that jaguars have rarely been reported to attack humans in the wild. It seems that despite all the local stories circulating about jaguars' inclination to hunt people in Bajo Atrato, jaguars do not regard humans as prey and are, according to zoologists and biologists, the least likely of all the big cats to attack humans.

Cases of man-eating big cats have been well-documented in Africa and India. Some recent figures show that in southeastern Tanzania alone, at least 600 people have been killed by lions since 1990 (Frank et al. 2006). One of the most well-known cases in Africa is that of the Tsavo River lions during the construction of the Kenya-Uganda railway in 1898 (Frank et al. 2006; J. H. Patterson 1907; B. Patterson 2004). It is believed that about 135 railroad workers were killed by two lions and that this behavior was mainly provoked by the decimation of game and of some inadequate human burials—at the time, the Hindu railroad workers performed some kind of abbreviated cremation for the people who died during the railway construction, attracting hungry lions who acquired the taste for human flesh (B. Patterson 2004). In India, home of the world's largest population of tigers, it has been estimated that about eighty-five people are killed or injured each year by these animals (Mazoomdaar 2014). Jim Corbett, a famous British Indian hunter who between 1907 and 1938 hunted down about twelve man-eating tigers and leopards that were "collectively blamed for more than 1,500 human deaths" in Northern India (Bellows 2008, ¶10), noticed that most of these predators were suffering from wounds or disease. According to Corbett, "a man-eating tiger is a tiger that has been compelled, through stress of circumstances beyond its control, to adapt to a diet alien to it. The stress of circumstances is, in nine cases out of ten, wounds, and in the tenth case, old age" (1946, xiii). All documented cases involving big cats killing humans, or even livestock, have to do with a drastic switch of diet from natural prey to domesticated animals, which are easier to catch. This change is associated with a failure of these animals to recover from wounds, a severe decrease in access to game, or simply even the feline's age—either too old or too young (Beveridge 2014; Corbett 1946; Dickinson 2004). Specialists agree that there is nothing in such behavior—tigers, lions, or jaguars feeding on people—that resembles natural animal instinct but rather that these big cats are trying to adapt to a combination of abruptly changing circumstances that leave them little choice but to pursue unusual prey. It seems then that only under a set of exceptional circumstances a jaguar may actually turn into a man-eating creature. Can war favor these circumstances?

Prominent Pets

In 2004 photojournalist Jesús Abad Colorado took the photo shown in figure 6.1 during the demobilization of paramilitary soldiers in Tierralta. A jaguar cub no more than a few months old walks among the backpacks and

FIGURE 6.1. Demobilization of paramilitary soldiers, attended by a jaguar cub. Photo: Jesús Abad Colorado (2004). Source: Rueda 2016, 33.

semiautomatic rifles of soldiers standing in line formation. The men and their military equipment are all perfectly aligned, yet the uniformity of their formation is interrupted by this juvenile jaguar's insouciance. The men's weapons, military gear, and posture contrast with the presence of a wild animal wearing two wide and thick leather collars: indications that taming has been attempted. But jaguars, zoologists argue (Brown and López 2001; Rabinowitz and Nottingham 1986; Zeller 2007), cannot be tamed in the manner that lions or tigers can. People who have worked with captive jaguars describe them as unreliable, secretive, unpredictable, and untamable (Rabinowitz 2014, 178): "You'll never see a jaguar tamer in the circus. If you do, buy a ticket, because that'll be a one-time show" (Mahler 2009, 32). Even in zoos, they are not good exhibition animals, and aspects of their jaguarness are beautifully captured by a Ted Hughes poem in which he describes the jaguar who "on a short fierce fuse" acts as if "there's no cage to him" since "his stride is wildernesses of freedom" (1957, 4).

While looking at the photo, one understands that although the cub has been adopted as a pet, something about its walking and sniffing at ease reveals that this indomitable creature will never be like some of the disciplined military dogs that one sees, for instance, in parades. Of course, the paramilitaries are not an ordinary army, just as jaguars are not common pets. Keeping a pet like a jaguar may be a demonstration of one's status or wealth, or an opportunity to enhance one's image. This was, after all, the role of private royal menageries: demonstrations of an emperor or king's power and wealth (Berger 1980), for after all, who can afford to care for and provide for exotic animals? Keeping a jaguar as a pet might say something about the kind of masculinity these soldiers want to project, considering the skills that are necessary to capture such a magnificent predator. In the case of paramilitary soldiers, a jaguar's presence is symbolically powerful because the animal embodies particular values with which the paramilitaries identify themselves: stateliness, bravery, and strength. However, what if these characteristics are not merely used to symbolize desirable values but are also mobilized as a weapon? If we take another look at the picture, we find that among the soldiers, rifles, and military backpacks, the jaguar seems like just another war device—but what kind exactly?

In May 2003, the first time I set foot in the region, I saw a caged jaguar in the headquarters of the Seventeenth Brigade, a military unit headed between 1995 and 1997 by General Rito Alejo del Río, a graduate of the US Army School of the Americas who later was sent to prison for systematically arming, equipping, and assisting paramilitary death squads. The jaguar was on public display, and its cage was visible just beside some buildings and assault training fields. When I asked about that jaguar, the first answer I got from several sources was that it was the brigade's mascot. A questionable mascot indeed, but it was not at all rare that a battalion trained to wage war in the forest had found a jaguar. When I asked some local residents about that particular jaguar, it came up several times that the animal was used by the army in some dubious activities, which I learned were connected to the sinister allegations hanging over the Seventeenth Brigade—namely, its complicity with the paramilitaries who "pacified" the region. The jaguar, some people whispered, was used to eliminate the corpses of people secretly imprisoned and tortured in that military unit. I was shocked to hear this but later realized that such a terrible thing was not unrealistic given the dirty war that had taken place during the 1990s in this region, when massacres, forced disappearance, tortures, and killings became common currency. Militaries raising a man-eating jaguar? Perhaps. We cannot know for sure. But I did see that caged jaguar every time I crossed in front of the Seventeenth Brigade's headquarters until one day, at the end of 2005, when the cage was empty. Nobody was able to tell me anything about the jaguar's whereabouts.

In 2014, shortly after the fishermen were devoured, another formerly caged jaguar was pointed to as the perpetrator. According to several sources in Bajo Atrato, a paramilitary commander had kept a jaguar on one of his ranches and then released the animal back into the forest of Los Katíos National Park before his property was confiscated by judicial authorities. That confiscation was part of the agreements that paramilitaries had accepted during their demobilization process, and its aim was to contribute to a victims' reparation fund. Rumors suggested that the paramilitaries had habituated this jaguar to a diet that helped these death squads get rid of the people they considered undesirable.

When at the beginning of 2015 the authorities from the regional environmental institution confirmed the deaths of three other people killed during new "feline attacks" (Corpourabá 2015), local hunters decided to take care of business, and they successfully hunted down the animal. Some media sources reported with indignation how the body of an endangered species had first become a children's toy (the skull was used by some children to play with), then dog food (dogs were fed the jaguar's flesh and bones), and finally a hunting trophy (the fur was hung on a wall) (*Teleantioquia Noticias* 2015). The reaction of local inhabitants was quite the opposite: relief that the jaguar that had caused so much trouble was finally dead. I can clearly remember the conversation I had with a friend about this. He told me that three hunters had succeeded in tracking and trapping the jaguar but that people were now concerned that the animal had left a female and three cubs that they believed had developed the same propensity for human flesh. The proof was that, after the supposed man-eating jaguar was killed, the attacks on poultry and dogs did not end.

When I asked one of my friends why the original jaguar, which had been killed, had developed such behavior in the first place, he grabbed my arm, took me to one of the empty rooms of the house we were in, and told me in a near whisper that the jaguar had belonged to a paramilitary chief who had kept the animal on one of his ranches and tried to raise it as a pet. This story, which was spread by word of mouth throughout the region, acquired more and more elements every time I asked about it. Some people held that the jaguar was used to kill, whereas others said that the paramilitary chief entertained himself by letting the jaguar clamp his teeth on people. In any case the animal learned not to be afraid of humans. But my friend's allegations went beyond run-of-the-mill gossip as he explained that the jaguar was used to do away with the bodies of those kidnapped and tortured by the paramilitaries.

Apparently, the jaguar, kept in a cage, was fed with pieces of human flesh. This means that in order to better dispose of these bodies, the paramilitaries would cut them up and throw the pieces to the jaguar, which had been starved for several days in advance. This is how the jaguar became accustomed to human flesh, a diet that he could not give up once he was set free.

Although there is no doubt that a hungry jaguar could devour meat and bones without leaving a trace, to make a whole human body disappear would require a significant and systematic effort because jaguars do not eat their prey all at once but instead return to consume the parts at different times (Brown and López 2001; Novack and Main 2012; Rabinowitz 2000). Moreover, they eat neither guts nor teeth (Mahler 2009; Shepherd, Mills, and Shoff 2014). Therefore, delivering an entire human body may not be the most efficient practice, a fact corroborated by the idea that the jaguar kept by paramilitaries was regularly fed with pieces of human flesh rather than with a whole body at a time. Such a ghastly method, though not very sophisticated, becomes more plausible once one examines other methods used by paramilitaries throughout the country. In 2009 several former fighters confessed that in regions of Antioquia and Norte de Santander, furnaces were built to cremate the bodies of their victims (*Espectador* 2009b; *Tiempo* 2009). The intention was to avoid having mass graves in regions under the paramilitaries' control, as well as eliminating any evidence that could be used by prosecutors. Mass murder is a business requiring much inventiveness, and animals were also used for this purpose. In 2008 former commander José Gregorio Mangones Lugo, known as Carlos Tijeras ("Scissorhands"), told local prosecutors that in order to avoid their men being accused of being perpetrators of mass killings, his paramilitaries used venomous snakes: in this way the deaths were counted by local authorities as natural accidents (*Tiempo* 2008; *Semana* 2009). According to the inhabitants of the region of San Onofre, Rodrigo Mercado Pelufo, the chief commander of the Mountains of Mary Heroes Front, had a lake on his ranch where he threw both dead and living human bodies in order to feed Alfredito, a six-meter-long caiman (*New Herald* 2009; *Semana* 2009). In March 2009, during the confiscation of the properties of Carlos Mario Jiménez, commander in chief of the Central Bolívar Bloc of the United Self-Defense Forces, authorities found a lion whose cage was located kilometers away from the closest house, proof of what local inhabitants of the municipality of Cáceres already knew: it was not a simple exhibition animal (Caracol Radio 2009; *Espectador* 2009a).

Thus, the jaguar killing and devouring people in Bajo Atrato was, so to speak, a paramilitary jaguar. He was doing the work of warlords and literally became one of the *mochacabezas*—a beheader or head chopper, as paramilitaries are often called in the region. Because this jaguar was accustomed to eating human flesh, once in the wild he was more likely to go after people. A paramilitary jaguar represents an even greater threat than an ordinary jaguar, and if this particular jaguar had hunted down people and was even teaching his cubs to do the same, then the danger was clearly increasing. The armed conflict has changed these jaguars' appetite for humans, and the ferocity of their attacks and boldness in going so close to human dwellings reveal traits exceeding those of ordinary wild jaguars. This altered jaguar has, sadly, been transformed into a war device, and his behavior has become an extension of the evil that people attribute to paramilitaries: strength, deadliness, greed, and lack of compunction. A jaguar accustomed to eating human flesh as the result of a paramilitary commander's training is, after all, a jaguar involved in the armed conflict. It seems that the municipal secretary of Turbo was indeed correct: the jaguar was killing civilians, and this was evidence of how forests and their sylvan inhabitants may run amok because of war.

A Jaguar and a Half, or Half a Jaguar?

Among the many conclusions that can be drawn from the incidents associated with this jaguar, I focus on the failures and successes of the actors involved. A warlord succeeded in designing a more or less efficient "device" for the disposal of bodies—a design that, once it was released in the forest, the people of Bajo Atrato experienced as an evil, ravenous jaguar. Environmental managers failed to recognize that creatures such as man-eating jaguars can indeed exist, although they were correct in pointing out the troublesome impact that human affairs may have on the life of jaguars. Biologists, zoologists, and ethologists tend to see jaguars simultaneously as tokens and type: when they study particular jaguars (tokens), they infer characteristics related to the species as a whole (type), so when the traits of some singular jaguars do not fit into what is known about the type, what results is perceived as just an anomaly: a jaguar that is man-eating has aberrant behavior that diverges from the commonly accepted nature of the entire species. This kind of singular natural order, which in the minds of natural scientists determines a limited set of relationships, is opposed to how people in Bajo Atrato consider jaguars: they are what they are, and they become what they become mainly "in flesh and in sign" (Metcalf 2008, 124)—that is, by virtue of the material-semiotic encounters that individual jaguars have with people (Haraway 2008). In this sense a jaguar in Bajo Atrato is rarely taken for granted as possessing a set of limited qualities or propensities that are presumed to be part of some predetermined natural order.

Local communities have long encountered jaguars and have learned to cultivate in their daily lives what Jacob Metcalf (2008) calls "intimacy without proximity." Jaguars and humans participate in a social entanglement, yet despite their shared history and place, their mutual flourishing attains better results when there is no actual spatial proximity, given the fact that during close encounters, each one might prove dangerous to the other. In Bajo Atrato, people realize how their lives intersect with jaguars, and awareness of their own edibility surpasses any urge to become the master of one of these animals. The possibility of dominion seems to have been discarded by those living close to jaguars, and it is precisely in this respect that the warlord and paramilitaries who adopted the jaguar as a pet have failed: they forced a proximity without intimacy, without cohabitation, without mutual knowledge and recognition (Metcalf 2008). They tried to bring into their own all-too-human domain a being with a nature that is, and here I prefer once again the words of the poet, "wildernesses of freedom" (T. Hughes 1957, 4). Finally, those who failed the most, if failure can even describe their lamentable fate, were those who died in the forest under the claws and fangs of a creature indifferent to the laws governing war. They were victims, although a veil of uncertainty will always obscure their fate: Victims of what? Were they victims of "feline attack," as described by media, the unlucky prey of an endangered species showing a lack of interest in human affairs? Or did they experience the outrageous aftermath of a perverse plan perpetrated by particular warlords? The jaguar forces us to look attentively at the wonders and terrors of a war deeply entangled in forests and forcefully entangling their sylvan inhabitants. The jaguar asks us to consider the amplified aftermaths that war creates and how war's effects still reverberate even after the demobilization of armed groups and the signing of peace accords.

In my attempt to make sense of these events, one question still haunts me: was this a jaguar and a half, by which I mean a being whose behavior exceeded the driving forces of his own jaguarness? Or was this animal the half of a Jaguar, a being that did not attain his true flourishing? This being was prone to hunting and eating more than what is normally observed in jaguars, exhibiting a behavior that transgressed what scientists know about jaguars as an animal species and even demonstrating traits and preferences that transcended how jaguars have historically conducted themselves in Bajo Atrato. A jaguar attracted to the taste of human flesh after being used by paramilitary armies as a device of war is no longer what local communi-

FIGURE 6.2. The public and private life of animals. Images by J. J. Grandville (1841).

ties recognize as an ordinary jaguar. A jaguar belonging to a warlord is more dreadfully rapacious than one living in the forest: a jaguar turned into a weapon is greedier than the ones people are used to encountering in the stories of Uncle Tiger. His predatory violence and aberrant appetite become an expression of excess: a jaguar and a half that not only manifests the pervasiveness of war but that also creates new forms of vulnerability among those who rely on forest resources for their livelihood. Yet I think that this excess does not only add but also subtracts. This is an excess that is not entirely of the jaguar and that, perhaps, makes him something less than an ordinary animal. Let me illustrate that half of a jaguar.

In his analysis of J. J. Grandville's illustrations (figure 6.2) published in *Scènes de la vie privée et publique des animaux* (1841–42), John Berger argues that, unlike some traditions in which the purpose of portraying a person as an animal was to reveal a particular aspect of their character—e.g., a lion to represent courage or a donkey to exemplify stubbornness—in these illustrations, animals are not moral metaphors. Instead, "they are being used *en masse* to 'people' situations" (1980, 17) and have become prisoners of social situations that are not their own. Similarly, the man-eating jaguar causing so much havoc was coerced into resolving the sinister business of people involved in a dirty war. It is this involvement in too-human worlds that makes me believe that the jaguar is actually the "half of a Jaguar": imprisoned in the situations of men and perverted by human affairs, his jaguarness faded away.

Perhaps this man-eating jaguar is one of those monsters of the Anthropocene, that new planetary epoch in which the magnitude of human activities has come to shape our planet's very composition and processes. The monstrosity of this jaguar is associated not so much with the fear he unleashed as with his power of dislocating the borders between human and nonhuman forces, environmental and social processes, predation and warfare. Hence this hybrid creature is neither more nor less than a jaguar. I feel that by framing the question in such terms, I am taking away his own agency. After all, it is through his own acts—hunting in a way that is both efficient and impeccable, raising and feeding cubs, successfully evading hunters—that the jaguar participates in the transformative relations which people in Bajo Atrato have experienced. Perhaps the jaguar is simultaneously both: a being exceeding the drives of his own condition and a being halfway away from his own jaguarness. And it is by affirming this hybridity and this multiplicity that we can better understand war and its afterlives.

7

A LIFE OF LEGAL CONCERN

During the last three decades, Colombia's internal armed conflict has seriously hindered the lives of Indigenous and Afro-Colombian peoples. Besides the violations to their fundamental human rights, some of the most flagrant harms these peoples have experienced are related to the exposure of their traditional territories to different forms of environmental damage, including depletion of natural resources, ecosystem pollution, and biodiversity loss, as well as dispossession and land conversion. Yet as the previous chapters have shown, war also causes fundamental damage to the territory when, for example, it provokes the anger of spirits, the madness of animals, or the proliferation of certain sylvan beings. Territory is harmed when human and other-than-human beings are prevented from maintaining the practices and relationships that help them sustain their worlds and their emplaced sense of being. This is why, for Indigenous and Afro-Colombian peoples, territory constitutes not only a space for living but also a living entity.

In order to tackle some of the harm provoked by war and as part of a suite of policies that paved the way for the recognition of rights for all victims of armed conflict, in 2011 the Colombian president signed the Victims and Land Restitution Law (Law 1448). It aimed to provide reparations to victims of human rights violations and to restore the stolen lands of the millions of peasant families who had been driven away from their homes. Although this law was a major step toward addressing the legacy of violence, it was strongly criticized by Indigenous and Afro-Colombian organizations because the government did not seek their prior and informed consent during its formulation, an obligation that the Colombian state accepted in 1989 as signatory of the Indigenous and Tribal Peoples Convention, also known as International Labour Organization Convention 169 (ILO-169). Additionally, these organizations argued that, given the fact that the armed conflict has affected Indigenous and Afro-Colombian peoples in disproportionate ways, the damage to their unique ways of being required different measures of rectification than those the government was intending to provide to other victims.

It is in this context of Indigenous organizations pressing for recognition of their particular experiences of war that these social movements and the state forged a set of legal measures specifically aimed to redress the damage inflicted upon Indigenous lives. Concretely, the Decree-Law 4633, simply referred to as the Victims' Law for Indigenous [peoples], expresses that alongside human beings and ways of life, traditional territories should also be considered victims of violence: "The territory, understood as a living entity and foundation of identity and harmony, in accordance with the very cosmovision of the indigenous peoples and by virtue of the special and collective link that they hold with it, suffers a damage when it is violated or desecrated by the internal armed conflict and its underlying and related factors" (Congreso de Colombia, Decreto-Ley 4633, Art. 45).

Besides pointing out that armed violence is an experience shared by human and other-than-human beings, this recognition turns Indigenous and Afro-Colombian territories into legal subjects with interests and needs of their own. This decolonizes justice because the law incorporates practices and concepts that have been historically silenced and kept out of the realm of law (Izquierdo and Viaene 2018). It also challenges dominant political and legal paradigms: more than just a tool to protect rights regarding land ownership, the law allows Indigenous and Afro-Colombian peoples to make into a matter of public concern the well-being of a set of entities including spirits or sentient places, which modern states typically recognize only as belonging to the religious sphere of certain ethno-cultural minorities. Put differently, when referring to the harm inflicted upon the other-than-human beings that contribute to the making of their traditional territories, these people are undermining the borders that secular politics sets between the living and the material, between subjects and objects, or between, broadly speaking, the realms of nature and culture.

So far, I have been building an ethnographic argument to illustrate that, following Indigenous and Afro-Colombian cosmopolitical endeavors, which involve sociality between human and other-than-human actors, the inclusion of territory as a victim paves the way for new contestations about what constitutes damage and what form of justice might be appropriate. This last chapter explores how far this legal tool goes and how short it falls in grasping and enabling reparations that respond to the specificity of Indigenous and Afro-Colombian territories. What sort of actions has the recognition of territory as victim prompted? In what sense do those actions reflect the modern understanding of harm and environmental issues, and to what extent do they respond to *Bajoatrateño* practices and conceptualizations? To address these questions, in the first part of the chapter I discuss how the Victims' Law for Indigenous [Peoples] embodies a unique opportunity to decolonize justice and decenter the human in our understanding of war and its aftermath. In the second part, I present another legal instrument recently issued in Colombia: a rule from the Constitutional Court that conferred legal personality to the Atrato River and granted it specific rights. This law stands as one of the greatest attempts to legally protect Indigenous and Afro-Colombian territories, yet this legal protection focuses on the river as a mere natural resource sustaining the life of local communities—that is, as a container for life rather than as a form of life itself. Inspired by the work of Julie Cruikshank (2005, 251), I wonder to what extent this focus on rivers as natural resources is not only narrow but also politically unjust. This chapter sustains a rather simple premise: what to do with the Atrato River and *Bajoatrateño* territory, legally and politically speaking, in order to redress the harm that has been inflicted on them depends on what the Colombian state considers the river and the territory to be, ontologically speaking.

Diplomatic Endeavors

In one of the official editions of the Victims' Law for Indigenous [Peoples], two high officials from the Colombian government state that the inclusion of the territory as a victim was possible because government and Indigenous authorities held a respectful *diálogo de saberes*: a dialogue among different ways of knowing (Presidencia de la República 2012, 8). For them, "this inclusion accounts for the sociopolitical recognition of the diversity of epistemologies and relations between man and Mother Earth that, with their different versions, take precedence in the indigenous way of thinking" (Presidencia de la República 2012, 9). When examining the Victims' Law from the perspective I offered throughout the previous chapters, the inclusion of the territory as a victim allows us to imagine various policies of attention and reparation that might result from taking into account a large diversity of other-than-human beings. My take here is that this inclusion represents a political victory for Indigenous and Afro-Colombian organizations in their quest for justice. However, when damage to territory is wrapped up in concepts such as cosmovision or "the diversity of epistemologies" that the aforementioned state officials referred to, the law adopts a tone in which the multicultural Colombian state simply ensures that they respect the worldviews of particular social actors recognized as legitimate others. The issue is that when those who experience the damage caused by war in terms, let us say, of spirits that have disappeared, snakes that have become more aggressive, or places that are now haunted, these people are not recognized as presenting claims about the very nature of the world and the human experience within it (Holbraad 2008), but merely as producing cultural interpretations of "real" facts. The idea that these experiences correspond to a particular worldview emerges in the epistemological process through which those local experiences are translated into modern terms for those who do not inhabit the worlds of spirits or of places endowed with agency.

When invoking, for example, spirits that have gone mad, communities of Bajo Atrato are calling upon different logics of how the universe is constituted (Handelman 2008, 181) and principles "of a being in the world and the orientation of such a being toward the horizons of experience" (Kapferer 1988, 79). In other words, they are referring to ontic and ontological questions about the constitution of the world and the logic of relationships among the beings that it comprises and not merely epistemological questions—the standing point from which one sees the world. Within the realm of transitional justice and the redressing of damage, this kind of awareness should imply a turn from the protection of the cultural frameworks through which Indigenous and Afro-Colombian peoples represent the world to the consideration of the realities that become possible once the human and its rights cease to be the predominant matter of legal and ethical concern. Until this slight difference is admitted, the kind of dialogue of knowledges that state officials invoke will be asymmetrical because the power relations that make this dialogue possible would never be called into question—by which I mean, the type of world and reality sanctioned by the modern institutions that make up the nation-state will not be admitted as itself subject to negotiation. This may have profound consequences for the policies of reparation to Indigenous peoples because if reparation policies are enclosed within a multicultural framework that would just putatively accommodate the plurality of existing cultural representations of the world, the type of damage invoked by

Indigenous and Afro-Colombian peoples would continue to be confined to the world of their beliefs, meaning that damage to territory would say nothing "real" about the suffering of the territory itself and much less about the impacts upon spirits or masters of game animals because none of these entities "really" exist, at least not in the way assumed by the positivist ontologies that back up modern states' politics. By embracing difference through its modern matrix of knowledge—within which things and events are allocated to either the realms of nature or culture, or of facts and values, as argued by Bruno Latour (2004)—the multicultural state circumscribes the possible forms of expression that Indigenous and Afro-Colombian cultural difference may adopt, foreclosing the potential that this "difference" might have to challenge both the terms that modern institutions mobilize to define reality and the power-laden structures that sustain said version of reality. Put differently, the state recognizes "cultural" differences as long as they do not undermine its own onto-epistemic tenets, bracketing off the question of the world itself from the realm of tolerable difference. In the context of damage to territory and the redress of its harm, this distinction between reality and worldviews limits our ability to effectively address the very definition of damage and its possibilities of reparation. If, within the multicultural paradigm, spirits or sentient places are allowed to exist only as social constructions, can the state deliver justice and reparations that are consistent with the experiences of Indigenous and Afro-Colombian peoples?

Bruce Braun and Sarah Whatmore (2010, ix) argue that the way different life-forms contribute to the world we all share must enter into our current understanding of politics. On the basis of this argument, the inclusion of the territory as a victim becomes akin to what philosopher Isabelle Stengers (2005a) describes as a cosmopolitical proposal: an endeavor to compose a common, political world in which the fissures between *kósmos* (the universe or, in another sense, the given, the immanent, the objective, the natural) and *politikós* (the particular, the instituted, the transcendent, the subjective, the social) are constantly negotiated. I thus interpret the arrival of territory into the realm of law as a seed liable to disrupt the way in which the multicultural state has been regulating the relationships—and building boundaries—between "the real" or the world itself and cultural representations or worldviews. Concretely, this seed would be capable of inhibiting a human-centric approach to justice and creating a slightly different awareness of the damage provoked by war and, therefore, the possibilities of reparation. According to this framework, transitional justice would be based on a less human-centric ethics, an ethics not necessarily related to the extension of moral considerations toward other-than-humans. Rather, it would take as its starting point the human condition of living with and for other-than-human entities. Besides forcing us to reconsider certain ontological distinctions among people, places, and other beings, this also reminds us that the existence of humans, other-than-humans, and places is always mutually nurtured.

When considering war as an experience shared by different kinds of beings, the Victims' Law invites us to assume a sort of diplomatic stance toward the realities experienced by Indigenous and Afro-Colombian peoples, on one hand, and the kind of reality sanctioned by the modern state, on the other. Diplomacy here means something different than legal indulgences regarding the beliefs or practices of Indigenous and Afro-Colombian communities. More than concessions made by the state in its consideration of the way in which these peoples think of themselves as actors in the world, or about the kinds of beings they believe can or do exist, or of the actions these peoples believe they themselves and these beings can perform, diplomacy in this case becomes a kind of "generative excess" (I. Vargas 2020, 245): an agreement reached by parties with radically different ways of understanding the world yet who compromise by accepting the absence of a common or absolute ontology as the ground for politics (Stengers 2005b, 194). Here I follow once again the ideas of Stengers (2005b), who sees diplomacy as something other than the adoption of subtle tact in dealing with those who represent another point of view. Rather, for her, diplomacy is a kind of "positive pluralism" (Stengers, 2002, 261), an agreement reached by parties that, representing radical ways of understanding the world, compromise in accepting the absence of an ontological sovereign (Stengers 2005b, 194).

The well-known example of the wasp and the orchid, discussed by Deleuze and Guattari (2004), is useful to understand the outcomes of this kind of diplomacy. According to these authors, the encounter of an orchid that lures a male wasp by mimicking a female wasp is not just one of imitation—a deceptive flower that has evolved to resemble female versions of a pollinator insect for the propagation of its own species. It is, rather, an instance of becoming: through a mutual capture of shape and rules of engagement, both entities compose a new reality, a rhizomatic association in which the boundaries of one cannot be thoroughly distinguished from the boundaries of the other. Stengers holds that such an encounter does not create any sort of wasp-orchid unity, rather that "wasps and orchids give each other quite another meaning to the relation that takes place between them" (2010, 29). A diplomatic event would be exactly that: a generative excess in which each party entertains its own version. As a potential diplomatic event, the Victims' Law becomes thus an achievement in which the state and Indigenous peoples can accept an agreement without undermining their own practices and values. In this sense the law would allow the state to protect the rights of Indigenous and Afro-Colombian communities without having to compromise its own regime of truth (i.e., to accept the positivist existence of the kinds of spiritual beings that Indigenous and Afro-Colombian peoples have seen affected by war) while also allowing these communities to advocate for the protection of the other-than-human beings that constitute their territories, without having to constrain their demands to the language of human and environmental rights. Within this context I see my own ethnographic endeavor as an act of cosmopolitical diplomacy (Kohn 2020; Latour 2004) that allows other-than-human beings, in this case those affected by war, a mode of expression that can be intelligible within modern legal and political idioms without being necessarily constrained by them.

If the recognition of territory as a victim is an entente that might disrupt the orders of the public—the interests, practices, and values promoted in the name of secular, scientific knowledge—and the private—the interests, practices, and values attributed to the so-called sociocultural constructions of reality embodied by certain peoples—such recognition may also expand what philosopher Jacques Rancière identifies as the regime of the perceptible. According to him, the core of political action is shaped by an a priori "system of self-evident facts of sense perception" that conditions what is possible to say and think, to see and hear (2000, 12). He calls this the *distribution of the sensible*: the condition of possibility for perception, thought, and, of course, political action. It is by virtue of this distribution of the sensible that forms of inclusion and exclusion are established within a political community. When the other-than-human beings that have been left unaccounted for by traditional legal systems break into the realm of law, a new distribution of the sensible takes place, one in which the expressions of those entities affected by war might start to be heard as a voice rather than as noise (Povinelli 2015). In addition, this voice can also trigger a decolonizing effect because it potentially paves the way for new subjects to irrupt and become matters of common interest, slowing down that modern tendency, assumed as universal and necessary in politics and law, that draws a neat cut between subjects and objects, the sacred and the secular, reality and beliefs. Although spirits, sentient places, or animals endowed with conscious intent still struggle to find their place in the common political arena, the insistence of taking into consideration their fate within a transitional justice framework can only increase the chances of enlarging that arena. And this, I am convinced, entails ethical and political questions capable of transforming beliefs and practices regarding social justice, as well as of shaping our everyday relations to ourselves, to others, and to the world (White 2001).

A Fluid Subject of Rights

In January 2016 the Colombian Constitutional Court, the country's highest tribunal, visited Quibdó—the capital of Chocó—and Paimadó, the heart of one of the municipalities most affected by the pollution associated with alluvial gold mining. It was the first time that this tribunal held a session in situ. Holding several hearings with local communities, the goal of the court was to corroborate a situation denounced countless times by *Chocoano* organizations: the dramatic contamination produced by dredges and excavators, as well as by cyanide and mercury, used in the illegal mines operated or defended by armed organized criminals along the Atrato River and its tributaries. During its four-day visit and after collecting several testimonies of local experts and communities, the court assessed the extent to which mining and logging were compromising the rights to "life, health, water, food security, healthy environment, culture, and territory" of local populations (Corte Constitucional ¶2.10: 7). Shortly after, the court issued Sentence T-622, which recognized the Atrato River as a bearer of rights. This was a watershed decision, one that by considering the river worthy of respect and protection challenged those bedrock beliefs, entrenched at the core of Western legal systems, according to which humans are the only rights holders and the natural world is but a collection of resources to be owned and managed (Boyd 2017).

The recognition of the Atrato River as a rights-bearing subject is added to the long series of national jurisprudence regarding the protection of Indigenous and Afro-Colombian territories. Somehow this ruling follows the path initially paved by the Law of Victims when it considered these territories to be a victim of armed conflict. The underlying logic is simple: that which can be described as a victim might be considered a subject, one whose nature and rights are henceforth delineated by the Constitutional Court. The new legal status of the Atrato represents a major change in terms of policies regarding use and care of this river and its tributaries. Concretely, the court gave one year to the national government and to regional and local environmental authorities to set in motion a plan to neutralize the harm provoked by logging and mining companies in Chocó, decontaminate water sources, recover damaged ecosystems, and support the recuperation of traditional forms of subsistence. Requiring the full participation of local communities at every stage of this plan, the ruling also ordered the creation of a body of guardians, which would include a member of the local communities and a delegate from the national government, and which would act as the legal representatives of the river basin. Along with a panel of experts headed by the Office of the Inspector General of Colombia—the main public institution overseeing the correct functioning of government agencies and institutions—and comprising experts from Indigenous and Afro-Colombian communities, as well as of academic and social organizations, these "Guardians of the Atrato" would monitor the implementation of the judicial decision and keep all riverine communities informed about the advances of the policies to be designed in the aforementioned safeguard plan.

In its detailed and extensive ruling, the court engages with a large body of national and international jurisprudence regarding Indigenous peoples and environmental rights in order to assert how deeply *Chocoano* communities depend on the river for their physical, cultural, and spiritual sustenance. Hence, the ruling also constitutes an important step for the protection of the rights of Indigenous and Afro-Colombian peoples, for it recognizes that their cultures cannot be understood without considering the "special relationships they have with their natural environment" or the "use, conservation, and administration of their natural resources" (Corte Constitucional ¶3.2: 5). Adopting an alternative approach regarding the collective rights of ethnic communities, the ruling includes so-called biocultural rights: "the rights that result from the recognition of the deep and intrinsic connection that exists between nature, its resources, and the culture of the ethnic and Indigenous communities that inhabit them, which are interdependent with each other and cannot be understood in isolation" (Corte Constitucional ¶5.11: 1). Based on this interdependency, the court understands that it is not possible to effectively defend and protect these peoples without implementing measures for the protection of their territory and its biophysical components.

According to Elizabeth Macpherson (2019), these biocultural rights are not necessarily new rights for the ethnic communities but a way of tying together cultural rights and rights to stewardship over their lands. But moving a step further than these biocultural rights, the court adopts what it describes as an eco-centric approach: the interconnectedness of humans with nature, which means that the latter does not belong to humankind but quite the opposite—that humans are but a species among many others. According to the ruling, this approach implies that "in no way are [humans] the owners of other species, biodiversity, natural resources, or the fate of the planet. Consequently, this [eco-centric] theory sees nature as a true subject of rights that must be recognized by the States and exercised under the tutelage of its legal representatives, such as, for example, by the communities that inhabit nature or that have a special relationship with it" (Corte Constitucional ¶5.9: 2).

The consideration of the environment and living organisms as entities worthy of protection "not just for the simple material, genetic or productive utility that these can represent to humans" (Corte Constitucional ¶9.27: 4) thus entails a shift from interdependency (a human-centered approach that sees the conservation of nature as a means to secure human well-being) to interconnectedness (a nature-centered approach that does not see humans as the sole bearer of intrinsic value). This shift also entails the recognition of nature as a bearer of interests and the human obligation to protect such supreme interests. This is why the court granted legal personhood to the Atrato River and determined conservation, protection, maintenance, and restoration to be its specific rights. As the Law of Victims does, the declaration of this new nonhuman subject of rights overcomes the legal divide between persons (capable of having rights) and property (unable to possess rights). As observed by Mari Margil, recognizing the rights of rivers, forests, and nature in general needs to be done by breaking "away from legal strictures that were never intended to apply to nature" (2018). Likewise, David Boyd (2017) argues that the recognition of these kinds of rights underscores the fact that all life has intrinsic value and that humans have a moral responsibility regarding nature, which undermines the kind of anthropocentrism that has historically distinguished modern thought—the idea that humans are separated from, and are superior to, the natural world.

Although conferring legal personhood to a river may sound counterintuitive or even futile, given, for example, the impossibility of a river to express itself in courts or sue those who violate its rights, it is no stranger than the kind of personhood that many legal systems already accord to family trusts, companies, or incorporated societies, which, through a common legal technique of make-believe known as legal fiction (Moglen 1990), are treated as persons, meaning that they may enter into contracts, buy and sell land, sue and be sued, or commit torts just as natural persons do (Schane 2006). Companies are even, under the legal personhood granted by US jurisprudence, entitled to the constitutional right to free speech (Boyd 2017). Facing the urgent need to create conditions of intelligibility through which the voice of the river can be heard, the court acknowledges that the rights of the Atrato basin are better exercised under the tutelage of those who have cultivated a special relationship with the river. And that is precisely the role to be played by the guardians' commission.

The composition of the Guardians of the Atrato River was a matter of tension between *Chocoano* organizations and the national government. Initially conceived of as a body of two representatives (one from the state and the other from local communities), Indigenous and Afro-Colombian social organizations challenged this kind of configuration, arguing that in order to better represent the river's interest, it was imperative to adopt a more participatory approach; otherwise, a single representative could distort the will of both the river and its riverine communities. The rationale of this demand was based on the characteristics of the river itself. Along its 650 kilometers (404 miles) and hundreds of tributaries, this river meets a high diversity of communities that, though sharing a riverine pattern of life, encounter diverse versions of the Atrato. As pointed out by Diego Cagüeñas and colleagues (Cagüeñas, Galindo, and Rasmussen 2020), upstream, near its source, the crystalline but rough waters of the Atrato have little in common with the deep, silent, and muddy river one finds in Bajo Atrato. Whereas the basin offers gold and platinum in its middle course, fish and wood predominate near the river's mouth. In the same vein, the children who play at the shores, the women who do laundry and gut fish on the rafts, the elders who distinguish the presence of *fieras*, the *jaibanas* who summon aquatic spirits, or the log drivers who move timber downstream do not necessarily meet the same kind of river. This multiplicity contrasts with the single, monolithic river depicted in the legal ruling, where the language of sustainable exploitation and conservation of natural resources tends to stabilize the ontological status of the Atrato. Attending then to the diverse modes of being coalescing around the Atrato and under the premise that all communities are indeed guardians of the Atrato River, the seven *Chocoano* social organizations representing Indigenous and Afro-Colombian peoples proposed the commission of guardians to be constituted by fourteen delegates, half of them women. This unprecedented and groundbreaking move challenged the initial scope that the ruling gave to the body of guardians because, from the beginning, local organizations understood that through these guardians, communities could enforce their autonomous decisions regarding their territories (Macpherson 2019) and that they were the ones who could undertake legal actions to protect the river from further environmental threats. I think that, given the participatory approach that local organizations aimed to bestow to the task of the river's representation, it would have been desirable to enlarge political participation by including children and elders among the guardians as well.

At first glance, the granting of rights to the Atrato River seems to evoke the "biocentric turns" (Gudynas 2009, 34) of the Ecuadorian and Bolivian constitutions, which, drawing from Indigenous ontologies, challenged dominant economic paradigms in order to stress how fundamentally important it was that humans live in harmony with nature. The Ecuadorian constitution dedicates its entire seventh chapter to the rights of Nature (Pacha Mama), emphasizing its right to "integral respect for its existence and the maintenance and regeneration of its life cycles, structure, functions, and evolutionary processes" (Political Constitution of Ecuador, Art. 71). In its preamble the Bolivian Constitution recognizes "the existing plurality of all things," including mountains, rivers, and lakes, emphasizing the importance of recognizing Mother Earth's rights to redress contemporary environmental issues and construct alternatives to capitalism. However, it is important to highlight that the Colombian case is different because it is a "culturally located" case, meaning that the river's rights are "a consequence of the recognition of the [human] rights of indigenous and tribal peoples as river communities" (Macpherson and Clavijo Ospina 2018, 284). It is important to understand what this difference entails.

The Bolivian and Ecuadorian models have been criticized because their legal systems did not specify which tools and pathways to use when applying rights to nature (Kauffman and Martin 2017) or who should act as nature's representative (Boyd 2017; Fish 2013). For example, Laurel Fish has shown how in Ecuador, claims on behalf of nature have not always been made by local communities to fight back against corporations or developers, which was the original intention, but have also been made by powerful economic actors to simply relocate development projects to places that best suited their own interests. The problem, explains Fish, is that by invoking nature as something abstract and universal, the Ecuadorian Constitution portrays the environment as a homogeneous, harmonious entity with a single set of needs that always align with the interests of idealized, disfranchised communities that have nature's best interest at heart (Fish 2013, 7–9). Similarly, Craig Kauffman and Pamela Martin (2017) have underscored how lawsuits presented in the name of rights of nature have served in some cases to undermine the state's extractive development agenda but in other cases to strengthen the power of private companies or actors that maintain that their activities are carried out in nature's general interest. Given that the Atrato

River cannot represent itself in the legal system, the Colombian model, inspired by the recognition of rights to the Whanganui River in New Zealand, attempted to solve this problem by connecting the rights of the river to the human rights of the riverine communities. This is precisely why the designation of guardians who speak and act on behalf of the river is intended to engender enforceability (Macpherson and Clavijo Ospina 2018).

But the intermingling of river and human rights can be criticized precisely for the anthropocentrism that the eco-centric approach adopted by the ruling aims to overcome. As explained before, the Colombian court holds that it is developing an approach in which this river has intrinsic worth and possesses fundamental rights, and that the granting of said rights is consequential with the recognition of Afro-Colombian and Indigenous ways of life. Lawyers Elizabeth Macpherson and Felipe Clavijo Ospina explain that this means that the specific rights of the river are tied up with the collective rights these communities have to traditional stewardship of their territories, in a way which is similar to how other Latin American countries have protected Indigenous lands "by expanding the right to 'property'" (2018, 292). In other words, even if recognition of the rights of the Atrato River seems to be the highest form of legal protection, this protection is based on an approach that, as noted by geographer Nick Mount, privileges rationalism rather than existentialism, meaning that the rights awarded to the river have to do with "what it provides for human life" and not the fact that its very existence "should be equated with human life" (Mount 2017) or any living being's life. To say it differently, as transcendental as this ruling is, the specific granted rights seem to enact another version of the nature-culture divide (I. Vargas 2020): the Atrato River is a fundamental resource in the lives and cultural practices of Indigenous and Afro-Colombian peoples, a feature of nature to which attaching adequate practices of conservation, protection, maintenance, and restoration is important. In this way, as pointed out by Fish, the conflation of human rights with the river's rights "undermines the very premise of ecocentric policies" (2013, 9) because the river is not protected by virtue of its own inherent value but for what it offers to people. In addition, the fact that only the communities who have developed a culturally-specific relationship with the river can speak on its behalf raises the question of whether or not the rights of this river can exist outside of a given specific cultural context (Macpherson and Clavijo Ospina 2018, 291).

The court ruling successfully delineates a path of actions that slow down neoliberal and extractivist agendas, establishing a framework through which new ethical relations with the natural world might emerge. However, when considering the rights of the river as one would human rights, only certain legal measures are possible. What can be done to redress, let us say, the harm done to *fieras*? The rights conferred to the Atrato enact thus a particular version of this river, one in which it exists as an element upon which local peoples unfold their own particular cultures: the river emerges as a container for life rather than as a form of life itself, as evidenced by the language adopted in the ruling: "In the case under review, these communities are allegedly being threatened by the intensive activities of illegal mining with toxic chemical substances and heavy machinery in the Atrato River Basin. . . . This mineral exploitation would put in imminent risk not only their physical existence, the perpetuation and reproduction of their ancestral traditions and culture, but also the habitat and the natural resources of the place where the identity of the communities is built, strengthened, and developed" (Corte Constitucional de Colombia ¶6.11: 1).

Inspired by the work of Julie Cruikshank on the agency of glaciers and on how Indigenous knowledge about this subject is seen as irrelevant to the modern world (2005, 251–58), I wonder to what extent this focus on rivers as natural resources is not only narrow but also politically unjust. The emphasis on what rivers provide to locals disregards the fact that communities engage in relations that help produce rivers, as examined in the first part of this book. This is why, in a framework where rivers are seen as an element of the natural world in need of protection, the compromised existence of *fieras* or aquatic spirits can only be accepted—and therefore defended—as a cultural belief about rivers, but not as beings that actually populate the rivers. Such an approach can provide only minimal reparation to the lifeworlds of human and other-than-human local communities.

In the ruling, the Atrato River is depicted through page after page as a key natural resource that offers all that is needed "to reproduce life and recreate culture" (Corte Constitucional de Colombia ¶1: 3). Moreover, the language of rights does not merely acknowledge the de facto existence of a river in need of conservation, protection, maintenance, and restoration. Rather, the ruling creates a new subject, a new kind of legal person that, stabilized ontologically as a "natural resource," "environment," or "nature," comes to share partial connections (Strathern 2004) with the kind of being that local communities meet in their daily lives. This stabilization can never account for the multiplicity of rivers that people meet in their daily lives, as the experiences with *palizadas*, *fieras*, or *madres de agua* demonstrate. In this sense the kind of personhood the ruling ascribes to the river is more prescriptive than descriptive: the court's decision presents what the river ought to be (a natural resource in good health) but not the kind of being that local communities recognize. But to be fair, rendering intelligible the kind of being the river is should be one of the tasks that the guardians eventually address (Cagüeñas, Galindo, and Rasmussen 2020), one that, following the kind of "polyphonic sensibility" (Castillo 2020, 252) that the river and its other-than-human beings propitiate, would allow to the river modes of expression that are not reducible to either those specific to the human or those allocated to natural resources.

When bringing to attention how the traditional productive practices of local communities have helped preserve "the natural and ecological heritage of the Nation" (Corte Constitucional de Colombia ¶5.28), the court aims to reinforce a version of the river aligned with the principles of sustainable development, which ends up resonating with that too-modern tendency of seeing constituents of the natural world such as mountains or lakes as containers of life but not as beings themselves. Let me be clear. The protection of rights of Indigenous and Afro-Colombian peoples through either the recognition of the rights of the Atrato River or of their territories as victims of armed violence is a way to enforce the interdependency that exists between these communities and their traditional territories. However, conceiving of rivers as resources in need of protection and not as beings in their own right leads us back to that modern tenet that separates life and being from nonlife and matter. Here I refer to the ideas of Elizabeth Povinelli (2015, 2016) on geontological power, a form of power that she identifies as the real trademark of modern governance.

Povinelli (2016) explains that the ontology through which "being" has been traditionally understood is, as a matter of fact, a bio-ontology: one that reinstates the idea of life as the capacity to grow, reproduce, change continually, and die. Within this ontology, life is heavily grounded on a "carbon imaginary": life is dependent on biological processes made up of chemical reactions sustained by carbon, the chemical element most abundant on Earth. Within this construct, biological life is dependent on the being's ability to give birth, reproduce, and die, which constitutes the integral differentiation between the living and the inanimate. The category of nonlife lacks all the qualities attributed to life, and this crucial distinction underpins the moral and political calculations of modern states. Unlike biopower, defined as "a power to foster life or disallow it to the point of death" (Foucault 1990, 138), Povinelli argues that geontopower operates through the maintenance "of the self-evident distinction between life and nonlife" (2015, 429). Because of this foundational distinction, all those existences associated with the realm of *geo*—earth, rocks, water—are described as susceptible to being consumed, depleted, or exhausted but never killed. Thus they have a political and ethical standing that allows for particular procedures for their accumulation and exploitation—and in some cases their preservation, but only insofar as they provide for human life. The point is that when the law follows the so-called eco-centric approach, it effectively calls into question human superiority over other forms of life, but it misses the opportunity to let other forms of existence dispute the taken-for-granted difference between *bio* and *geo*, life and nonlife, being and resource (Povinelli 2015, 441). In its place, the rights granted to the river just extend the forms, modes of engagement, and relations that already exist within the modern framework, saturating in this way the Atrato River with a set of familiar ontological qualities that strengthen its standing as a natural resource.

As progressive as the ruling might seem, it still operates within a framework in which the river is essentially conceived of as a natural resource in need of adequate stewardship, not as an existence whose ontological status should be reconsidered. I do not pretend to argue that the lives of *fieras* or rivers should be equated with human life, only that by actualizing the divide between beings and their environing worlds, the law misses the opportunity to call into question the too-modern way of thinking that places human modes, qualities, and forms of being at the hierarchical apex through which other modalities of being are then asserted. I therefore wonder if awarding rights to the Atrato River is the best way of protecting *fieras* and other similar forms of existence, given the fact that within the current multicultural framework, the reality embodied by these beings cannot be asserted as anything more than a cultural belief. Ultimately, what is at stake with *fieras* or *madres de agua*, as well as with rivers, is not something that people believe in or something that people have but something that *is,* something whose particular modalities of existence render people—and rivers—what they are.

To a certain degree, the law becomes a subtle form of ontological occupation (Escobar 2015). The recognition of the rights of the Atrato River does not just validate the existence of a set of prerogatives to which rivers have a just claim; rather, the law captures the local lifeworlds of rivers and peoples by using the cultural, political, economic, material, spatial, and temporal patterns of a rights framework. This framework allows us to grieve and care for a vital resource that enriches the life of local communities, but the language of rights and their universal pretensions does not challenge the modern cultural assumptions of those political systems that do not allow us to conceive of, or relate with, rivers other than as natural resources. In other words, by deploying a discourse of rights and a set of policies for their reinforcement, the law inadvertently diminishes the possibilities of relating with, and being accountable for, other-than-human beings, including rivers, in ways that are not prescribed by modern legal systems. The rights framework disregards the set of local relations that renders possible, for example, the existence of *fieras* or *madres de agua*, relations that, as I have explained, resist the translation of these beings into cultural beliefs and of rivers into mere natural resources. To put it in another way, the rights framework might end up obliterating some of the earnest endeavors of human and other-than-human existences to be and exist otherwise. To effectively protect the lives that the Atrato River embodies, the granting of rights may prove insufficient if the ontology of the legal system does not change. In sum, by recognizing the Atrato as a legal person, the court intends to portray the river as something different than a resource to meet human needs, yet by leaving unquestioned the categories that sustain the idea of rights and foregrounding the *bio* at the expense of the *geo*, the court in fact simply creates another type of natural resource, a resource with a thin varnish of person (I. Vargas 2021).

Although to protect, preserve, maintain, and restore the river is the best way the court found to defend the rights of Indigenous and Afro-Colombian communities, the ruling gave very little space to the discussion of the actual content of this river's rights, which gives rise to questions about when or under what circumstances the river's rights should be protected or how far its rights will reach (Macpherson 2019). For example, is it only in relation to its material status as a natural resource that the river should be protected? What about the impact that intangible and yet powerful forces such as spirits, the dead, or *fieras* may have? And who should be held accountable for large-scale threats, such as climate change or global markets, that are not easily localizable? What if some riverine communities see their own human rights jeopardized on account of, let us say, the right that the Atrato may have to flow? But the fact that the ruling does not give content to the actual rights of the river is not wrong per se because it opens up the possibility for local communities, through the guardians of the river, to give visibility to the kinds of beings they meet in their daily lives to those who just see a natural resource.

In a place where the very lives of Afro-Colombian and Indigenous peoples are overwhelmingly subjugated to various forms of necropower, a power that deploys war in the interest of maximum destruction, defining "who matters and who does not, who is *disposable* and who is not" (Mbembe 2003, 27), and where the lives sustained by these territories are deemed, in the best of cases, to not be grievable enough (Butler 2009), a law that recognizes the rights of a river should be celebrated for what it enables—the safeguard of a vital constituent of people's territories and the protection of the human lives entangled with it—and not for what it forecloses. It is also important to recognize the kind of generative political space that the court's decision creates, for it also has the potential to reinvent what philosopher Jacques Rancière refers to as "the commons." This idea refers here not so much to the set of shared material goods accessible to all members of a given society as to the political configuration through which "some affairs are seen as common affairs and subjects are given the capacity to deal with those affairs" (Rancière 2012, ¶1). To Rancière, the commons is simultaneously all that people share in common in relation to a given element (for example, a river and the realization of how important it is to sustain the life of people) and the rhetorical and aesthetic "system of self-evident facts of sense perception" (Rancière 2000, 12) by virtue of which some properties of this element are foreclosed (for example, the regimes of truth that render said river a natural resource but not a living being). Precisely, seeing rivers as legal persons allows new subjects to irrupt and to become matters of public concern, opening spaces in the political arena to "new voices to appear and to be heard" (Rancière 2010, 60). Along these lines, territories recognized as rightful victims of war and rivers endowed with an ethical standing make visible that which, until then, had no reason to be seen; they force a new distribution of the sensible by provoking a perceptual alteration and therefore a political rearrangement about "what is seen and what can be said," about "who has the ability to see and the talent to speak" (Rancière 2004, 13), about a language in which "what was only audible as noise" starts "to be heard as speech" (Rancière 2011, Thesis 8). It is in this way that *madres de agua*, spirits, or *fieras* might reach a political status in which their lives matter for how they enrich the world and not just for what they represent within particular worldviews.

More than simply finding ways of turning human-environment relationships into more sustainable endeavors, what would be at stake in this new "commons" would be the generation of conditions through which rivers and forests (and their modes of expression) find their place within the public sphere as persons whose interests and concerns may overcome those of the communities living near and in them. Because the recognition of the personhood of rivers or of territories as victims cannot be an end in itself, but rather a means to establish a common ground in which the worlds of Indigenous peoples, modern institutions, and *terrivertories* may converge, at least partially, it is important to draw ethnographic attention to the sphere of the local relationships and stories that have conferred, in the first place, a status to rivers as something other than natural streams of water and a status of territory as more than a piece of land used for cultural reproduction. *Fi-*

eras, madres de agua, palizadas, as well as jaguars, rubble, wandering spirits, and the material and onto-epistemic conditions through which all of them emerge, may provide some of the necessary elements to design the political field where that common world can be forged.

Although the ruling that gives rights to the Atrato River depicts the relationship between this river and people as one of intimate interconnections, it does so in a way that still conceives of river and people as two discrete domains. But the heart of the relations between humans and the other-than-humans inhabiting the river is not interconnectedness—which is the tenet of the eco-centric approach employed by the legal system—but rather co-constitution and co-emergency: the very modes of being through which each of them exist become the condition of each other's flourishing. Political and ethical considerations of existences such as those of rivers or *fieras* should therefore not radically differ from the considerations of recognizable other-than-human forms of life, such as some animals, mainly because the potentiality of being that Indigenous and Afro-Colombian communities define as true and estimable for themselves is hardly conceivable without the existence of entities like *fieras,* spirits, or rivers.

Even if the ruling that recognizes the Atrato River's rights provides only limited legal personhood to this constituent of Indigenous and Afro-Colombian territories, it nevertheless provides us with a series of elements that should be taken into consideration when enforcing any transitional justice policy. If recognition of the territory as a victim was an important cornerstone in the decolonization of certain paradigms of transitional justice, allowing for the inclusion of damage that war causes to other-than-humans, the granting of rights to the Atrato River may help translate into public policy the necessary actions to redress the destruction inflicted on *Bajoatrateño* territories. Transitional justice offers thus a historic opportunity to reconcile in a single framework of practices—by which I mean practices of reparation—what modernity has stubbornly maintained as two divergent ontological domains: nature and culture, *kósmos* (the inherent and objective) and *pólitikos* (the instituted and social). But for this to happen, a truly diplomatic gesture is needed, one in which, by letting forests, rivers, and people flourish in their relentless entanglements, *terrivertories* come to inhabit the realm of modern politics as something other than physical enclosures that enable biological and cultural life. In this way, justice and reparations would be enacted as part of a large "ecology of selves" (Kohn 2013) or "meshwork of lifeworlds" (I. Vargas 2021) capable of accounting for the kinds of harm that diverse forms of geontopower and biopower have provoked.

Uncommon Diplomacy

Demands for justice for the harm done to territories and their other-than-human dwellers have been articulated in other Latin American contexts. In Ecuador the Inter-American Court of Human Rights accepted the testimony of a spiritual leader (*yachak*) who spoke on behalf of the spirits affected by seismic exploration in Sarayaku, in the Amazon, as evidence of the damage caused by oil companies to the living forest (*Kawsak Sacha*) (Melo 2014). In a scenario of transitional justice, the Mayan Q'eqchi' peoples in Guatemala raised concerns about the poor health with which both their corn and poultry grew years after the repressive campaigns carried out by military death squads during the dictatorship of General Rios Montt (Izquierdo and Viaene 2018; McAllister and Nelson 2013). In Colombia the Special Jurisdiction for Peace (JEP), which is the post-conflict transitional justice system created as part of the peace agreement with the FARC, explicitly promotes "harmonization of the territory" as a means to achieve reconciliation and healing between victims and perpetrators (Jurisdicción Especial para la Paz 2018, General Regulation, Art. 44). In a more recent case, the JEP Chamber for Recognition of the Truth—a body responsible for investigating the most emblematic cases of Colombia's long war—resolved in January 2020 that the territories of the Afro-Colombian and Awá people living in Nariño, as well as the territory of Nasa peoples in Cauca, should be recognized as victims of armed conflict, meaning that these territories have the same rights to justice, truth, reparation, and guarantees of nonrepetition that every victim formally has. All of these are examples not of demands made in the name of respect for the worldviews embodied by Indigenous peoples but of attempts to incorporate Indigenous perspectives into the realm of law and, through this, to promote open discussions about the kinds of realities that are at stake once the human is decentralized as the only possible locus of law and rights.

Both the recognition of the territory as a victim and the granting of rights to the Atrato River are the seeds of what might become a powerful diplomatic arrangement, particularly because these legal arrangements force into visibility that modern onto-epistemic constraint which deters the possibility of seeing rivers and forests as anything other than the background of human will. As argued before, diplomacy is not merely a compromise intended to eliminate antagonisms; after all, antagonism, as Chantal Mouffe recalls it, is an inherent condition of politics, understood as the practices that seek "to establish a certain order and organize human coexistence in conditions that are always potentially conflictual" (2000, 101). Instead, a diplomatic event produces a "positive pluralism" (Stengers, in Zournazi 2002, 261), bringing about a specific set of practices and obligations under which each involved party—the state and *Chocoano* communities, for example—is capable of entertaining its own version of an agreement without surrendering their values and the attachments that these values generate (Stengers 2005b). In this way, when redressing the damage undergone by the territory in Bajo Atrato the diplomatic entente would allow the state to repair the harm that local communities situate in more-than-human worlds while allowing Indigenous and Afro-Colombian peoples to voice their painful experiences of war in a way that is not constrained by the expressions that the language of human and environmental rights has created. Diplomatic agreements should then be the foundation on which transitional justice, with its aim of enhancing the participation of the most vulnerable and promoting the fair reparation of past wrongs, is built. The diplomatic arrangement that both the Victims' Law and the decision of the Colombian Constitutional Court embody is not an end in and of itself but a means to establish a common ground in which the worlds of Indigenous peoples and modern institutions may, at least partially, converge and find a common course of action. But for transitional justice to become a true diplomatic agreement, modern states and mainstream society must transform their ethical obligations and underlying practices, thereby generating the conditions of possibility under which humans may appropriately inhabit that damaged world that we share with many kinds of more-than-human others.

The diplomatic momentum that arose out of the consideration of Indigenous territories as victims of armed conflict has contributed to bringing into the public arena the effects of war upon the environment. Based on the idea that the environment has been both backdrop and victim of the long war waged in Colombia, new interest in understanding both war's environmental impacts and the way that land and natural resources fuel the conflict have arisen. "Nature," said the minister of environment and sustainable development in 2017, "was a silent victim of the conflict" (Rodríguez 2017). This opinion, also shared even by the JEP Chamber for Investigation and Accusation (JEP 2019), encapsulates the way the damage that war produces in more-than-human worlds is currently being addressed by state institutions: an atomistic and passive nature in need of rescue. Even if it is true that key ecosystems and protected areas have been theaters of military operations, that the exploitation of natural resources has contributed to filling armed actors' pockets, or that pollution and biodiversity loss often succeed war, the damage undergone in Indigenous and Afro-Colombian territories is far from being limited to the environmental sphere, as the previous chapters have demonstrated. Even though the consideration of the environment as a victim may help dislocate the anthropocentrism that characterizes most of the current understanding of war, locating the harm in a "silent nature" reproduces an onto-epistemic divide that, endowing the declarations of *palizadas*, jaguars, or *rastrojos* with a status of noise rather than voice, does not necessarily account for what happens in places like Bajo Atrato.

Considering that in its execution, impetus, and aftermaths, war is seldom an exclusively human experience, different scholarly approaches have been tackling the environmental impacts associated with war preparation and postwar activities (Machlis and Hanson 2008), the ecological footprint of warfare and the military-industrial complex (Belcher et al. 2020; Crawford 2019), the kind of relations and beings that arise out of ruined ecologies and heavily polluted places (Masco 2004), and the inclusion of animal and vegetal species as loci of militarized destruction (Johnson 2019; Pugliese 2020). However, emphasizing the environmental pole of the nature-culture divide or enlarging the community of beings harmed by war might prove insufficient to grasp the accumulative, entangled, hybrid, and rhizomatic effects of armed violence, especially if, when discussing community, we insist on setting distinctions between the realms of *bio* and *geo* or between these and the spiritual worlds. This is why I have relied on a framework that, acknowledging the living arrangements that human and other-than-human subjectivities undertake in Bajo Atrato, has allowed me to move my ethnographic description away from the nature-culture divide. I am convinced that detouring this divide is the first step to doing full justice to the experiences that Indigenous and Afro-Colombian communities derive from their territories.

I first met Lewis in 2003. At the time, I was working with a human rights organization, and I was on my way to a hamlet located next to the Gengadó River, where communities from all over Bajo Atrato were organizing a regional meeting to discuss political strategies for limiting the effects of armed violence. We had stopped at Carmen del Darién, a small town by the Atrato River, to announce to the local youth committee that we would be holding a meeting with them in the coming days. The committee was in the middle of a rehearsal, preparing their traditional dances for the coming festivities. Lewis was playing drums, leading the band while several young people danced around them. When we arrived, the music and the dance livened up. This was the way they welcomed us. I was amazed by the rhythm and the grace of those sweaty bodies. When they finished, I was introduced to Lewis and shook the callused and blistered hand of a proficient drummer and hard-working fisherman. He was the leader of the youth committee, a role he had assumed shortly after the paramilitaries had caused the forced disappearance of one of his older brothers in 2000. That was not the first loved one that Lewis's family had lost because of war. Sometime before the disappearance of his brother, another of his older brothers had been taken away and his stepfather killed, also by paramilitaries. Eight years before this tragedy, guerrillas had killed his grandfather. Before that, his mother's brother and his father's cousin had been victims of the armed conflict. This long list of deaths continued to grow after we met. In 2009 his brother Manuel, a social leader with whom I was friendly, was tortured and killed by the FARC guerrillas. Along with Manuel, his friend Graciano and Jair, a fourteen-year-old boy, were also killed. Those deaths still pain me. The last time I saw Lewis in 2016, I gave him a couple of photos I had taken of Manuel and asked him to give one to his mother, Socorro. I was not in the mood to pay her a visit and bring a gift that would likely open a poorly healed wound.

In an interview Lewis granted to a journalist at the end of 2017, after having participated in a workshop on reconciliation and transitional justice, he described the unflagging struggle that his community and his own family have undertaken to stay in their ancestral territory. Despite their losses and the fear provoked by the two forced displacements of which they were victims, they had always managed to return to their lands and rivers. They knew that their presence in their homeland and in their *homeriver* was the only means to keep both themselves and the territory alive. "Our main victory," said Lewis, "has been staying in our territory, because without people, everything will be at the mercy of obscure forces" (*Espectador* 2017b). What a triumph it is indeed to find thousands of Indigenous and Afro-Colombian families holding their ground and resiliently facing the violence of war and poverty because without communities taking care of places, cultivating values, nurturing existences, and fostering worlds, there would be no territory at all. That has been the duty of Lewis, his ancestors, and his kin as long as the rivers have flowed and the forests have grown. What a triumph it is indeed to stay alive despite an overwhelming war machine that has employed all means to destroy the modes of being that these peoples embody. Because without Indigenous and Afro-Colombian peoples, Bajo Atrato would be but a piece of land ready to be ravaged by obscure forces. At the same time, without territory, deprived of the care and nurturing it provides and of the possibilities of being it enables, Lewis and all his kin would possibly become simple folk, perhaps the kind of ordinary mainstream citizens imagined by the Colombian state before the right to cultural difference was granted to Afro-Colombians in 1991.

The day I met Lewis and his later interview reveal two powerful aspects of life in Bajo Atrato. On one hand, our first encounter reveals to what extent music, dance, party, ritual, and carnival are not just essential components of daily life but, in many cases, a condition for political organization, as I was reminded later in that hamlet near the Gengadó River during the festivities that followed the creation of the Great Community Council of Bajo Atrato (ASCOBA). More importantly, when a youth committee rehearses its performance even during the armed occupation of their land, one is struck by the fact that war, despite its pervasiveness and overwhelming power, is not the only force organizing people's lives. It is erroneous to assume that violence shapes the repertoire of people's actions, as if Indigenous and Afro-Colombian communities have simply constructed their lives for the purposes of responding to the evils embodied by armed groups and colonial forces. This is my critique against some of the research on violence among Afro-

Colombian and Indigenous populations, and the way I have found to demarcate my work from other research that has made armed conflict the bread and butter of its ethnographic inquiry. I hope my writing reflects my resistance to the temptation to reify violence, by which I mean to make it an analytical ground from which all conclusions are drawn. What I have done instead is to render war one of the possible forces shaping the set of social relations that, in Bajo Atrato, are made of human and other-than-human entanglements.

On the other hand, Lewis's words—without us, the territory would be exposed to murky forces—contain great power because they accurately capture how people and their practices contribute to bringing territory into existence, conveying the idea that territory is always verging on the actual, something in continual production. That has been precisely the approach of this book: territory is an aggregation of relations rather than something that merely grounds human practices; it is an intersection of human and other-than-human assemblages weaving together a collectivity of life able to flourish, if I can borrow Povinelli's poetic words, through "the coordination" of their own "habits of being" (2016, 138). More a "domain of entanglement" (Ingold 2006, 14) than a substance, more an event than a passive recipient of people's will, territory is constantly made and remade; it is simultaneously constituted by human and other-than-human selves, and it is what results from the very act of their assembling. That considered, one might state that beings—human and other-than-human—and the territory itself are in every instance of each relation a different kind of entity. A territory that is not homogeneous but multifarious is therefore vulnerable to many presences on many scales. This is why *palizadas* and oil-palm monocultures are not just producing environmental damage, or why the wrath of *madres de agua* and the restlessness of spirits are not just collective traumas wrapped in the language of cultural beliefs. Forced displacement, as I have shown, goes beyond the threat against the human rights of Indigenous and Afro-Colombian peoples: without the warmth that human presence and labor create, places decayed, and animals were marooned; without communities taking care of their rivers, the waters diverged, floods became a constant, and forests and rivers disappeared. The effects provoked by the abandonment of fond places shows to what extent the territory was left, as anthropologist Angela Lederach beautifully expresses it, "to cry out for her people" (2017, 593). This cry is but the realization of how communities and their territories, along with their different more-than-human constituents, become the possibility for each other's existence. In a scenario of transitional justice, where the experience of victims is put at the center of what circulates within the public sphere (Sotelo 2020), failure to recognize this existential co-constitutionality between human and other-than-human beings, or a stubborn maintenance of the divide between people and their enmeshed worlds, can only provoke more harm to Indigenous and Afro-Colombian peoples and make it harder to redress the suffering contained within their territories.

If we agree that territory emanates from the relations that different beings entertain, then in the context of justice and reparations, rather than simply restoring things to a former state or position, what should be repaired is the set of relations that favor the coming into existence of said territory. This is why "flow" and its instantiations are common threads throughout this book. Flow, as Hugh Raffles (2014, 100) reminds us, is not "extraneous and abstractable from existence," meaning that flow is material, too: the changes in the flow of rivers, as well as the impossibilities that people face when trying to *embarcar*—that is, to travel and circulate—are the main problems resulting from *palizadas*, showing that flow is not only a condition of rivers but also is their very form; it is the shape that rivers' flow adopts that favors the presence of *fieras*; it is because of the lack of circulation of people and their warmth that the rot found a fertile ground to spread and produce ruins and rubble; it is the incapacity of flowing with the rhythms of life and death that turned dead people into spirits stagnating in space and time. Flow leads us also to consider that the places that compose these territories can be conceptualized as moments in the organization of things (Ingold 1993). Take into account, once again, dammed rivers, trails doomed to perdition, abandoned gardens, and decayed houses. All of them are arrangements favored by the presence of other-than-human forces such as *palizadas*, *rastrojos*, and *avichuchos*. By keeping these presences at bay, people show that, through daily practices of care and work, they may insert themselves into these arrangements, favoring versions of their territories that are most amenable to human endeavors. But when there is a change in the usual disposition and flow of the elements that compose a given arrangement (like an agglomeration of the beings that people tend to consider pernicious, such as wasps, cockroaches, weeds), new kinds of places emerge.

Considering the role that other-than-human forces play in the making and unmaking of places, one realizes that the obscure powers Lewis refers to are not just of a political, economic, or military nature, even if socioeconomic, cultural, and environmental transformations are some of their most evident manifestations. The occupation of Bajo Atrato by the war machine unleashed a series of events that overturned the possibilities of being and becoming that humans and other-than-humans had historically profited from in these territories. This is why the most fundamental dimension of the struggles of Indigenous and Afro-Colombian peoples in defense of their territories is ontological: these peoples are not just defending something they have but also an entity with whom their very way of being becomes possible. This ontological dimension is palpable when one examines the difficulties that these communities face in enacting their own worlds—those that exist beyond the dominant world-building practices of modernity—as well as when one becomes aware of the transformations that war has produced in ecologies made of human and other-than-human entanglements. Specifically, the transformation of the world-making arrangements that humans and other-than-humans entertain—often exhibiting care and reciprocity, sometimes animosity and contention, but always wonder and mutual recognition—comes to define the qualities of places and the possibilities that their inhabitants, human and otherwise, find to dwell there together.

The damage of war tends to exceed the kind of deterministic aims so often ascribed to the actions perpetrated by armed actors. Not all violence is instrumental, nor are all the forces capable of transforming the qualities of these peoples' territories external in their origin or imposed by alien presences. Dammed rivers, restless ghostly presences, wandering evil spirits, and wicked jaguars are afterlives of war, no doubt. However, *palizadas*, jaguars, *fieras*, spirits, and *madres de agua* were all present prior to the armed violence in this region. By this I mean that these are presences that belong to the ordinary world of these peoples and with which they have learned to coexist or, in some cases, to keep at bay. These are the kinds of existences that, without the presence of people—as Lewis's powerful statement suggests—would have made Bajo Atrato a quite different kind of territory. What is new in the context of war is a disruptive arrangement of forces, an arrangement that amplifies their destructive propensities and their potential estrangement from their worlds (like *madres de agua*), from their own former selves (like the jaguar), or from fellow humans (like the spirits of Caño Claro). This amplification, this excess, is what causes forest and river ecologies to run amok and is what ultimately leads us to consider the territory as a victim. And it is in this respect that concepts such as human rights violations, trauma, and environmental damage account for only part of what people and territories have experienced.

I have shown that the recognition of Indigenous territories as victims (an unprecedented move in the jurisprudence of war) ought to mean more than simply assuring the full enjoyment of the land-ownership rights that these peoples are entitled to. Such recognition has in fact paved the way for Indigenous and Afro-Colombian organizations to put into evidence the flaws of modern and anthropocentric conceptualization of victimization and to reaffirm that when war hits their territories, the violent transformation of the very conditions through which human and other-than-human beings flourish and sustain their mutually constituted lives are at stake. This realization compels us to consider a form of justice in which the framework of human rights and its human-centrism is problematized. War has without doubt compromised human and environmental rights, but something in the way Indigenous and Afro-Colombian peoples experience harm exceeds these rights-based frameworks, mainly because the myriad beings affected stand in a relation to the domains of nature and culture in a way that cannot be framed in terms of either "and" or "or" (de la Cadena 2016). In this same vein, rivers and forests embody forms of being whose modes of expression cannot be reducible to those that modern ontology allocates to them as natural resources (or containers of life, at best). When considered in relational and emergentist terms, the rivers and forests that constitute Indigenous and Afro-Colombian territories (or *terrivertories*) become assemblages of emplaced relationships that resist containment within the borders that the legal system has set up for them.

In the legal arena, the struggles that Indigenous and Afro-Colombian social organizations have undertaken to get their territories recognized as victims of armed conflict should not necessarily result in new rights for the affected beings. The language of rights is not ecological enough, for it is strongly embedded in a liberal conception of the individual, enacting a neat separation between beings and the material environments with which they are entangled, as well as overlooking the lively relationalities through which humans, places, and other-than-humans are mutually constituted and emerge as large communities of life (Schlosberg 2014). In this way, policies of reparation are not reducible to those specific to the human. In the context of transitional justice, intended to redress the legacies of past wrongs against Indigenous and Afro-Colombian communities and their territories, failure to consider other-than-human beings will simply reproduce a hegemonic approach to justice heavily embedded within colonial structures.

A legal arrangement like the one that confers legal personhood to the Atrato River brings to the fore the importance of extending moral and ethical considerations to these other existences with whom Afro-Colombian and Indigenous peoples' modes of being are so entangled. But the recognition of the Atrato as a bearer of rights, or of territory as victim, might not really challenge the human-culture divide that remains pervasive in the legal framework if the ontological characteristics that locals give to entities, including forests and rivers, are not incorporated into reparation practices. The recognition of the suffering experienced by other-than-human beings is indispensable to the decolonization of justice and to the design of reparations capable of extending beyond humanitarian assistance and rights restitution. If reparation policies are embedded within a multicultural framework that putatively accommodates the plurality of existing cultural representations of the world, the type of damage invoked by Indigenous and Afro-Colombian communities would continue to be confined to the world of their beliefs, meaning that damage to territory would say nothing "real" about the suffering of the territory itself and much less about the impacts upon spirits, man-eating jaguars, or *madres de agua* because none of these entities "really" exist, at least not in the way a modern state understands their existence. By embracing difference within a matrix of knowledge where things and events are allocated to either the realm of nature or of culture, the multicultural state circumscribes the possible forms of expression that Indigenous and Afro-Colombian peoples may adopt, foreclosing the possibility that this "difference" has to challenge both the terms that modern institutions mobilize to define damage and the power-laden structures that sustain its means of reparation. If, within the multicultural paradigm, living *terrivertories* are only allowed to exist as sociocultural constructions, transitional justice institutions will have a great deal of difficulty delivering a form of justice attuned to the experiences that these peoples derive from their territories.

The kinds of ecologies disrupted, but also created, by the latent damaging forces associated with irregular warfare are what constitute afterlives: the effects of war engraved upon ecologies made of human and more-than-human entanglements, as well as the way these effects unfold in the emplaced arrangements whereby entities forge their own habits of being. Afterlives are accretive, ramify in many directions and at different intervals, affecting collectivities of life in ways that are not always obvious. As with *madres de agua*, man-eating jaguars, or *fieras*, people face a violence that does not follow any simple path, that cannot be easily mapped, whose effects cannot be assigned to any single correspondence, and that ends up intensifying, in multiple ways, prior forms of vulnerability and precarity. Afterlives are incremental in that they leave in their wakes a form of harm that stays with people and more-than-human beings long after the destructive actions carried out by armies are over. Take *palizadas*, rubble, military remnants, and wandering spirits. They all embody a form of violence that is not immediate or focused around one single event. Afterlives also show how hybrid and multiple war is. Consider the violence that wicked jaguars, witness trees, evil spirits, or even abandoned villages represent. This is a hybrid and a heterogeneous violence because it brings together apparently disconnected realms: the natural and the fabricated, the human and the nonhuman, the tangible and the invisible, the vibrant beings of living forests and the ruinous materialities of warfare. Because they are multiple and hybrid, afterlives are not always bound within bodies, which means that their effects are mainly traced through the associations woven between two or more subjects. Take, for instance, the way that the death of soldiers who had harassed and displaced local communities transformed the attributes of places and the possibilities the living found to dwell in them. This transformation also illustrates the rhizomatic logic of war: the always ramified, interwoven, and yet elusive ways in which violence sits and propagates in *Bajoatrateño* territories. In sum, afterlives show that war cannot be understood as a singular, well-demarcated event because its effects are widely distributed: in time it is slow and elongated, in space it is derivative, and among assemblages of beings it is ecological. In the context of poverty, structural forms of racism, and high marginalization in which Indigenous and Afro-Colombian lives are so entrenched, the afterlives of war become what Naveeda Khan calls "threat multipliers" (2016, 190), instances of a violence that exacerbate issues of vulnerability, precarity, and dispossession.

Afterlives compel us to reconsider conceptually what war and wartime are, as well as the common grounds—material and otherwise—for understanding and redressing their legacy. International humanitarian law and jurisprudence have tried to humanize war through the creation of a vast set of norms to regulate the means and methods of warfare, taking into consideration moral concerns about how to not inflict unnecessary pain and suffering on both combatants and civilians (Bartelson 2018). Although warfare tends to expose the most barbarous aspects of the human condition, the efforts to minimize suffering have made hostile enemies into subjects of humane treatment without canceling their antagonisms. The nonanthropocentric and ecological approach to war I advocate might be seen as another attempt to humanize war, but not merely through the incorporation of other-than-humans as subjects of moral concern. As Jane Bennett (2010) and Karen Barad (2011) argue, the aim of considering humans and other-than-humans together is not just to eliminate ontological distinctions in order to reach a perfect equality among all of us, but to open new venues for being and living in this shared world. Similarly, what I have attempted here is to situate these other-than-human beings as actors whose interests and concerns may make and unmake humans and propel us in new directions. Tainted felines, ruinous *palizadas*, fierce *fieras*, and wicked spirits should not be perceived as exotic anomalies experienced by radical others who belong to an incomparable place apart. Quite the opposite. They compel us to see the worlds to which we humans give life in entangled and emplaced forms, and to see how any human act of destruction always carries seeds capable of altering the course of many other-than-human lives.

The legal fight for the recognition of the harm inflicted upon Indigenous and Afro-Colombian territories is a struggle that these peoples undertake in order to render more fluid the means by which the territory is produced as a matter of public concern. At stake is the expansion of who the territory's legitimate interlocutors might be, as well as of the means and expressions that can be used to convey the harm inflicted upon these whole ecologies. A shift from the violations of the human rights of Indigenous and Afro-Colombian communities to the disruption of ecologies made of human and other-than-human entanglements might also imply a change in politics, something akin to what Elizabeth Grosz (2002) describes as a shift from a politics of identity (a politics of recognition and identity formation through the affirmation of the culture that others embody, in this case Indigenous and Afro-Colombian peoples) to a politics of responsibility toward the imperceptible: a politics concerned with events, forces, entanglements, and the impersonal, in this case ecologies and assemblages. This would thus entail a kind of politics in which what is central is the being of becoming rather than the becoming of being (Grosz 2002, 466).

The becoming of being, with its emphasis on the politics of recognition and identity, has become the emblem of modern multiculturalism (Taylor 1992), for it acknowledges the worth of distinct cultural traditions and the collective identities shaped by ethnicity, race, religion, or sexuality. Facing the challenge of including damage that Indigenous and Afro-Colombian peoples locate in their traditional territories, the Colombian multicultural state aims to be sensitive to the territorial realities harmed by war, but it does so mainly by strengthening the rights of these ethno-cultural communities. This is but a way of tying all cultural difference to epistemological difference and reifying nature and culture as two divergent ontological domains. The recognition of territory as victim calls into question the way that the multicultural state tends to conflate certain experiences regarding territories with particular ethnic identities. This means that the afterlives of war involving and affecting the set of relationships that people cultivate with the living places they inhabit is not an experience circumscribed to those ethnic groups that the Colombian state recognizes as legitimate others (Indigenous and Afro-Colombian peoples in this case). In fact, war has been an experience shared by many rural, peasant societies who are officially excluded from the framework of ethnic rights and cultural recognition. The relational framework I have adopted in this book and its emphasis on what I just described as the being of becoming might help us track how certain meanings and experiences arise as a consequence of certain practices, of the cultivation of particular sensitivities and ways of relating with the living world, which are not necessarily confined to certain ethnic identities. Last, and although the legal system does not consider it, the possibility of experiencing the territory as a victim is a kind of experience that transcends any of the social conditions that the multicultural state has recognized only for certain ethno-cultural affiliations.

If the war waged in the forests and rivers of Bajo Atrato shows to what extent our own human lives are existentially entangled with other sets of beings, this violence should then compel us to be aware of the many extra-human elements that must be present in any effort to deliver justice and build lasting peace. Because the afterlives of war require that we think about territory in terms of ecologies made of co-constitutional beings and emergent relationalities, we must therefore also think of justice in these terms. And this, once again, does not entail any kind of symmetrical correspondence between the rights of human and other-than-human entities, or the blurring of all their ontological differences. Rather, it is an attempt to lay the foundations of a polity (Jane Bennett 2010) or a *demos* (Povinelli 2015) in which a new arrangement of the "common" is possible (Rancière 2000): a political system with new ethical sensibilities toward, and more venues of communication between, its human and other-than-human members. This common, which might or might not coincide with the interests of that majority often described as "we the people," waits to be created. But in order to arise in a way that would let life flourish, it must be composed in the company of those other-than-human agents that participate in the making of a more humane and cosmopolitan life. Indigenous and Afro-Colombian peoples have shown us that such an arrangement is not only already possible but that other-than-humans have always made it possible. And transitional justice—which encapsulates the will of a society to establish a new social contract, bringing to the forefront some of the hardest questions regarding politics and law—is an outstanding opportunity to build a new kind of collectivity in which the lives and beings of rivers and forests are allowed to flourish.

Throughout this book I have made a simple argument: what to do in legal and political terms in order to redress the harm inflicted on Indigenous and Afro-Colombian territories depends on what local communities, on one hand, and the Colombian state, on the other, consider the territory to be. Therefore, justice would be delivered according to the kinds of ententes that these actors are capable of achieving. To aid this process, I have broken down certain divides currently pervading most interpretations of war. The after-lives of armed violence in the Bajo Atrato region show how the distinctions between people and their surrounding worlds, subjects and objects, animate and inert, the real and the believed, are not always adequate to understand what has reverberated. More than bringing to light the intimate relationships that people in Bajo Atrato cultivate with their territories and the myriad other-than-human beings that these places harbor—which would simply serve to once again actualize the divide between humans and nature—what I have endeavored here is a depiction of the deep relationalities of being and becom-ing, of life and death, that create territory and in which humans and other-than-humans actively participate. The damage unleashed by war compels us then to reconsider how we do justice to more-than-human worlds and how inadequate a transitional justice framework that reifies that neat multicul-tural distinction between "reality" and the so-called cultural representations of said reality might be. In the face of this, the possibilities of redressing the harm experienced by territorialities made of human and other-than-human entanglements do not reside in the design of new measures to redress the rights of a portrayed "radically exteriorized Other"—Indigenous and Afro-Colombian communities, in this case—but require the cultivation of new forms of responsibility: new abilities to respond to and to account for other forms of more-than-human distinctiveness (Barad 2011; Haraway 2008). The path I followed to address the afterlives of violence in Indigenous and Afro-Colombian territories led me to understand the differential experiences of war not in terms of the cultural frameworks that these peoples mobilize to rep-resent their suffering but in terms of the kinds of worlds that we humans, in the company of beings that call into question our exceptionality, are able to bring into life and live within.

References

ACIA (Consejo Comunitario Mayor de la Asociación Campesina Integral del Atrato). 2002. *Medio Atrato: Territorio de Vida*. Bogotá: Red de Solidaridad Social.

Almario, Oscar. 2001. "'Tras Las Huellas de Los Renacientes: Por El Laberinto de La Etnicidad e Identidad de Los Grupos Negros o 'Afrocolombianos' del Pacífico Sur." In *Acción Colectiva, Estado y Etnicidad en El Pacífico Colombiano*, edited by Mauricio Pardo, 15–39. Bogotá: Instituto Colombiano de Antropología e Historia, Colciencias.

Álvaro, Miriam. 2009. "De Las Armas a La Desmovilización: El Poder Paramilitar en Colombia." *Revista Internacional de Sociología* 67 (1): 59–82.

Alves, Jaime Amparo. 2019. "'Esa Paz Blanca, Esa Paz de Muerte': Peacetime, Wartime, and Black Impossible Chronos in Postconflict Colombia." *Journal of Latin American and Caribbean Anthropology* 24 (3): 653–71.

Alves, Jaime Amparo, and João Costa Vargas. 2017. "On Deaf Ears: Anti-Black Police Terror, Multiracial Protest and White Loyalty to the State." *Identities* 24 (3): 254–74.

Amorth, Gabriele. 1999. *An Exorcist Tells His Story*. San Francisco: Ignatius.

Anderson, Ben. 2009. "Affective Atmospheres." *Emotion, Space and Society* 2 (2): 77–81.

Appelbaum, Nancy. 2016. *Mapping the Country of Regions: The Chorographic Commission of Nineteenth-Century Colombia*. Chapel Hill: University of North Carolina Press.

Arbeláez, Mónica. 2001. "Comunidades de Paz del Urabá Chocoano: Fundamentos Jurídicos y Vida Comunitaria." *Controversia* 177:11–40.

Asher, Kiran. 2009. *Black and Green: Afro-Colombians, Development, and Nature in the Pacific Lowlands*. Durham, NC: Duke University Press.

Azevedo, Fernando, and Dennis Murray. 2007. "Spatial Organization and Food Habits of Jaguars (*Panthera onca*) in a Floodplain Forest." *Biological Conservation* 137:391–402.

Barad, Karen. 2003. "Posthuman Performativity: Towards an Understanding of How Matter Comes to Matter." *Signs* 28 (3): 801–31.

Barad, Karen. 2011. "Nature's Queer Performativity." *Qui Parle* 19 (2): 121–58.

Barnet, Miguel. 1968. *Biography of a Runaway Slave*. Willimantic, CT: Curbstone.

Bartelson, Jens. 2018. *War in International Thought*. Cambridge: Cambridge University Press.

Belcher, Oliver, Patrick Bigger, Ben Neimark, and Cara Kennelly. 2020. "Hidden Carbon Costs of the 'Everywhere War': Logistics, Geopolitical Ecology, and the Carbon Boot-Print of the US." *Transactions of the Institute of British Geographers* 45 (1): 65–80.

Bellows, Jason. 2008. "A Large-Hearted Gentleman." *Damn Interesting*, April 2008. https://www.damninteresting.com/a-large-hearted-gentleman.

Benjamin, Andrew. 2015. *Towards a Relational Ontology: Philosophy's Other Possibility*. Albany: SUNY.

Bennett, Jane. 2001. *The Enchantment of Modern Life: Attachments, Crossings, and Ethics*. Princeton, NJ: Princeton University Press.

Bennett, Jane. 2010. *Vibrant Matter: A Political Ecology of Things*. Durham, NC: Duke University Press.

Bennett, Judith. 2004. "Pests and Disease in the Pacific War: Crossing the Line." In *Natural Enemy, Natural Ally: Toward an Environmental History of War*, edited by Richard Tucker and Edmund Russell, 217–51. Corvallis: Oregon State University Press.

Benson, Elizabeth. 1998. "The Lord, the Ruler: Jaguar Symbolism in the Americas." In *Icons of Power: Feline Symbolism in the Americas*, edited by Nicholas Saunders, 53–76. London: Routledge.

Berger, John. 1980. *About Looking*. New York: Pantheon.

Berque, Augustin. 1987. *Écoumène: Introduction à l'Étude Des Milieux Humains*. Paris: Belin.

Bessire, Lucas, and David Bond. 2014. "Ontological Anthropology and the Deferral of Critique." *American Ethnologist* 41 (3): 440–56.

Beveridge, Candida. 2014. "Face to Face with a Man-Eating Tiger." BBC News, November 12, 2014. https://www.bbc.com/news/magazine-29987187.

Bingham, Nick. 2006. "Bees, Butterflies, and Bacteria: Biotechnology and the Politics of Nonhuman Friendship." *Environment and Planning* 38 (3): 483–98.

Blaser, Mario. 2009. "Political Ontology." *Cultural Studies* 23 (5): 873–96.

Blaser, Mario. 2013a. "Notes towards a Political Ontology of 'Environmental' Conflicts." In *Contested Ecologies: Dialogues in the South on Nature and Knowledge*, edited by Lesley Green, 13–27. Cape Town: HSRC.

Blaser, Mario. 2013b. "Ontological Conflicts and the Stories of People in Spite of Europe." *Cultural Anthropology* 54 (5): 547–68.

Böhme, Gernot. 1993. "Atmosphere as the Fundamental Concept of a New Aesthetics." *Thesis Eleven* 36 (1): 113–26.

Boyd, David. 2017. *Rights of Nature: A Legal Revolution That Could Save the World*. Toronto: ECW.

Brady, Lisa. 2008. "Life in the DMZ: Turning a Diplomatic Failure into an Environmental Success." *Diplomatic History* 32 (4): 585–611.

Braun, Bruce, and Sarah Whatmore. 2010. "The Stuff of Politics: An Introduction." In *Political Matter: Technoscience, Democracy, and Public Life*, edited by Bruce Braun and Sarah Whatmore, ix–xxxviii. Minneapolis: University of Minnesota Press.

Brown, David, and Carlos López. 2001. *Borderland Jaguars: Tigres de La Frontera*. Salt Lake City: University of Utah Press.

Bushnell, David. 1993. *The Making of Modern Colombia: A Nation in Spite of Itself*. Berkeley: University of California Press.

Butler, Judith. 2009. *Frames of War: When Is Life Grievable?* London: Verso.

Cagüeñas, Diego, María Isabel Galindo, and Sabina Rasmussen. 2020. "El Atrato y Sus Guardianes: Imaginación Ecopolítica Para Hilar Nuevos Derechos." *Revista Colombiana de Antropología* 56 (2): 169–96.

CAMAWA (Asociación de Autoridades Wounaan del Pacífico). 2005. *Cosmovisión Wounaan y Siepien*. Docordó: Instituto de Investigaciones Ambientales del Pacífico.

Campbell, Joseph, and Michael Toms. 1990. *An Open Life: Joseph Campbell in Conversation with Michael Toms*. New York: Perennial.

Caracol Radio. 2009. "Alias 'Macaco' cobraba a sus deudores con un león hambriento." March 14, 2009. https://caracol.com.co/radio/2009/03/13/judicial/1236979320_777931 .html.

Carroll, Leah Anne. 2011. *Violent Democratization: Social Movements, Elites, and Politics in Colombia's Rural War Zones, 1984–2008*. Notre Dame, IN: University of Notre Dame Press.

Casey, Edward. 1996. "How to Get from Space to Place in a Fairly Short Stretch of Time." In *Senses of Place*, edited by Steven Feld and Keith Basso, 13–52. Santa Fe: School of American Research Press.

Castaño, Daniel, and Gabriel Ruiz. 2019. "'Con El Jesús en La Boca': Miedo y Vida Cotidiana en Sociedades en Guerra. El Caso de Tumaco (Nariño, Colombia)." *Horizontes Antropológicos* 25 (54): 23–50.

Castillo, Camilo. 2020. "Encuentros Entre Antropología y Estudios de Ciencia y Tecnología en Colombia: Una Respuesta al Dossier 'Conflicto y Paz En Colombia, Más Allá de Lo Humano.'" *Maguaré* 34 (1): 245–67.

Castrillón, Héctor. 1982. *Chocó Indio*. Medellín: Centro Pastoral Indígena.

Castrillón, Héctor. 2010. *Mitos y Tradiciones Chamí*. Medellín: Misioneros Claretianos Provincia Occidental.

Centro Cultural Mama-U. 2002. "El Cuento Afroatrateño: Una Expresión de La Oralitura." *Revista Mama-U* 3:1–28.

Cheucarama, Fidel, Nélson Yabur, and Ciro Pineda. 2006. *Jaibanás, Tongueros y Yerbateros: Sabios Ancestrales Indígenas del Bajo Atrato-Chocó*. Riosucio: Instituto de Investigaciones Ambientales del Pacífico.

Chica Jiménez, Felipe, Paco Gómez Nadal, and Ana Luisa Ramírez Flórez. 2017. *Las Heridas de Riosucio: 1996–2017*. Cali: Universidad Autónoma de Occidente.

Chomsky, Noam. 2006. *Failed States: The Abuse of Power and the Assault of Democracy*. New York: Owl.

CINEP (Centro de Investigación y Educación Popular). 2016. Banco de Datos, Noche y Niebla. Accessed January 26, 2016. https://www.nocheyniebla.org.

Clark, Nigel. 2010. *Inhuman Nature: Sociable Life on a Dynamic Planet*. London: Sage.

Clatterbuck, Wayne. 2011. "Tree Wounds: Response of Trees and What You Can Do." University of Tennessee Extension Publications, no. SP683: 1–5.

Clayton, Philip. 2006. "Conceptual Foundations of Emergence Theory." In *The Reemergence of Emergence: The Emergentist Hypothesis from Science to Religion*, edited by Philip Clayton and Paul Davies, 1–31. Oxford: Oxford University Press.

CNMH (Centro Nacional de Memoria Histórica). 2015. "Indígenas se reúnen en la Sierra Nevada por sus víctimas y la memoria." March 6, 2015.

https://www.centrodememoriahistorica.gov.co/noticias/noticias-cmh/indigenas-se
-reunen-en-la-sierra-nevada-porsus-victimas-y-la-memoria.

Colombiano. 2012. "Polémica por declaraciones de diputado Rodrigo Mesa." May 8,
2012. https://www.elcolombiano.com/historico/rodrigo_mesa_la_plata_que_uno_le
_meta_al_choco_es_como_meterle_un_perfume_a_un_bollo-AVEC_181100.

Comisión Intereclesial de Justicia y Paz. 2005. *La Tramoya: Derechos Humanos y
Palma Aceitera, Curvaradó y Jiguamiandó.* Bogotá: CINEP y Comisión Intereclesial
de Justicia y Paz.

Comisión Intereclesial de Justicia y Paz. 2012. "Taponamiento río Jiguamiandó." YouTube
video, March 12, 2012. https://www.youtube.com/watch?v=UKS4xakNLZ4&spfreload=5.

Contagio Radio. 2015. "Taponamiento del río Jiguamiandó en Chocó afecta a más de
6000 personas." January 30, 2015. https://www.contagioradio.com/taponamiento
-del-rio-jiguamiando-en-choco-afecta-a-mas-de-6000-personas-articulo-4094.

Coole, Diana, and Samantha Frost. 2010. "Introducing the New Materialisms." In *New
Materialisms: Ontology, Agency, and Politics,* edited by Diana Coole and Samantha
Frost, 2–43. Durham, NC: Duke University Press.

Coppola, Francis Ford, dir. 1979. *Apocalypse Now.* Paramount Pictures.

Corbett, Jim. 1946. *Man-Eaters of Kumaon.* New York: Oxford University Press.

Corpourabá. 2015. "Jaguar muerto en el corregimiento del Bocas del Atrato." Accessed
August 2, 2016. http://web.corpouraba.gov.co/jaguar-muerto-en-el-corregimiento-de
-bocas-del-atrato.

Costa, Luiz, and Carlos Fausto. 2010. "The Return of the Animists: Recent Studies of
Amazonian Ontologies." *Religion and Society: Advances in Research* 1:89–109.

Crawford, Neta. 2019. *Pentagon Fuel Use, Climate Change, and the Costs of War.* Provi-
dence: Watson Institute for International and Public Affairs, Brown University.

Cruikshank, Julie. 2005. *Do Glaciers Listen? Local Knowledge, Colonial Encounters, and
Social Imagination.* Vancouver: University of British Columbia Press.

Cuesta Romaña, Elmer. 2010. *Monografía del Municipio Carmen Del Darién.* Medellín:
Lealon.

DANE (Departamento Administrativo Nacional de Estadísticas). 2010. *La Visibili-
zación Estadística de Los Grupos Étnicos Colombianos.* Bogotá: Imprenta Nacional.

DANE (Departamento Administrativo Nacional de Estadísticas). 2018. "Medida de
pobreza multidimensional municipal de fuente censal 2018." https://www.dane.gov
.co/index.php/estadisticas-por-tema/pobreza-y-condiciones-de-vida/pobreza-y
-desigualdad/medida-de-pobreza-multidimensional-de-fuente-censal.

Das, Veena. 1998. "Wittgenstein and Anthropology." *Annual Review of Anthropology*
27:171–95.

De Friedemann, Nina S. 1974. "Minería del Oro y Descendencia: Güelmambí, Nariño."
Revista Colombiana de Antropología 16:9–52.

De Friedemann, Nina S. 1985. "*Troncos* among Black Miners in Colombia." In *Miners
and Mining in the Americas,* edited by Thomas Greaves and William Culver, 204–25.
London: Manchester University Press.

De Friedemann, Nina S., and Alfredo Vanín. 1994. *Entre La Tierra y El Cielo: Magia y
Leyendas del Chocó.* Bogotá: Planeta.

de la Cadena, Marisol. 2015. *Earth Beings: Ecologies of Practice across Andean Worlds.* Durham, NC: Duke University Press.

de la Cadena, Marisol. 2016. "Uncommoning Nature: Stories from the Anthropo-Not-Seen." *E-Flux* 56.

Deacon, Terrence. 2006. "Emergence: The Hole at the Wheel's Hub." In *The Re-emergence of Emergence: The Emergentist Hypothesis from Science to Religion,* edited by Philip Clayton and Paul Davies, 111–50. Oxford: Oxford University Press.

Debret, Jean-Baptiste. (1834) 2014. *Voyage Pittoresque et Historique au Brésil.* Paris: Actes Sud.

Defensoría del Pueblo, República de Colombia. 2002. "*Amicus Curiae,* Explotación de Madera y Derechos Humanos." Bogotá: Defensoría del Pueblo.

Defensoría del Pueblo, República de Colombia. 2014. "*Amicus Curiae,* Explotación de Madera en El Bajo Atrato." Bogotá: Defensoría del Pueblo.

del Toro, Guillermo, dir. 2001. *The Devil's Backbone.* Warner Bros.

Deleuze, Gilles. 2001. *Pure Immanence: Essays on a Life.* New York: Zone.

Deleuze, Gilles, and Félix Guattari. (1991) 1996. *What Is Philosophy?* New York: Columbia University Press.

Deleuze, Gilles, and Félix Guattari. (1980) 2004. *A Thousand Plateaus: Capitalism and Schizophrenia.* London: Continuum.

Dickinson, Daniel. 2004. "Toothache Made Lion Eat Humans." BBC *News,* October 19, 2004. http://news.bbc.co.uk/2/hi/africa/3756180.stm.

Douglas, Mary, and Baron Isherwood. 1979. *The World of Goods: Towards an Anthropology of Consumption.* New York: Norton.

Dufort, Philippe. 2014. "The Dual Function of Violence in Civil Wars: The Case of Colombia." *Colombia International* 81:205–35.

Dufrenne, Mikel. (1953) 1973. *The Phenomenology of Aesthetic Experience.* Evanston, IL: Northwestern University Press.

Duncan, Gustavo. 2007. *Los Señores de La Guerra: De Paramilitares, Mafiosos y Auto-defensas.* Barcelona: Planeta.

Earl, Riggings. 1993. *Dark Symbols, Obscure Signs: God, Self, and Community in the Slave Mind.* New York: Orbis.

Echevarría, Juan Manuel, dir. 2013. *Requiem NN.* Documentary film. Lulo Films.

Escalón, Sebastián. 2014. "Palma Africana: nuevos estándares y viejas trampas." *Plaza Pública,* January 9, 2014. https://www.plazapublica.com.gt/content/palma-africana-nuevos-estandares-y-viejas-trampas.

Escobar, Arturo. 1997. *Biodiversidad, Naturaleza y Cultura: Localidad y Globalidad en Las Estrategias de Conservación.* Mexico DF: UNAM and CIICH.

Escobar, Arturo. 2001. "Culture Sits in Places: Reflections on Globalism and Subaltern Strategies of Localization." *Political Geography* 20:139–74.

Escobar, Arturo. 2005. *Más Allá del Tercer Mundo: Globalización y Diferencia.* Bogotá: Instituto Colombiano de Antropología e Historia.

Escobar, Arturo. 2007. "Worlds and Knowledges Otherwise: The Latin American Modernity/Coloniality Research Program." *Cultural Studies* 21 (2–3): 179–210.

Escobar, Arturo. 2008. *Territories of Difference: Place, Movements, Life*, Redes. Durham, NC: Duke University Press.

Escobar, Arturo. 2015. "Territorios de Diferencia: La Ontología Política de Los 'Derechos al Territorio.'" *Cuadernos de Antropología Social* 41:25–38.

Escobar, Arturo. 2016. "Thinking-Feeling with the Earth: Territorial Struggles and the Ontological Dimension of the Epistemologies of the South." *Revista de Antropología Iberoamericana* 11 (1): 11–32.

Escobar, Arturo. 2020. *Pluriversal Politics: The Real and the Possible*. Durham, NC: Duke University Press.

Espectador. 2009a. "El león de los paramilitares." March 13, 2009. https://www.elespectador.com/impreso/judicial/articuloimpreso127254-el-leon-de-los-paramilitares.

Espectador. 2009b. "Los hornos del horror en el Catatumbo." May 9, 2009. https://www.elespectador.com/impreso/salvatore-mancuso/articuloimpreso140079-los-hornos-del-horror-el-catatumbo.

Espectador. 2015. "Por desnutrición y diarrea aguda han muerto más de 20 niños en Chocó." March 4, 2015. https://www.elespectador.com/noticias/nacional/desnutricion-y-diarrea-aguda-han-fallecido-20-menores-c-articulo-547587.

Espectador. 2017a. "Los sobrevivientes del río San Juan." August 7, 2017. https://colombia2020.elespectador.com/territorio/los-sobrevivientes-del-rio-san-juan.

Espectador. 2017b. "La resiliencia de 'Lewis' Moya, líder social del Bajo Atrato." December 26, 2017. https://colombia2020.elespectador.com/justicia/la-resiliencia-de-lewis-moya-en-el-bajo-atrato.

Espinosa, Nicolas. 2012. "Impactos del Paramilitarismo en La Región Urabá/Chocó 1998–2006." *El Ágora U.S.B.* 12 (2): 289–327.

Ferguson, Adam. (1767) 1995. *An Essay on the History of Civil Society*. Cambridge: Cambridge University Press.

Fish, Laurel. 2013. "Homogenizing Community, Homogenizing Nature: An Analysis of Conflicting Rights in the Rights of Nature Debate." *Stanford Undergraduate Research Journal*, 6–11.

Foucault, Michel. 1990. *History of Sexuality*. New York: Vintage.

Franco, Vilma, and Juan Restrepo. 2011. "Empresarios Palmeros, Poderes de Facto y Despojo de Tierras en El Bajo Atrato." In *La Economía de Los Paramilitares: Redes de Corrupción, Negocios y Política*, edited by Mauricio Romero, 269–410. Bogotá: Corporación Nuevo Arco Iris.

Frank, Laurence, Graham Hemson, Hadas Kushnir, and Craig Packer. 2006. "Lions, Conflict and Conservation in Eastern and Southern Africa." Background Paper for the Eastern and Southern Africa Lion Conservation Workshop, Johannesburg, South Africa, January 11–13, 2006. http://static.wixstatic.com/ugd/87ac64_dcc32ba6c03845f2957b61eff0916206.pdf.

Freud, Sigmund. (1901) 2003. *Psychopathology of Everyday Life*. New York: Dover.

Frost, Robert. 1942. *A Witness Tree*. New York: Henry Holt.

Gagné, Karine, and Mattias Borg Rasmussen. 2016. "Introduction—An Amphibious Anthropology: The Production of Place at the Confluence of Land and Water." *Anthropologica* 58 (2): 135–49.

Gates, Henry Louis. 1988. *The Signifying Monkey: A Theory of Afro-American Literary Criticism.* New York: Oxford University Press.

Gentry, Alwyn. 1986. "Species Richness and Floristic Composition of the Chocó Region Plant Communities." *Caldasia* 15:71–91.

Georgiou, Ion. 2003. "The Idea of Emergent Property." *Journal of the Operational Research Society* 54:239–47.

Giraldo, Carlos. 1997. *El Desplazamiento en Colombia: Relatos e Imágenes.* Bogotá: CINEP.

Giray, Tugrul, Manuela Giovanetti, and Mary Jane West-Eberhard. 2005. "Juvenile Hormone, Reproduction, and Worker Behavior in the Neotropical Social Wasp *Polistes canadensis.*" *Proceeding of the National Academy of Sciences of the United States of America* 102 (9): 3330–35.

Gordillo, Gastón. 2004. *Landscapes of Devils: Tensions of Place and Memory in the Argentinian Chaco.* Durham, NC: Duke University Press.

Gordillo, Gastón. 2014. *Rubble: The Afterlife of Destruction.* Durham, NC: Duke University Press.

Gordillo, Gastón. 2019. "Ambient Thickness: The Atmospheric Materiality of the Anthropocene." Paper presented at the Institute for the Study of International Development, McGill University. Montreal, April 3.

Graeber, David. 2015. "Radical Alterity Is Just Another Way of Saying 'Alterity.'" *Hau: Journal of Ethnographic Theory* 5 (2): 1–41.

Groombridge, Brian, and Martin Jenkins. 2002. *World Atlas of Biodiversity: Earth's Living Resources in the 21st Century.* Berkeley: University of California Press.

Grosz, Elizabeth. 2002. "A Politics of Imperceptibility: A Response to 'Anti-racism, Multiculturalism and the Ethics of Identification.'" *Philosophy & Social Criticism* 28 (4): 463–72.

Gudynas, Eduardo. 2009. "La Ecología Política del Giro Biocéntrico en La Nueva Constitución de Ecuador." *Revista de Estudios Sociales* 32:34–47.

Guynup, Sharon. 2009. "Jaguar." BBC *Wildlife, Portfolio,* 26–37. Accessed October 3, 2016. http://sharonguynup.com/Sharon_Website/Articles_files/BBC%20Wildlife%20-%20Jaguars.pdf (no longer available).

Halperin, Rhoda. 1994. *Cultural Economics: Past and Present.* Austin: University of Texas Press.

Handelman, Don. 2008. "Afterword: Returning to Cosmology—Thoughts on the Positioning of Belief." *Social Analysis* 52 (1): 181–95.

Haraway, Donna. 2008. *When Species Meet.* Minneapolis: University of Minnesota Press.

Hastrup, Kirsten. 2010. "Emotional Topographies: The Sense of Place in the Far North." In *Emotions in the Field: The Psychology and Anthropology of Fieldwork Experience,* edited by James Davies and Dimitrina Spencer, 191–211. Stanford, CA: Stanford University Press.

Heddon, Deirdre. 2008. *Autobiography and Performance.* Basingstoke: Palgrave Macmillan.

Henig, David. 2012. "Iron in the Soil: Living with Military Waste in Bosnia-Herzegovina." *Anthropology Today* 28 (1): 21–23.

Hernández, Nicolás. 2008. "Campesinos Sin Tierras: La Historia de Los Desplazados del Bajo Atrato." Bachelor in Journalism, Pontifica Universidad Javeriana.

Hertz, Robert. (1909) 1960. *A Contribution to the Study of the Collective Representation of Death*. Glencoe: Free Press.

Hoffmann, Odile. 2004. *Communautés Noires dans Le Pacifique Colombien: Innovations et Dynamiques Ethniques*. Paris: IRD and Karthala.

Holbraad, Martin. 2008. "Definitive Evidence, from Cuban Gods." *Journal of the Royal Anthropological Institute* (n.s.): S93–109.

Hornborg, Alf. 2017. "Artifacts Have Consequences, Not Agency: Toward a Critical Theory of Global Environmental History." *European Journal of Social Theory* 20 (1): 95–110.

Hristov, Jasmin. 2009. *Blood and Capital: The Paramilitarization of Colombia*. Athens: Ohio University Press.

Hughes, Christina, and Celia Lury. 2013. "Re-turning Feminist Methodologies: From a Social to an Ecological Epistemology." *Gender and Education* 25 (6): 786–99.

Hughes, Ted. 1957. *The Hawk in the Rain*. London: Faber and Faber.

Human Rights Watch. 2010. *Paramilitaries' Heirs: The New Face of Violence in Colombia*. New York: Human Rights Watch.

Hyde, Lewis. 1998. *Trickster Makes This World: Mischief, Myth, and Art*. New York: Farrar, Straus and Giroux.

IAHCR (Inter-American Commission on Human Rights). 1999. "Third Report on the Human Rights Situation in Colombia. OEA/Ser.L/V/II.102 Doc. 9 Rev.1."

IAHCR (Inter-American Commission on Human Rights). 2004. "Report on the Demobilization Process in Colombia. OEA/Ser.L/II.120 Doc. 60."

IAHCR (Inter-American Commission on Human Rights). 2008. "Follow-Up on the Demobilization Process of the AUC in Colombia. OEA/Ser.L/V/II CIDH/INF.2/07."

IAHCR (Inter-American Commission on Human Rights). 2013. "Case of the Afro-Descendant Communities Displaced from the Cacarica River Basin (Operation Genesis) v. Colombia. Judgment of November 20."

IGAC (Instituto Geográfico Agustín Codazzi). 1992. *Atlas de Colombia*. Bogotá: Instituto Geográfico Agustín Codazzi.

Ingold, Tim. 1993. "The Temporality of the Landscape." *World Archaeology* 25 (2): 152–74.

Ingold, Tim. 2000. *The Perception of the Environment: Essays on Livelihood, Dwelling and Skill*. New York: Routledge.

Ingold, Tim. 2006. "Rethinking the Animate, Re-animating Thought." *Ethnos* 71 (1): 9–20.

Ingold, Tim. 2011. *Being Alive: Essay on Movement, Knowledge and Description*. London: Routledge.

Instituto Colombiano de Cultura Hispánica. 1992. *Geografía Humana de Colombia: Región del Pacífico*. Vol. 9. Bogotá: Instituto Colombiano de Cultura Hispánica.

Internal Displacement Monitoring Centre. 2007. *Resisting Displacement by Combatants and Developers: Humanitarian Zones in North-West Colombia*. Geneva: Internal Displacement Monitoring Centre and Norwegian Refugee Council.

Isacsson, Sven-Erik. 1975. "Biografía Atrateña: La Formación de Un Topónimo Indígena Bajo El Impacto Español." *Indiana* 3:93–109.

Izquierdo, Belkis, and Lieselotte Viaene. 2018. "Decolonizing Transitional Justice from Indigenous Territories." *Peace in Progress* 34 (June 27, 2018). https://dplfblog.com /2018/06/27/decolonizing-transitional-justice-from-indigenous-territories/.

Jaramillo-Villa, Úrsula, and Luz Jiménez-Segura. 2008. "Algunos Aspectos Biológicos de La Población de *Prochilodus magdalenae* en Las Ciénagas de Tumaradó (Río Atrato), Colombia." *Actualidades Biológicas* 30 (88): 55–66.

Jeanne, Robert. 2004. "Construction and Utilization of Multiple Combs in *Polistes canadensis* in Relation to the Biology of a Predaceous Moth." *Behavioral Ecology and Sociobiology* 4 (3): 293–310.

JEP (Justicia Especial para la Paz). 2018. "Reglamento General. Acuerdo No. 001 de 2018." March 9, 2018. https://www.jep.gov.co/salaplenajep/Acuerdo%20ASP %2001%20de%202018.pdf.

JEP (Justicia Especial para la Paz). 2019. "Comunicado 009: Unidad de Investigación y Acusación de La JEP 'Reconoce Como Víctima Silencosa El Medio Ambiente.'" June 5, 2019. https://www.jep.gov.co/SiteAssets/Paginas/UIA/sala-de-prensa /Comunicado%20UIA%20-%20009.pdf.

JEP (Justicia Especial para la Paz). 2021. "Comunicado 019 de 2021: La JEP Hace Pública la estrategia de Priorización dentro del Caso 03, conocido como el de 'Falsos Positivos.'" December 19, 2021. https://www.jep.gov.co/Sala-de-Prensa/Paginas/La -JEP-hace-p%C3%BAblica-la-estrategia-de-priorizaci%C3%B3n-dentro-del-Caso -03,-conocido-como-el-de-falsos-positivos.aspx.

Johnson, Penny. 2019. *Companions in Conflict: Animals in Occupied Palestine.* New York: Melville House.

Kalyvas, Stathis. 2003. "The Ontology of 'Political Violence': Action and Identity in Civil Wars." *Perspectives on Politics* 1 (3): 475–94.

Kapferer, Bruce. 1988. *Legends of People, Myths of State: Violence, Intolerance, and Political Culture in Sri Lanka and Australia.* Washington: Smithsonian Institute Press.

Kauffman, Craig M., and Pamela L. Martin. 2017. "Can Rights of Nature Make Development More Sustainable? Why Some Ecuadorian Lawsuits Succeed and Others Fail." *World Development* 92:130–42.

Kelly, Marcella, and Scott Silver. 2009. "The Suitability of the Jaguar (*Panthera onca*) for Reintroduction." In *Reintroduction of Top-Order Predators*, edited by Matt Hayward and Michael Somers, 187–205. Oxford: Wiley-Blackwell.

Kent, Lia. 2016. "Sounds of Silence: Everyday Strategies of Social Repair in Timor-Leste." *Australian Feminist Law Journal* 42 (1): 31–50.

Khan, Naveeda. 2016. "Living Paradox in Riverine Bangladesh: Whiteheadian Perspectives on Ganga Devi and Khwaja Khijir." *Anthropologica* 58 (2): 179–92.

Kim, Eleana. 2016. "Toward an Anthropology of Landmines: Rogue Infrastructure and Military Waste in the Korean DMZ." *Cultural Anthropology* 31 (2): 162–87.

Kohn, Eduardo. 2007. "How Dogs Dream: Amazonian Natures and the Politics of Transspecies Engagement." *American Ethnologist* 34 (1): 3–24.

Kohn, Eduardo. 2013. *How Forests Think: Toward an Anthropology beyond the Human.* Berkeley: University of California Press.

Kohn, Eduardo. 2020. "Anthropology as Cosmic Diplomacy: Toward an Ecological Ethics for Times of Environmental Fragmentation." In *Living Earth Community: Multiple Ways of Being and Knowing*, edited by Sam Mickey, Mary Evelyn Tucker, and John Grim, 55–65. Cambridge: Open Book.

Kwon, Heonik. 2008. *Ghosts of War in Vietnam*. Cambridge: Cambridge University Press.

Laakkonen, Simo. 2004. "War—An Ecological Alternative to Peace? Indirect Impacts of World War II on the Finnish Environment." In *Natural Enemy, Natural Ally: Toward an Environmental History of War*, edited by Richard Tucker and Edmund Russell, 175–94. Corvallis: Oregon State University Press.

Latour, Bruno. 1999. *Pandora's Hope: Essays on the Reality of Sciences Studies*. Cambridge, MA: Harvard University Press.

Latour, Bruno. 2004. *Politics of Nature: How to Bring the Science into Democracy*. Cambridge, MA: Harvard University Press.

Latour, Bruno. 2005. *Reassembling the Social: An Introduction to Actor-Network Theory*. New York: Oxford University Press.

Law, John. 2007. "Actor-Network Theory and Material Semiotics." In *The New Blackwell Companion to Social Theory*, edited by Bryan Turner, 141–58. Oxford: Blackwell.

Law, John. 2015. "What's Wrong with a One-World World?" *Distinktion: Journal of Social Theory* 16 (1): 126–39.

Leal, Claudia. 2018. *Landscapes of Freedom: Building a Postemancipation Society in the Rainforests of Western Colombia*. Tucson: University of Arizona Press.

Leal, Claudia, and Eduardo Restrepo. 2003. *Unos Bosques Sembrados de Aserríos: Historia de La Extracción Maderera en El Pacífico Colombiano*. Medellín: Universidad de Antioquia.

Le Billon, Philippe. 2001. "The Political Ecology of War: Natural Resources and Armed Conflicts." *Political Geography* 20:561–84.

Lederach, Angela. 2017. "'The Campesino Was Born for the Campo': A Multispecies Approach to Territorial Peace in Colombia." *American Anthropologist* 119 (4): 589–602.

Leeming, David. 1991. *The World of Myth*. Oxford: Oxford University Press.

LeGrand, Catherine. 2003. "The Colombian Crisis in Historical Perspective." *Canadian Journal of Latin American and Caribbean Studies* 28 (55–56): 165–210.

Leopold, Aldo. 1972. *Wildlife of Mexico*. Berkeley: University of California Press.

Levine, Lawrence. 1977. *Black Culture and Black Consciousness: Afro-American Folk Thought from Slavery to Freedom*. New York: Oxford University Press.

Lévi-Strauss, Claude. 1962. *Le Totémism Aujourd'hui*. Paris: Presses Universitaires de France.

Lien, Marianne, and John Law. 2011. "'Emergent Aliens': On Salmon, Nature, and Their Enactment." *Ethnos* 76 (1): 65–87.

López, Claudia. 2005. "Del Control Territorial a La Acción Política." *Arcanos* 11:39–47.

Losonczy, Anne-Marie. 1993. "De Lo Vegetal a Lo Humano: Un Modelo Cognitivo Afro-Colombiano Del Pacífico." *Revista Colombiana de Antropología* 30:38–57.

Losonczy, Anne-Marie. 2006a. *La Trama Interétnica: Ritual, Sociedad y Figuras de Intercambio entre Los Grupos Negros y Emberá Del Chocó*. Bogotá: Instituto Colombiano de Antropología e Historia and Instituto Francés de Estudios Andinos.

Losonczy, Anne-Marie. 2006b. *Viaje y Violencia: La Paradoja Chamánica Emberá*. Bogotá: Universidad Externado de Colombia.

Lynch, John D. 2015. "The Role of Plantations of the African Palm (*Elaeis guineensis Jacq.*) in the Conservation of Snakes in Colombia." *Caldasia* 37 (1): 169–82.

Lyons, Kristina. 2019. "Ríos y Reconciliación Profunda: La Reconstrucción Socio-Ecológica en Tiempos de Conflicto y 'Transición' en Colombia." *Maguaré* 33 (2): 209–45.

Machlis, Gary, and Thor Hanson. 2008. "Warfare Ecology." *BioScience* 58 (8): 729–36.

Macpherson, Elizabeth. 2019. *Indigenous Water Rights in Law and Regulation: Lessons from Comparative Experience*. Cambridge: Cambridge University Press.

Macpherson, Elizabeth, and Felipe Clavijo Ospina. 2018. "The Pluralism of River Rights in Aotearoa, New Zealand and Colombia." *Journal of Water Law* 25:283–93.

Mahler, Richard. 2009. *The Jaguar's Shadow: Searching for a Mythic Cat*. New Haven, CT: Yale University Press.

Mameli, Paola. 2014. "Etnografías de Cocinas: El Espacio Acuático en Riosucio, Chocó." Bachelor's thesis, Pontificia Universidad Javeriana.

Mann, Thomas. (1924) 1958. *The Magic Mountain*. New York: Alfred A. Knopf.

Margil, Mari. 2018. "Our Laws Make Slaves of Nature: It's Not Just Humans Who Need Rights." *Guardian*, May 23, 2018. https://www.theguardian.com/commentisfree /2018/may/23/laws-slaves-nature-humans-rights-environment-amazon.

Martínez Arango, Rodrígo. 2013. "Un jaguar mató a un pescador en Urabá." *Colombiano*, May 24, 2013. https://www.elcolombiano.com/historico/un_jaguar_mato_a _un_pescador_en_uraba-MBEC_243690.

Masco, Joseph. 2004. "Mutant Ecologies: Radioactive Life in Post–Cold War New Mexico." *Cultural Anthropology* 19 (4): 517–50.

Mazoomdaar, Jay. 2014. "Why Are India's Tigers Killing Humans?" BBC *News*, January 20, 2014. https://www.bbc.com/news/world-asia-india-25755104.

Mbembe, Achille. 2003. "Necropolitics." *Public Culture* 15 (1): 11–40.

McAllister, Carlota, and Diane Nelson. 2013. "Aftermath: Harvests of Violence and Histories of the Future." In *War by Other Means: Aftermath in Post-genocide Guatemala*, edited by Carlota McAllister and Diane Nelson, 1–45. Durham, NC: Duke University Press.

Mejía, Carlos Arturo. 1995. *Fauna de La Serranía de La Macarena*. Bogotá: Amazonas Editores, Ediciones Uniandes.

Melo, Mario. 2014. "Voces de La Selva en El Estrado de La Corte Interamericana de Derechos Humanos." *Sur: Revista Internacional de Derechos Humanos* 20:291–99.

Merleau-Ponty, Maurice. (1945) 2002. *Phenomenology of Perception*. London: Routledge.

Metcalf, Jacob. 2008. "Intimacy without Proximity: Encountering Grizzlies as a Companion Species." *Environmental Philosophy* 5 (2): 99–128.

Mingorance, Fidel, Flaminia Minelli, and Hélène Le Du. 2004. *El Cultivo de La Palma Africana en El Chocó: Legalidad Ambiental, Territorial y Derechos Humanos*. Quibdó: Human Rights Everywhere and Diócesis de Quibdó.

Mitchell, Sandra. 2012. "Emergence: Logical, Functional and Dynamical." *Synthese* 185: 171–86.

Mittermeier, Russell, Patricio Robles Gil, Michael Hoffman, John Pilgrim, Thomas Brooks, Cristina Goettsch, John Lamoreux, and Gustavo Da Fonseca. 2005. *Hotspots Revisited: Earth's Biologically Richest and Most Endangered Terrestrial Ecoregions*. Chicago: University of Chicago Press.

Moglen, Eben. 1990. "Legal Fictions and Common Law Legal Theory: Some Historical Reflections." *Tel Aviv University Studies in Law* 10:33–62.

Mol, Annemarie. 1999. "Ontological Politics: A Word and Some Questions." In *Actor Network Theory and After*, edited by John Law and John Hassard, 74–89. Boston: Blackwell.

Mol, Annemarie. 2002. *The Body Multiple: Ontology in Medical Practice.* Durham, NC: Duke University Press.

Mouffe, Chantal. 2000. *On the Political.* New York: Routledge.

Mount, Nick. 2017. "Can a River Have Legal Rights? A Different Approach to Protecting the Environment." *Independent*, October 13, 2017. https://www.independent.co.uk /environment/river-legal-rights-colombia-environment-pacific-rainforest-atrato -river-rio-quito-a7991061.html.

National Security Archive. 2010. "US. Embassy Colombia Cable, 1998 Bogota 9345." http://nsarchive.gwu.edu/NSAEBB/NSAEBB327/doc01_19980813.pdf.

Navaro-Yashin, Yael. 2009. "Affective Spaces, Melancholic Objects: Ruination and the Production of Anthropological Knowledge." *Journal of the Royal Anthropological Institute* 15:1–18.

Navaro-Yashin, Yael. 2012. *The Make-Believe Space: Affective Geography in a Postwar Polity.* Durham, NC: Duke University Press.

New Herald. 2009. "Paras alimentan fieras con los restos de sus víctimas." August 23, 2009. https://www.elnuevoherald.com/noticias/mundo/america-latina/colombia-es /article1998424.html.

Nieto, Patricia. 2012. *Los Escogidos.* Medellín: Alcaldía de Medellín and Sílaba Editores.

Niiler, Eric. 2014. "After Protecting Habitat for Jaguars, Expert Believes the Species Can Adapt and Survive." *Washington Post*, December 22, 2014. https://www .washingtonpost.com/national/health-science/after-protecting-habitat-for-jaguars -expert-believes-the-species-can-adapt-and-survive/2014/12/19/10b2591e-6f5c-11e4 -8808-afaa1e3a33ef_story.html.

Noticias Uno. 2014. "No dejan cazar jaguar que ha matado a cinco personas." YouTube video, May 10, 2014. https://www.youtube.com/watch?v=mGdmxgCYaWw.

Noticias Urabá. 2013. "Tigre se come a dos campesinos en dos meses en Bocas del Atrato (Turbo)." YouTube video, May 25, 2013. https://www.youtube.com/watch?v =mAhnzCyBcxs.

Novack, Anthony, and Martin Main. 2012. *Jaguar: Another Threatened Panther.* Gainesville: University of Florida Press.

Observatorio del Programa Presidencial de Derechos Humanos. 2003. *Panorama Actual del Chocó.* Bogotá: Presidencia de la República, Ministerio del Interior.

Offen, Karl. 2018. "Environment, Space, and Place: Cultural Geographies of Colonial Afro-Latin America." In *Afro-Latin American Studies: An Introduction*, edited by Alejandro de la Fuente and George Reid Andrews, 486–534. Cambridge: Cambridge University Press.

Ogden, Laura, Billy Hall, and Kimiko Tanita. 2013. "Animals, Plants, People, and Things: A Review of Multispecies Ethnography." *Environment and Society: Advances in Research* 4:5–24.

Ojeda, Diana. 2016. "Los paisajes del despojo: propuestas para un análisis desde las reconfiguraciones socioespaciales." *Revista Colombiana de Antropología* 52 (2): 19–43.

Oslender, Ulrich. 2003. "Discursos Ocultos de Resistencia: Tradición Oral y Cultura Política En Comunidades Negras de La Costa Pacífica Colombiana." *Revista Colombiana de Antropología* 39:203–35.

Oslender, Ulrich. 2004. "Fleshing Out the Geographies of Social Movements: Colombia's Pacific Coast Black Communities and the 'Aquatic Space.'" *Political Geography* 23: 957–85.

Oslender, Ulrich. 2008. *Comunidades Negras y Espacio en El Pacífico Colombiano: Hacia Un Giro en El Estudio de Los Movimientos Sociales.* Bogotá: Instituto Colombiano de Antropología e Historia, Universidad Colegio Mayor de Cundinamarca and Universidad del Cauca.

Oslender, Ulrich. 2016. *The Geographies of Social Movements: Afro-Colombian Mobilization and the Aquatic Space.* Durham, NC: Duke University Press.

Oxford Dictionary of English Etymology. 1966. "Ecumene." Edited by C. T. Onions, G. W. S. Friedrichsen and R. W. Burchfield. Oxford, UK: Clarendon Press.

Pardo, Mauricio, and Manuela Álvarez. 2001. "Estado y Movimiento Negro en El Pacífico Colombiano." In *Acción Colectiva, Estado y Etnicidad en El Pacífico Colombiano,* edited by Mauricio Pardo, 229–58. Bogotá: Instituto Colombiano de Antropología e Historia and Colciencias.

Pardo Pedraza, Diana. 2022. "Landscapes of Suspicion: Minefields and Cleared-Lands in Rural Colombia." *Fieldsights,* January 25, 2022. https://culanth.org/fieldsights /landscapes-of-suspicion-minefields-and-cleared-lands-in-rural-colombia.

Patterson, John Henry. 1907. *The Man-Eaters of Tsavo and Other East African Adventures.* London: Macmillan.

Patterson, Bruce. 2004. *The Lions of Tsavo: Exploring the Legacy of Africa's Notorious Man-Eaters.* New York: McGraw-Hill.

Perea, Nevaldo. 2012. *Soy Atrato: Vida y Amargos Recuerdos de Un Líder Negro.* Santander: Otramérica.

Perera, Sasanka. 2001. "Spirit Possessions and Avenging Ghosts: Stories of Supernatural Activity as Narratives of Terror and Mechanisms of Coping and Remembering." In *Remaking a World: Violence, Suffering, and Recovery,* edited by Arthur Kleinman, Veena Das, Margaret Lock, Mamphela Ramphele, and Pamela Reynolds, 157–200. Berkeley: University of California Press.

Pineda, Ciro. 2002. *Cuentos Tradicionales del Atrato: Embera, Catío, Chamí, Wounan, Tule.* Riosucio: Cabildo Mayor Indígena del Bajo Atrato y del Darién Chocoano.

Pinto García, Constancio. 1978. *Los Indios Katíos: Su Cultura, Su Lengua.* Medellín: Granamerica.

Plumwood, Val. 2000. "Being Prey." In *The Ultimate Journey: Inspiring Stories of Living and Dying,* edited by Sean O'Reilly, James O'Reilly, and Richard Sterling, 128–46. San Francisco: Travelers Tale.

Polak, Micbal. 1993. "Competition for Landmark Territories among Male *Polistes canadensis* (L.) (Hymenoptera: Vaspidae): Large-Size and Alternative Mate-Acquisition Tactics." *Behavioral Ecology and Sociobiology* 4 (4): 325–31.

Polisar, John, Ines Maxit, Daniel Scognamillo, Laura Farrell, Melvin E. Sunquist, and John Eisenberg. 2003. "Jaguars, Pumas, Their Prey Base, and Cattle Ranching: Ecological Interpretations of a Management Problem." *Biological Conservation* 109: 297–310.

Povinelli, Elizabeth. 2012. "The Will to Be Otherwise/The Effort of Endurance." *South Atlantic Quarterly* 111 (3): 453–75.

Povinelli, Elizabeth. 2015. "The Rhetorics of Recognition in Geontopower." *Philosophy & Rhetoric* 48 (4): 428–42.

Povinelli, Elizabeth, 2016. *Geontologies: A Requiem to Late Liberalism.* Durham, NC: Duke University Press.

Presidencia de la República. 2012. Decreto Ley de Víctimas No. 4633 de 2011. *Colección Cuadernos Legislación y Pueblos Indígenas de Colombia No. 3.* Bogotá: Imprenta Nacional de Colombia.

Price, N. S. 1995. "The Origin and Development of Banana and Plantain Cultivation." In *Bananas and Plantains*, edited by S. Gowen, 1–12. London: Chapman & Hill.

Proyecto Biopacífico. 1998. *Informe Final General.* Vol. 1. Bogotá: Ministerio del Medio Ambiente y Proyecto Biopacífico.

Pugliese, Joseph. 2020. *Biopolitics of the More-Than-Human: Forensic Ecologies of Violence.* Durham, NC: Duke University Press.

Quiceno, Natalia. 2016. *Vivir Sabroso: Luchas y Movimientos Afroatrateños en Bojayá, Chocó.* Bogotá: Universidad del Rosario.

Rabinowitz, Alan. 2000. *Jaguar: One Man's Struggle to Establish the World's First Jaguar Preserve.* Washington, DC: Island.

Rabinowitz, Alan. 2014. *An Indomitable Beast: The Remarkable Journey of the Jaguar.* Washington, DC: Island.

Rabinowitz, Alan, and B. G. Nottingham Jr. 1986. "Ecology and Behaviour of the Jaguar (*Panthera onca*) in Belize, Central America." *Journal of Zoology* 210: 146–59.

Raffles, Hugh. 2014. "Flow: A Concept to Travel With." *Suomen Antopologi: Journal of the Finnish Anthropological Society* 39 (2): 99–100.

Ramos, Alcida Rita. 2012. "The Politics of Perspectivism." *Annual Review of Anthropology* 41:481–94.

Ramos, Alcida Rita. 2022. "El Giro Que No Gira o Esto No Es Una Pipa." In *Humanos, Más Que Humanos y No Humanos: Intersecciones Críticas En Torno a La Antropología y La Ontología*, edited by Daniel Ruiz-Serna and Carlos Del Cairo, 394–403. Bogotá: Pontificia Universidad Javeriana.

Rancière, Jacques. 2000. *Le Partage Du Sensible: Esthétique et Politique.* Paris: La Fabrique-éditions.

Rancière, Jacques. 2004. *The Politics of Aesthetics: The Distribution of the Sensible.* London: Continuum.

Rancière, Jacques. 2010. *Dissensus: On Politics and Aesthetics.* London: Bloomsbury.

Rancière, Jacques. 2011. "Ten Theses on Politics." *Theory and Event* 5 (3).

Rancière, Jacques. 2012. "Occupation." *Political Concepts* 3.

Rangel, Orlando. 2015. "La Biodiversidad de Colombia: Significado y Distribución Regional." *Revista de La Academia Colombiana de Ciencias Exactas, Físicas y Naturales* 39:176–200.

Rasmussen, Mattias Borg. 2015. "Deep Time and Shallow Waters: Configuration of an Irrigation Channel in the Andes." In *Waterworlds: Anthropology in Fluid Environments*, edited by Kirsten Hastrup and Frida Hastrup, 203–18. New York: Berghahn.

Restall, Matthew, and Kris Lane. 2011. *Latin America in Colonial Times*. Cambridge: Cambridge University Press.

Restrepo, Diego. 2018. "Tumaco, Un Posconflicto Armado." *Razón Pública* 22 (January). https://razonpublica.com/tumaco-un-posconflicto-armado/.

Restrepo, Eduardo. 1995. "Los Tuqueros Negros del Pacífico Sur Colombiano." In *Renacientes del Guandal: Grupos Negros de Los Ríos Satinga y Sanquianga*, edited by Eduardo Restrepo and Jorge Del Valle, 243–348. Medellín: Biopacífico, Universidad Nacional de Colombia.

Restrepo, Eduardo. 1996. "Cultura y Biodiversidad." In *Pacífico: ¿Desarrollo o Biodiversidad? Estado, Capital y Movimientos Sociales en El Pacífico Colombiano*, edited by Arturo Escobar and Álvaro Pedrosa, 220–41. Bogotá: CEREC.

Restrepo, Eduardo. 2013. *Etnización de La Negridad: La Invención de Las "Comunidades Negras" Como Grupo Étnico en Colombia*. Popayán: Universidad del Cauca.

Rodríguez, Emiliano. 2017. "Nature: The Silent Victim of Colombia's Armed Conflict." *Earth Journalism Network*, July 27, 2017. https://earthjournalism.net/stories/nature-the-silent-victim-of-colombias-armed-conflict#:~:text=%22Nature%20was%20a%20silent%20victim,in%20Cartagena%2C%20last%2023%20July.

Roldán, Mery. 1998. "Violencia, Colonización y La Geografía de Diferencia Cultural en Colombia." *Análisis Político* 35:3–26.

Romero, Manuel. 2005. *Canaguaro: La Guerra de Los Tigreros*. Bogotá: Parature Editores.

Romero, Mauricio. 2002. "Democratización Política y Contrarreforma Paramilitar en Colombia." *Política y Sociedad* 39 (1): 273–92.

Rose, Deborah Bird. 1992. *Dingo Makes Us Human: Life and Land in an Aboriginal Australian Culture*. Cambridge: Cambridge University Press.

Rueda, Santiago. 2016. "Hoy tenemos, mañana no sabemos: Jesús Abad Colorado—La fotografía y la guerra." *ArtNexus* 147 (June-August): 32–36.

Ruiz González, Luis. 2012. "Análisis de Las Rupturas y Continuidades Estratégicas en Sus Ámbitos Económicos, Social y Político Entre El Bloque Élmer Cárdenas de Las AUC (2002–2006) y La Banda Criminal Los Urabeños (2006–2010) Presentes en El Urabá Chocoano." Facultad de Ciencia Política y Gobierno, Universidad Colegio Mayor de Cundinamarca.

Ruiz-Serna, Daniel. 2005. "El Estado llega con los ricos: Lo que está en juego en el Bajo Atrato." *Cien días vistos por CINEP* 12 (57): 19–21.

Ruiz-Serna, Daniel. 2006. "Nuevas Formas de Ser Negro: Consideraciones Sobre Las Identidades entre La Gente Chilapa y Negra del Bajo Atrato Chocoano." In *Identidades Culturales y Formación del Estado en Colombia*, edited by Ingrid Bolívar, 209–48. Bogotá: Ediciones Uniandes.

Russell, Edmund, and Richard Tucker. 2004. "Introduction." In *Natural Enemy, Natural Ally: Toward an Environmental History of War*, edited by Richard Tucker and Edmund Russell, 1–14. Corvallis: Oregon State University Press.

Safford, Frank, and Marco Palacios. 2002. *Colombia: Fragmented Land, Divided Society*. New York: Oxford University Press.

Salinas, Yamile, and Juan Zarama. 2012. *Justicia y Paz: Tierras y Territorios en Las Versiones de Los Paramilitares*. Bogotá: Centro de Memoria Histórica and Organización Internacional para las Migraciones.

Salomon, Frank, and Stuart Schwartz. 1999. "New Peoples and New Kinds of People: Adaptation, Readjustment, and Ethnogenesis in South American Indigenous Societies (Colonial Era)." In *The Cambridge History of the Native Peoples of the Americas*, Vol. 3, edited by Frank Salomon and Stuart Schwartz, 443–94. New York: Cambridge University Press.

Sánchez, John Antón. 2002. *Entre Chinangos: Experiencias de Magía y Curación entre Comunidades Negras del Pacífico*. Quibdó: Instituto de Investigaciones Ambientales del Pacífico, Fundación Cultural y Ambiental Las Mojarras and Federación de Organizaciones de Comunidades Negras del San Juan.

Saunders, Nicholas. 1998. "Architecture of Symbolism: The Feline Image." In *Icons of Power: Feline Symbolism in the Americas*, edited by Nicholas Saunders, 12–52. London: Routledge.

Savoy, Eric. 1995. "The Signifying Rabbit." *Narrative* 3 (2): 188–209.

Schane, Sanford. 2006. *Language and the Law*. London: Bloomsbury.

Schlosberg, David. 2014. "Ecological Justice for the Anthropocene." In *Political Animals and Animal Politics*, edited by Marcel Wissenburg and David Schlosberg, 75–89. London: Palgrave Macmillan.

Schmidt, Justin. 2016. *The Sting of the Wild*. Baltimore: Johns Hopkins University Press.

Seigworth, Gregory, and Melissa Gregg. 2010. "An Inventory of Shimmers." In *The Affect Theory Reader*, edited by Melissa Gregg and Gregory J. Seigworth, 1–25. Durham, NC: Duke University Press.

Semana. 2005. "Habla Vicente Castaño. El verdadero jefe de las autodefensas le da la cara al país por primera vez." June 16, 2005. https://www.semana.com/portada/articulo/habla-vicente-castano/72964-3.

Semana. 2006. "El Führer de Urabá." October 31, 2006. https://www.semana.com/nacion/articulo/el-fhrerde-uraba/80185-3.

Semana. 2007. "Pacto con el diablo: ¿Qué significa para el país la revelación del explosivo documento firmado por políticos y jefes paramilitares?" January 20, 2007. https://www.semana.com/nacion/articulo/pacto-diablo/83048-3.

Semana. 2009. "Fiscalía investiga sórdidas prácticas paramilitares." December 12, 2009. https://www.semana.com/nacion/justicia/articulo/fiscalia-investiga-sordida-practicas-paramilitares/104067-3.

Serje, Margarita. 2005. *El Revés de La Nación: Territorios Salvajes, Fronteras y Tierras de Nadie*. Bogotá: Universidad de los Andes.

Serrano, José. 1994. "Cuando Canta El Guaco: La Muerte y El Morir en Poblaciones Afrocolombianas Del Río Baudó, Chocó." Bachelor's thesis, Universidad Nacional de Colombia.

Sharp, William. 1976. *Slavery on the Spanish Frontier: The Colombian Chocó 1680–1810*. Norman: University of Oklahoma Press.

Sharpe, Christina. 2016. *In the Wake: On Blackness and Being*. Durham, NC: Duke University Press.

Shepherd, Suzanne, Angela Mills, and William Shoff. 2014. "Human Attacks by Large Felid Carnivores in Captivity and in the Wild." *Wilderness and Environmental Medicine* 25:220–30.

Shigo, Alex. 1984. "Compartmentalization: A Conceptual Framework for Understanding How Trees Grow and Defend Themselves." *Annual Review of Phytopathology* 22 (1): 189–214.

Sotelo, Luis Carlos. 2010. "Looking Backwards to Walk Forward: Walking, Collective Memory and the Site of the Intercultural in Site-Specific Performance." *Performance Research* 15 (4): 59–69.

Sotelo, Luis Carlos. 2020. "Not Being Able to Speak Is Torture: Performing Listening to Painful Narratives." *International Journal of Transitional Justice* 14 (1): 220–31.

Spence, Jocelyne, David Frohlich, and Stuart Andrews. 2013. "Performative Experience Design: Where Autobiographical Performance and Human-Computer Interaction Meet." *Digital Creativity* 24 (2): 96–110.

Stengers, Isabelle. 2002. "A 'Cosmo-Politics': Risk, Hope, Change." Interview by Mary Zournazi. In *Hope: New Philosophies for Change*, edited by Mary Zournazi, 244–72. London: Routledge.

Stengers, Isabelle. 2005a. "The Cosmopolitical Proposal." In *Making Things Public*, edited by Bruno Latour and Peter Weibel, 994–1003. Cambridge: MIT Press.

Stengers, Isabelle. 2005b. "An Ecology of Practices." *Cultural Studies Review* 11 (1): 183–96.

Stengers, Isabelle. 2010. "Including Nonhumans in Political Theory: Opening the Pandora's Box." In *Political Matter: Technoscience, Democracy, and Public Life*, edited by Bruce Braun and Sarah Whatmore, 3–33. Minneapolis: University of Minnesota Press.

Stewart, Kathleen. 2007. *Ordinary Affects*. Durham, NC: Duke University Press.

Stoler, Ann Laura. 2008. "Imperial Debris: Reflections on Ruins and Ruination." *Cultural Anthropology* 23 (2): 191–219.

Stoler, Ann Laura. 2013. "The Rot Remains." In *Imperial Debris: On Ruins and Ruination*, edited by Ann Laura Stoler, 1–35. Durham, NC: Duke University Press.

Strathern, Marilyn. 2004. *Partial Connections*. Oxford: Altamira.

Strathern, Marilyn. 2005. *Kinship, Law and the Unexpected: Relatives Are Always a Surprise*. Cambridge: Cambridge University Press.

Sumner, Seirian, Hans Kelstrup, and Daniele Fanelli. 2010. "Reproductive Constraints, Direct Fitness and Indirect Fitness Benefits Explain Helping Behaviour in the Primitively Eusocial Wasp, Polistes Canadensis." *Proceedings of the Royal Society B* 277 (1688): 1721–28.

Taussig, Michael. 1992. *The Nervous System*. New York: Routledge.

Taylor, Charles. 1992. *Multiculturalism and the Politics of Recognition*. Princeton, NJ: Princeton University Press.

Teleantioquia Noticias. 2014. "Campesinos tras la caza de un jaguar." YouTube video, May 7, 2014. https://www.youtube.com/watch?v=_VLZa0456Bo.

Teleantioquia Noticias. 2015. "Habitantes de Bocas del Atrato cazan y se comen a un jaguar que mató a tres pescadores." YouTube video, February 24, 2015. https://www.youtube.com/watch?v=gto1NrVVbNc.

Thrift, Nigel. 2008. *Non-representational Theory: Space, Politics, Affect*. New York: Routledge.

Tiempo. 2008. "Paras usaron serpientes venenosas para matar a sus víctimas, reveló desmovilizado a la Fiscalía." March 3, 2008. https://www.eltiempo.com/archivo/documento/CMS-3984686.

Tiempo. 2009. "Cambio conoció los hornos crematorios que construyeron los paramilitares en Norte de Santander." May 20, 2009. https://www.eltiempo.com/archivo/documento-2013/CMS-5235387.

Tiempo. 2015. "Unos 655 colombianos desplazados por choques entre grupo armado y ELN." March 5, 2015. https://www.eltiempo.com/archivo/documento/CMS-15342697.

Tilley, Christopher. 2006. "Introduction: Identity, Place, Landscape and Heritage." *Journal of Material Culture* 11:7–32.

Todd, Zoe. 2016. "An Indigenous Feminist's Take on the Ontological Turn: 'Ontology' Is Just Another Word for Colonialism." *Journal of Historical Sociology* 29 (1): 4–22.

Trujillo Molano, Jimena. 2012. "Escribir Sobre Lo Intangible: Vivir Lo Sagrado." In *Etnografías Contemporáneas: Trabajo de Campo*, edited by Sandra Murillo, Myriam Jimeno, and Marco Martínez, 181–208. Bogotá: Universidad Nacional de Colombia.

Tsing, Anna Lowenhaupt. 2012. "On Nonscalability: The Living World Is Not Amenable to Precision-Nested Scales." *Common Knowledge* 18 (3): 505–24.

Tsing, Anna Lowenhaupt. 2013. "More-Than-Human Sociality: A Call for Critical Description." In *Anthropology and Nature*, edited by Kirsten Hastrup, 27–42. New York: Routledge.

Tucker, Richard. 2004. "The Impact of Warfare in the Natural World: A Historical Survey." In *Natural Enemy, Natural Ally: Toward an Environmental History of War*, edited by Richard Tucker and Edmund Russell, 15–41. Corvallis: Oregon State University Press.

Turner, Terry. 2009. "The Crisis of Late Structuralism. Perspectivism and Animism: Rethinking Culture, Nature, Spirit, and Bodiliness." *Tipití: Journal of the Society for the Anthropology of Lowland South America* 7 (1): 3–42.

UNCHR (United Nations Commission on Human Rights). 1998. "Report of the UN High Commissioner for Human Rights on the Human Rights Situation in Colombia. UN Doc E/CN.4/1998/16."

Unruh, Jon, Nikolas Heynen, and Peter Hossler. 2003. "The Political Ecology of Recovery from Armed Conflict: The Case of Landmines in Mozambique." *Political Geography* 22:841–61.

Valencia, Armando. 2005. "Territorio e Identidad Cultural." *Selva y Río* 2:15–36.

Valencia, Armando. 2013. "Alternativas Organizativas Ante La Guerra y El Desplazamiento en El Bajo Atrato." *Revista de Estudios del Pacífico Colombiano* 1:57–81.

Vargas, Iván. 2020. "Forest on Trial: Towards a Relational Theory of Legal Agency for Transitions into the Ecozoic." In *Liberty and the Ecological Crisis: Freedom on a Finite Planet*, edited by Christopher Orr, Kaitlin Kish, and Bruce Jennings, 234–50. London: Routledge.

Vargas, Iván. 2021. "Conjuring Sentient Beings and Relations in the Law: Rights of Nature and a Comparative Praxis of Legal Cosmologies." In *From Environmental to Ecological Law*, edited by Kirsten Anker, Peter Burdon, Geoffrey Garver, Michelle Maloney, and Carla Sbert, 119–34. New York: Routledge.

Vargas, Jennifer. 2016. "Despojo de Tierras Paramilitar en Riosucio, Chocó." In *El Despojo Paramilitar y Su Variación: Quiénes, Cómo, Por Qué*, edited by Francisco Gutiérrez and Jennifer Vargas, 121–46. Bogotá: Universidad del Rosario.

Vargas, Patricia. 1993. *Los Embera y Los Cuna: Impacto y Reacción Ante La Ocupación Española. Siglos XVI y XVII*. Bogotá: CEREC and Instituto Colombiano de Antropología.

Vargas, Patricia. 2016. *Historias de Territorialidades en Colombia: Biocentrismo y Antropocentrismo*. Bogotá: Autores Independientes.

Vasco, Luis Guillermo. 1985. *Jaibanás: Los Verdaderos Hombres*. Bogotá: Banco Popular.

Velásquez, Rogelio. 1959. "Cuentos de Raza Negra." *Revista Colombiana de Folclor* 3: 3–63.

Velásquez, Rogelio. (1961) 2000. "Ritos de La Muerte en El Alto y Bajo Chocó." In *Fragmentos de Historia, Etnografía y Narraciones Del Pacífico Colombiano Negro*, 127–71. Bogotá: Instituto Colombiano de Antropología e Historia.

Vilaça, Aparecida. 2005. "Chronically Unstable Bodies: Reflections on Amazonian Corporalities." *Journal of the Royal Anthropological Institute* 11:445–64.

Villa, William. 2013. "Colonización y Conflicto Territorial en El Bajo Atrato: El Poblamiento de Las Cuencas de La Margen Oriental." *Revista de Estudios del Pacífico Colombiano* 1:9–56.

Viveiros de Castro, Eduardo. 1998. "Cosmological Deixis and Amerindian Perspectivism." *Journal of the Royal Anthropological Institute* 4 (3): 469–88.

Wade, Peter. 1990. "El Chocó: Una Región Negra." *Boletín del Museo del Oro* 29: 121–49.

Wade, Peter. 2016. "Mestizaje, Multiculturalism, Liberalism, and Violence." *Latin American and Caribbean Ethnic Studies* 11 (3): 323–43.

Werner, Erik. 2000. *Ni Aniquilados Ni Vencidos: Los Emberá y La Gente Negra del Atrato Bajo El Dominio Español. Siglo XVIII*. Bogotá: Instituto Colombiano de Antropología.

West, Robert. 1957. *The Pacific Lowlands of Colombia: A Negroid Area of the American Tropics*. Baton Rouge: Louisiana State University Press.

White, Stephen. 2001. *Sustaining Affirmation: The Strengths of Weak Ontology in Political Theory*. Princeton, NJ: Princeton University Press.

Whitten, Norman. 1974. *Black Frontiersmen: A South American Case*. New York: Schenkman.

Wildman, Wesley. 2010. "An Introduction to Relational Ontology." In *The Trinity and an Entangled World: Relationality in Physical Science and Theology*, edited by John Polkinghorne and John Zizioulas, 55–73. Grand Rapids: Eerdmans.

Wilk, Richard. 1996. *Economies and Cultures*. Boulder: Westview.

Wilk, Richard, and Lisa Cligget. 2007. *Economies and Cultures: Foundations of Economic Anthropology*. Boulder: Westview.

Williams, Caroline. 2005. *Between Resistance and Adaptation: Indigenous Peoples and the Colonisation of the Chocó, 1510–1753*. Liverpool: Liverpool University Press.

Wolfe, Patrick. 1999. *Settler Colonialism and the Transformation of Anthropology: The Politics and Poetics of an Ethnographic Event*. London: Bloomsbury.

Zeller, Kathy. 2007. *Jaguars in the New Millennium Data Set Update: The State of the Jaguar in 2006*. New York: Wild Conservation Society.

national army, 25, 63, 110, 120, 186; violations of human rights, 26, 63, 65, 158–160, 181n, 202. *See also* Seventeenth Brigade (Colombian army); connivance, official army and paramilitaries

nature-culture divide, 2–3, 24, 31, 70, 210, 221, 227–28; and its legal consequences, 20, 23, 73–74, 88–89, 210–12, 222–30, 234–39, 241

necropolitics, 26, 67, 225

oil-palm plantations, 1, 16, 147–51, *148*, 155–56, 161–62, 165, 179, 233

omens, 91, 96, 99, 172

ontological occupation, 24–26, 28–29, 149, 151, 224, 235

ontology, 3–4, 21–22, 86, 212–14, 220, 223, 225, 236, 190. *See also* relational ontology

Operación Génesis, 26, 159. *See also* Seventeenth Brigade (Colombian army)

oral traditions, 73, 190–91, 193–96. *See also* Uncle Tiger and Uncle Rabbit

outboard motors, 49, 53, 56, 84–85, 132

palizadas, 1, 38, 53–60, *59*, *60*, *54*, 62–66; place making and cleaning, 53, 56–62, 68–70

palms, 42, 100, 172–73. *See also* oil-palm plantations

paramilitary armies, 1, 6, 14, 20, 25–28, 62–66, 72, 80, 87, 101–9, 113, 115, 131, 135, 139, 148–50, 183, 200–206. *See also* ACCU (Peasant Self-Defense Forces of Córdoba and Urabá); AGC (Gaitanista Self-Defense Group of Colombia); human corpses: of soldiers

Pavarandó, 72, 161

peccaries, 18, 122, 152, 197

personhood, 2, 3; legal, 22, 218, 222, 225–27, 236. *See also* territory: as a victim

phenomenology, 73, 82, 111

pilde. See psychotropic plants

pillory, 90–91

places: affective, 109–112, *109*, *114*, 142, 152–53, 169, 179, 182; and memory, 43, 110–11, 140, 169; co-constitution, 111–12, 175, 214, 223; making of, 56–60, 70, 123, 125–26, 134–35, 233; phenomenological approaches, 70, 111–12, 135; sense of, 16–17, 43–44, 51, 61, 135, 175, 209

plantain, 41–42, 86, 102, 133, *134*, 136, *137*, 156; gardens, 17, 128, 134–35

political ontology, 23–25

politics: beyond the human, 4, 153, 177, 180, 212–15, 226–27, 239–40 (see also *ecumene*); of identity, 14, 29–30, 239

poultry. *See* livestock

poverty, 6, 26, 29, 67, 171, 232, 238

predator-prey relationships, 185, 188, 192–94, 200

pregnant women, 94–96

priests, 8, 16, 74, 106–8

protected areas, 162, 186–87, 203, 229. *See also* Katíos National Park

psychotropic plants, 100, 115

quícharos. See fish

quiebrapatas. See land mines

rafts, 46–47, *46*, 57, 65, 71, 147, 219

rain, 17, 36, 53–54, 58, 64–65, 67

rastrojo, 126–28, *129*, *130*, *156*, 230, 234. *See also* forest: ruination

reconciliation, 169, 180, 183, 228, 232

relational ontology, 3–4, 17–21, 24–25, 29–31, 69–70, 121–24, 142, 227, 236, 240

renacientes, 85–87, 123, 172. *See also* relational ontology

reparations, 2–4, 21–23, 29–33, 70, 73, 131, 163, 203, 209–13, 222, 227–29, 234–37

resguardos, 8, 10, 90, 221. *See also* collective land tenure

rights: anthropocentrism, 20, 23–25, 212–13, 218, 221, 230, 236–37; cultural, 10, 13–14, 16, 22, 89, 215, 217, 220 (*see also* multiculturalism); beyond the human, 69, 89, 218–25, 236, 239–40; human, 1–2, 30, 34, 65, 69, 88, 162–66, 209, 220–25, 239; territorial, 11, 13, 14, 22–23 (*see also* collective land tenure)

rituals: birth, 15, 17; healing, 143, 145–47 (see also *jaibanas*); funerary, 100, 168, 170, 172–73, 184. *See also* exorcisms

rivers: agency, 48, 69, 73, 218, 222–27; bodily dispositions, 51, 73; dangers, 47–48, 56, 93; kinship relations, 37, 42–45, 51, 61; practices of care, 31, 38, 43–45, 53, 56–57, 60–61; relational aspects, 30, 37, 52, 61, 73, 79–81; ruination, 67–69, 99; social practices, 36–37,

42, 45–47, 49–50, 52; swirls, 71, 74–75, 77, 79–81, 84; travel, 35, 37, 38, 43, 54–56, 60–61 (*see also* embarking)

rot, 32, 53, 62, 66, 68, 110, 126, 234

rubble, 32, 68, 126, 128, 140, 227, 234, 237

ruination, 32, 69, 112, *118*, 120, 124–27, 156–57, 234, 238; triggered by nonhumans, *121*, 124–131, *125*,150–51, 234

runaway slaves, 42, 132

Salaquí River, 10, 38, 53, 56–58, 62–64, 77, 80, 101, 104, 120, 133–35, 152, 160–61

secretos. See snakebites

sedimentation, 60–61, 64–66, 69

serpent. *See* snakes

Seventeenth Brigade (Colombian army), 63, 159, 162, 202. *See also* connivance, official army and paramilitaries

shamanic aggression, 31, 91–95, 98–100

shamans. See *jaibanas*

sierpe. See snakes

skulls. *See* human corpses

slavery, 7, 40–42, 132, 196

snakebites, 143, 145–50, *144*

snakes, 1, 4, 13, 92, 97, 102, 108, 112, 197, 204, 212; *jepá*, 74; *mapana*, 58, 90–91, 146; *sierpe*, 75, 77–79, 86

sorcerers, 104–5, 108–9, 115, 147

souls in pain, 17, 154, 167–68, 171, 173, 177–78, 180–83. *See also* spirits: haunting

spirit possession, 104, 106–8, 113

spirits: evil, 1, 21, 30–32, 96–97, 99, 104–8, 113, 115–16, 235, 238; haunting, 110, 153–54, 158, 166–72, 174–78, 180–84, 227, 234–39; protectors of animals, 2, 4, 20, 213; sylvan, 17, 19, 21, 31, 91–94, 97–98, 102, 209–15, 225–28, 233

stagnation, 32, 62, 175; of time, 174, 234; of water, 38, 52, 61–62, 68

stingrays, 58, 75, 79–80

subject-object dichotomy, 2, 68–69, 74, 82–84, 112, 191, 210, 215, 241

substantialist ontology, 11, 18–19, 79. *See also* ontology

suffering, 2, 140, 148, 152, 167–72, 179–83, 241; nonhuman suffering, 15, 20–23, 29, 99, 174–75, 209, 213, 227, 234, 237–38

swamps, 8, 36, 39, 44, 49, 53–54, 63, 67, 93, 160

territory: healing the, 151, 153, 165–66, 177, 182–83; legal aspects, 10–13, 16, 44, 162; as a living entity, 2, 16, 21, 209; local conceptualizations of, 14, 16–17; relational attributes, 3, 16–20, 31, 69–70, 123, 135, 175, 232–33; spiritual relationship, 21, 217, 230; suffering of, 67, 179, 182, 213, 237 (*see also* nonhuman suffering); as a victim, 4, 20–24, 29, 33, 62, 209–10, 215, 235–36, 239–41

terrivertories, 69, 74, 226–27, 236–37

thanatopolitics. *See* necropolitics

thereness, 36–37, 62, 189

thunder, 102–103

timber companies, 11, 63–64, 66, 216; connivance with paramilitary armies, 31, 63, 161. *See also* war: economy of

tonga. See psychotropic plants

transitional justice, 2, 181–82, 211–15, 227–30, 232–37, 240–41

trauma, 2, 34, 168–70, 233, 235

travel. *See* embarking

trickster 193, 195. *See also* Uncle Tiger and Uncle Rabbit

Truandó River, 10, 38, 44, 63–64, 77, 97, 101, 135, 160–61, 192

turtles, 71, 75, 77, 197

unburied bodies, 1, 2, 113, 115, 158, 170, 178. *See also* human corpses

Uncle Tiger and Uncle Rabbit, 191–196, 207

underworld, 92, 94, 97, 103, 106, 108, 116

Urabá, 10, 161; Gulf of, 8, 39

vaca de agua. See *fieras*

victims and land restitution law, 21–23, 143, 209–11, 214–16, 218, 229

violence: against the territory, 1–2, 20–21, 32, 67, 72, 113, 133, 148–49 (*see also* territory: as a victim); ecological, 2, 23, 30–34, 89, 150, 238; embedded in places, 110, 152, 158, 168–69; structural, 6, 26–27 67, 232, 238. *See also* guerrilla armies; paramilitary armies; war

visiones, 92–93, 104. *See also* spirits

vulnerability, 33, 63, 69, 140–42, 207, 233, 237–38

vultures, 59, 154, 165, 177

wake, 33–34, 63, 152, 174. *See also* afterlives

wandering spirits. *See* spirits: haunting

war: conceptual aspects, 25, 69, 87–88, 195–96, 232–33, 235, 238–39; destructive production, 24, 29–30, 120–22, 126, 128–29, 141, 150; economy, 28, 31, 63–66, 148–50, 161–63, 216; environmental impacts (*see* environmental damage); historical aspects in Bajo Atrato, 25–30, 63, 101, 120, 131, 154–155, 158–164; impacts on other-than-human worlds, 1, 20, 24, 72, 113, 133, 148–49; pervasiveness, 25, 33, 207, 232; remnants of, 140, 157–58, 178; resistance against, 61, 101–103, 195–96

warmth: and coldness, 126, 130; and illness, 58; of people, 118–120, 126, 132, 136, 233–34; of plants, 145

wasps, 102, 119, 123–26, 214, 234

waterscapes, 31, 60, 62, 69, 92. *See also* floodplain lagoons; rivers; swamps; wetlands

wetlands, 8, 42, 61

wilderness, 17, 65, 93, 104, 131–32, 145, 160, 199

witness trees, 136, 138–40, *139*, *141*, 238

woody debris. *See* debris: woody; *palizadas*

Wounaan Indigenous people, 1, 7–8, 10, 20, 28, 73–75

zánganos, 93